Mad Mädchen

Mad Mädchen
Feminism and Generational Conflict in Recent German Literature and Film

Margaret McCarthy

berghahn
NEW YORK • OXFORD
www.berghahnbooks.com

First published in 2017 by
Berghahn Books
www.berghahnbooks.com

© 2017, 2019 Margaret McCarthy
First paperback edition published in 2019

All rights reserved. Except for the quotation of short passages for the purposes of criticism and review, no part of this book may be reproduced in any form or by any means, electronic or mechanical, including photocopying, recording, or any information storage and retrieval system now known or to be invented, without written permission of the publisher.

Library of Congress Cataloging-in-Publication Data

Names: McCarthy, Margaret, 1963- author.
Title: Mad madchen : feminism and generational conflict in recent German literature and film / Margaret McCarthy.
Description: New York : Berghahn Books, 2017. | Includes bibliographical references and index.
Identifiers: LCCN 2017014724 (print) | LCCN 2017024967 (ebook) | ISBN 9781785335709 (e-book) | ISBN 9781785335693 (hardback : alk. paper)
Subjects: LCSH: German literature--20th century--History and criticism. | Women in literature. | German literature--21st century--History and criticism. | Feminism and literature--Germany. | Motion pictures--Germany--History--20th century. | Women in motion pictures. | Feminism and motion pictures--Germany. | Motion pictures--Germany--History--21st century.
Classification: LCC PT151.W7 (ebook) | LCC PT151.W7 M43 2017 (print) | DDC 830.9/352--dc23
LC record available at https://lccn.loc.gov/2017014724

British Library Cataloguing in Publication Data

A catalogue record for this book is available from the British Library

ISBN 978-1-78533-569-3 hardback
ISBN 978-1-78920-499-5 paperback
ISBN 978-1-78533-570-9 ebook

To Joachim, Nico, and Nola Ghislain

Contents

List of Illustrations	viii
Acknowledgments	ix
Introduction	1
1. German Feminism in the 2000s: Brains, Bodies, and Bridges	25
2. Lost Objects, Monsters, and Melancholia in Zöe Jenny's *The Pollen Room* (1999), Alexa Hennig von Lange's *Relax* (1999), and Elke Naters's *Lies* (1999)	66
3. Dialogical and Borderline Selfhood in Charlotte Roche's *Wetlands* (2008) and *Wrecked* (2011)	101
4. Girls Gone Wild: Ulrike Meinhof, Uschi Obermaier, and Feminist Fantasies of '68	131
5. Counter-Cinema, Crossing Bridges, and Future Feminisms: Christian Petzold's *The State I Am In* (2000) and Fatih Akin's *The Edge of Heaven* (2007)	167
6. Mutable Mädchen: On Screen and in the Streets	206
Bibliography	237
Index	249

List of Illustrations

1.1	Bayenturm. Source: FrauenMediaTurm Köln	26
1.2	Cologne "Kranhäuser." Source: author's photo	27
1.3	Still: Alice Schwarzer and Verona Feldbusch on the Johannes B. Kerner talk show, 2001	44
2.1	Cover of *Relax*. Source: www.rowohlt.de	70
2.2	Vampirella Comic. Source: www.dynamite.com	71
3.1	*EMMA*, May/June 2001. Source: www.emma.de	102
4.1	Still: *The Baader Meinhof Complex* (2008)	144
5.1	Still: *The State I Am In* (2000)	176
5.2	Still: *The State I Am In* (2000)	177
5.3	Still: *The Edge of Heaven* (2007)	196
5.4	Still: *The Edge of Heaven* (2007)	197
6.1	*EMMA*, Spring 2011. Source: www.emma.de	212
6.2	*Missy Magazine*, April 2013. Source: www.missy-mag.de. Photo by Katharina Poblotzki	215

Acknowledgements

In 2008, as generational debates among German feminists began heating up between self-proclaimed "Mädchen" and Alice Schwarzer, I was excited that feminism suddenly mattered enough to warrant impassioned exchanges. At the same time I was also chagrined at a "repetition of the same," meaning old tensions flaring up in a new context. As someone who experienced lingering forms of second-wave feminism in college and more particularized third-wave approaches in graduate school, I found myself easily identifying with both sides, which became the inspiration for this volume.

In looking to literary and filmic protagonists confronted with conflicting forms of feminism, I discovered, however, responses quite different from mine. These extended from anger to neurosis and sometimes even madness. As in the debates of 2008, the mother/daughter trope provided a structuring principle, yet one that resonated beyond simple binaries and a younger generation's need to cast off maternal influence. Instead, the various power structures on display in the works this volume examines reveal the coexistence of affinities and differences—that is, both the need for nurturing and the basic differentiations that affirm existence via an individuated selfhood. Ideally, these two impulses would simply coexist, rather than provide the grounds for anger, disappointment, and conflict. But the novels and films I analyze in *Mad Mädchen* suggest otherwise, which of course provides the stuff of art and opens up often-wearying debates. At the same time, some of these works offer possibilities for conceptualizing solidarity in a manner that recognizes perennial conflict, yet continually reimagines it in order to preserve a larger whole.

In writing this volume, I was fortunate to experience the solidarity of female colleagues currently working on contemporary German feminism. Respondents such as Hester Baer and Katrin Sieg, who also subsequently read and commented on entire chapters, provided excellent feedback. On more than one occasion, Carrie Smith-Prei, Maria Stehle, and Hester Baer shared their work on popfeminism with me, which always charted territory I was only beginning to know, as well as set the standard for conceptual rigor. I'm also grateful to have worked with Birgit Mikus and Emily Spiers, whose comments on chapter two were extremely helpful. My Davidson College colleagues Caroline Weist, Robin Ellis, Anelise Shrout, and Suzanne Churchill have offered useful insights, pointed me in the direction of relevant scholarship, and made wonderful kaffeeklatsch companions. Early on I had a very useful email exchange with Christina Gerhardt, whose own reactions to feminist conflicts were both pointed and similar enough to mine to serve as a confidence builder. I am also indebted to Sonja Eismann, who generously provided access to *Missy Magazine* in online form. Finally, I am so lucky to have had three astute outside readers who offered invaluable suggestions.

Davidson College supported research in 2009, 2015, and 2016 at the FrauenMediaTurm in Cologne, where a neat pile of relevant print media resources always awaited me. I would especially like to thank Jasmin Schenk for working with me over the years. Ongoing conversations about feminism have long been a component of my friendship with Motria Procyk. Talking with her son, Stephan Snyder, about queer theory in the summer of 2015, was a real joy as well. (They may be the only mother/son duo I know who discuss—in the German sense of the word—gender and queer theory on a regular basis.) I'm also very indebted to my friend and colleague Vivian Shen who's my faithful sounding board for the tribulations of life at a small liberal arts institution in the South. My German friends Silvia Lastering, Werner Schmitz, and Sabine Bucholz have alerted me to key resources and also been part of the reason that summers in Cologne are so wonderful, as have Marion Hahn, Karl-Heinz Wiedemann, and Peter Dörpinghaus. On a yearly basis I get the much-needed reminder that there's so much more to life than work, including road trips to Wuppertal solely for the sake of riding the *Schwebebahn* from one end to the other. Thank you all for making the line between friends and family very fluid.

Of course family in the traditional sense has also made all the difference in my life. As a dean of students at a Catholic college in the 1970s, my father, Thomas N. McCarthy, was responsible for its transition to a coeducational institution. He hired their first female administrator and used Title IX as leverage against an old-boy athletic department. My mother, Ruth Patterson McCarthy, modeled for me not only the deep satisfactions of pursuing a career but also of losing herself in a novel at night, or in an embroidery or knitting project. She was both a do-ityourselfer and sophisticated *Schöngeist* who supplemented her professional identity with activities deeply pleasurable for the soul. Continued love and support from my brothers, Tommy, David, and Paul McCarthy, and sisters-in-law, Lisa Dumont, Marina Pacini, and Stella Tsai, have been a constant over the years. Most important of all, twenty-five years ago Joachim Ghislain came into my life. He and our children, Nico and Nola, became the center of my world, surrounding me with enough love and laughter to far outweigh the Sturm und Drang of family life. Not long into adolescence, Nico chastized me for singing along to "Blurred Lines," because, as he put it, the lyrics are "totally sexist." Nola remains my one and only mad but always charming Mädchen who will no doubt always be the boss of me. For his part, Joachim, whose many freely chosen domestic tasks include the laundry, once reminded me to use the little mesh bag because otherwise my bras would get stretched out. All kidding aside, he's the love of my life and the one who makes all things possible.

Introduction

Generational Divides and Difference(s)

On New Year's Day, 2016, I Skyped with a girlfriend who had attended a play the night before in Cologne, Germany. In passing she mentioned a chaotic scene on the subway platforms beneath the central train station, with aggressive revelers throwing firecrackers into the crowds. Within a few days, reports began to emerge of even more above-ground tumult instigated by roughly a thousand young men of Arab and North African origins. Their actions included attacking and sometimes sexually abusing young women as two hundred police officers largely failed to react. An appalling turn of events given Germany's attempts in the preceding months to welcome and integrate a million refugees, it further galvanized right-wing animosity, as well as reignited feminist debates on the cultural bases of misogyny.

By 5 January, elder feminist Alice Schwarzer published an article titled "The Consequences of False Tolerance" on her website.[1] In it she referred to the "gang bang party" at the Cologne Train Station as the means for immigrant men and their sons to "play hero like their brothers in the civil wars of North Africa and the Near East" and "make war in the middle of Europe." As the benefactors of false tolerance, she argued, these men embody the traditional, ingrained anti-Semitism and sexism of Arab culture that Schwarzer has long decried. Along now familiar lines, her rhetoric of "fathers, sons, and brothers" conjures an intergenerational ballast of patriarchal power seemingly impervious to liberal western mores.

Younger feminists Stefanie Lohaus and Anne Wizorek soon after published an article called "Immigrants Aren't Responsible for Rape Culture in Germany," in which they pointed to the yearly assaults and rapes at Oktoberfest celebrations.[2] According to a statistic they cite, 13 percent of

German women have reported experiencing sexualized violence, with many such acts never recorded at all. In essence, Lohaus and Wizorek challenged the notion that cultural beliefs "programmed" the attackers in Cologne, while critiquing the German legal system for the challenges it presents to women who have been assaulted.[3] In a later discussion with Schwarzer published in *Spiegel Online,* Wizorek also admonished male politicians otherwise uninterested in sexism for "instrumentalizing" it in order to stigmatize a particular group.[4]

If exposing false tolerance by the left, as well as the right's specious uses of sexism to bolster an anti-immigrant stance, provides the manifest content of these arguments, other comparative vantage points complicate familiar political divides. Less obvious to international readers are echoes of generational conflicts among German feminists in recent years. *Spiegel* alluded to this frame by describing Schwarzer as the "grande dame of German feminism" and Wizorek as "a prominent member of the new generation of feminists" who "often have different views about the direction the women's movement should take."[5] While *Spiegel Online* accurately describes a generational rubric embraced by some German feminists with particular fervor in the 2000s, media incarnations of this divide have often tangled up substantive arguments with hype. Schwarzer's 2001 debate with media icon Verona Feldbusch, dubbed "brain vs. body" by the talk show that provided the forum, provides one particularly egregious example. Opposing camps, of course, lend themselves to simplistic binaries, despite the layered resonances of the word "generation" within the German context. Though easily linked to Anglo-American feminist discourse, generational constructs have also buttressed the fraught parameters of German identity, imagined in alternately past and future-oriented, weighty and occasionally playful, terms. Given this larger, complex configuration of disjunctive elements, the feminist conflict that *Spiegel Online* alludes to in neutral tones in fact played out in Germany with particular force.

Within a larger feminist context, this framework shares ground with a cross-culturally ubiquitous trope of mother-daughter conflicts—what Astrid Henry has called "*the* central trope in depicting the relationship between the so-called second and third waves of US feminism."[6] In a recent essay, Birgit Mikus and Emily Spiers trace an even longer history among German feminists invested in a generational construct whereby daughters would continue to work towards the same overarching goals as their mothers. Significantly, they identify a "fractured legacy" between the first women's movement in mid-nineteenth-century Germany and contemporary feminists in both groups' understanding and uses of it: "From the very start, the founders and figureheads of the various political and social factions of the women's movement looked toward the future as the place where all of their demands, hopes, and dreams would be fulfilled, true equality between the sexes achieved, and women independent and self-determined beings."[7]

As much as feminist legacies are no doubt less unified than early German feminists optimistically imagined, their vision nonetheless presupposes enough commonalities to ensure a sustainable trajectory. Their optimism clearly warrants spotlighting for providing an antidote and implicit rebuke to divisiveness across the second and third waves. In Germany, such acrimony typically invokes, as Mikus and Spiers argue, the "1968 generation," which becomes "the object of affective displays of frustration and even intense dislike, as new German feminists accuse their forebears—Alice Schwarzer in particular—of prohibiting the progress they seek to secure."[8] This tendency shuts down interest in historical antecedents with potentially ameliorative effects, as in the quote above.[9] Along similar lines, an American focus solely on the second and third waves diverts attentions from a first wave that in fact extended across several generations. Such occluded knowledge reinforces what Henry calls the "persistent twoness of generations [that recalls] the mother-daughter relationship."[10] And "persistent twoness" in the German context, as I suggested above, has amplified itself to the point of a kind of culturally specific obstinacy.

As the quote above from Mikus and Spears indicates, German feminism from the 1970s is inextricably bound up with the student movement of 1968, out of which it arose. This touchstone both raises the stakes and sharpens the edges around generational affinities in Germany, which extend back to World War II and its aftermath. Those who came of age during the student movement created their own vigorously defined parameters of selfhood by challenging their parents to confront and work through the effects of their fascist past. They thus prompted the work of *Vergangenheitsbewältigung* (coming to terms with the past)—that is, the perpetually reflective, reformative measures vital to defining Germany as an enlightened democracy over and against its totalitarian alter ego. Given the persistence of guilt and trauma across the second half of the twentieth century, this process necessitated hard labor in the form of perpetual self-critique. Psychologically, its effects clearly counter the collective empowerment associated with social movements.

Over time, subsequent generations have attempted to differentiate themselves from a seemingly overarching parentalism that would correct rather than affirm identity. Miriam Gebhardt, author of *Alice in No-Man's-Land: How the German Women's Movement Lost the Women* (2012), pointedly frames her book-length critique of Alice Schwarzer in a manner that invokes the rhetoric of 1968: "Young women don't want to listen to another lesson in patriarchal feminism, they don't wish for the conscience police but rather solutions for concrete concerns."[11] Strikingly, generational affiliations in the new millennium have had effects far more enabling than admonitory. Since the 1990s, Germans have been able to choose from a wide variety of generational constructs, defining themselves temporally ("Generation 78," "Generation 89"), geographically ("Generation Berlin"), or more idiosyncratically by consumer choices and media forms ("Generation Golf," "Generation Ally"). As Hester Baer has argued, such affiliations manifest a "concurrent embrace and rejection of elements of German history."[12] On a deeper psychic level they prize individuation—in carefully chosen, sometimes highly particular terms—over collectivity.

This culturally specific backdrop thus reveals an intense investment in difference, often articulated within a familial rubric that pits children against parents and thus resonates in relation to feminism's trajectory in Germany. Whether articulated by its proponents or within the media echo chamber, it often appears as a largely bifurcated whole. This structure, of course, belies the web of diverse, often intersecting voices that have characterized the movement across different cultures. In addition, it perpetuates not only overused tropes of mothers and daughters but more specifically a notion of the third wave as more socially progressive and thus able to correct second-wave blind spots regarding white privilege. The feminist debates around the Cologne assaults cited above evoke precisely this tension, even if three white feminists debating on the origins of sexism looks a lot like racially tinged elitism. Given this irony, the logic informing a younger generation's imperatives deserves closer attention, particularly the negative consequences when difference alone steers feminist rhetoric and aims.

An ever-evolving third-wave sensitivity about cultural and racial difference—which does double duty by also demarcating a boundary against an older generation's less progressive purview—cannot escape the consequences of its own logic. An emphasis on difference—a younger generation knowing better than its predecessors and also trying to avoid a know-it-all attitude on racial issues—preprograms continual clashes. Knowledge itself implicitly takes opposing forms: the cumulative wisdom of an ever-more-enlightened perspective and the many subjectivities at any given moment that expose the former's universalizing tendencies. No matter how cautiously a younger generation stakes its claims about women, pushback inevitably ensues when difference provides its own kind of universal baseline for political discourse. Indeed, despite a third-wave embrace of multiple contrasting viewpoints, many nonwhite women entered the feminist arena in order to challenge continued blind spots regarding the overlapping effects of sexism and racism. Peggy Piesche's edited volume *Your Silence Does Not Protect You: Audre Lorde and the Black Women's Movement in Germany* (2012) includes many vital and influential voices, including May Ayim's. In an essay written over twenty-five years ago, she trenchantly critiqued the psychic toll of a women's movement that ignored racism, which she described as both "alarming and shocking."[13]

Valerie R. Renegar and Stacey K. Sowards have argued that society is "awash in false dichotomies," which define difference in terms of competing antithetical forces that have a way of reproducing themselves ad infinitum.[14] A third-wave need to expose and correct maternal parochialisms shares, of course, affinities with a Western imperative to inoculate Islamic culture against misogyny. Schwarzer's argument more overtly underscores this need, evoking what Fatima El-Tayeb has linked to a binary in which Europe is threatened by anti-Enlightenment migrant fundamentalism.[15] What gets "instrumentalized" in the process is not simply sexism as the justification for an anti-immigrant stance. Rather, an image of the fundamentalist Muslim immigrant serves as a stand-in for Europe's longer, suppressed history of anti-Semitism, racism, and gender inequality.[16] Consequently, a larger contradiction emerges between the "racelessness" of Europe's Enlightenment ideals and what El-Tayeb describes as a "not so subtle racialization of Europeanness as white and Christian and thus of racialized minorities as non-European."[17] In *European Others: Queering Ethnicity in Postnational Europe*, El-Tayeb traces a long history of transnational feminist frameworks' effects on European feminism, which, like Piesche's volume, spotlights Audre Lorde's shaping presence for the Afro-German movement. She documents women of color not only reacting to racism, but more specifically challenging the normative, exclusionary identity formations that prop up European identity, as well as Schwarzer's line of argument.

Within the longer history of feminism, Schwarzer's response to the Cologne attacks relies on a collectivizing impulse—in this case Arab men as the inverse of an oppressed, to a greater or lesser extent, female gender. A younger generation's logic, by contrast, exhibits more particularizing impulses, even if on the surface it appears to transplant Schwarzer's totalizing impetus to a German context. Less evident, however, are the kinds of sensitivities that inhibit the urge to speak for all women or all cultural others. As much as Wizorak and Lohaus speak back to German sexism as a pervasive force, their line of argument more subtly promotes the repair of self before others. This distinction, I would argue, reflects the trajectory of feminism from second-wave solidarity through the identity politics of the 1990s to contemporary awareness of whiteness as its own highly particular, rather than universal perspective.

What it Feels Like for a Mädchen

Despite the larger context provided here to identify, particularize, and of course critique dichotomous thinking, its presence and rhetorical force among German feminists in the new millennium have provided the launchpad for this volume. "Mad Mädchen" refers first and foremost to the kind of anger on display in debates that crested in 2008 when various younger feminists expressed their frustrations with an older generation, for whom Alice Schwarzer became exemplary. My title also draws on a "do or die" dynamic evident in what Madelyn Detloff has identified in an Anglo/American context as a "dynamic of contempt as the condition of autonomous selfhood."[18] Along similar lines, Astrid Henry's critique of generational rubrics underscores their biological connotations—that is, life cycles that inevitably pass out of existence. More concretely, my title also references some of the disgruntled voices of 2008 that referred to themselves as Mädchen. In doing so, they hoped to reprise 1990's girl culture, with its playfully performative approaches as an alternative to what was perceived as second-wave dogmatism.[19]

By attaching the adjective "mad" to Mädchen, however, I want to underscore the differences between then and now. Combining girlish ebullience with overt antipathies creates an odd affective dissonance that undercuts the subversive potential of ironic detachment. And when anger overrides girlishness as an antidote to maternal power, it precipitates precisely the kinds of high-stakes oppositions that preprogram factionalism. Equally important, the self-imposed parameters of rebellious daughters also run the risk of creating an arrested state of development, evident in white, educated, middle-class feminists' ignorance of oppression experienced by less privileged women. To wit: only a few years after the debates of 2008, some of the mad Mädchen of 2008 were confronted with evidence of their own racist blind spots in the globally linked forms of activism they subsequently pursued. Again, when always "knowing better" provides activism's modus operandi, limited awareness of experiences beyond one's own parameters of identity can undermine younger and older feminists alike. A larger ironic consequence is that "intersectionality" begins to look less like common ground among feminists than an across-the-board wielding of difference, but to various ends.

It perhaps goes without saying that this approach often shuts down an acknowledgement of affinities, which is striking given rhetorical strategies that historically united German women in pursuit of incipient feminist aims. As Myra Max Ferree has demonstrated in *Varieties of Feminism: German Gender Politics in Global Perspective,* German feminists since the nineteenth century have defined their project via an evolving concept of autonomy. She writes, "The central feminist self-definition as 'autonomous' critiqued the public gender order of the male breadwinner family in the West and the power of the Communist Party in the East."[20] As I will discuss in greater detail in chapter 1, this approach involved creating separate spaces for women in relation to the patriarchy. More recently, however, the same dynamic appears to have created wedges within the movement, evident in feminist voices of 2008 that proclaimed the advent of a new brand of feminism. Even if German feminists have lately been less inclined to conjure affinities across difference, a longer historical perspective reveals the kind of anger that has spurred collective action among young and old feminists alike.

Anger fired up German feminists to hurl a tomato at male student-movement activists indifferent to women's circumstances within a class-based critique of capitalist structures. And not only Schwarzer but also a wide range of feminists began to act collectively in the 1970s, forging alliances with the emerging Green Party that eventually led to actual changes in German laws that had disadvantaged women.[21] The kind of anger that initially energized German feminists in the 1970s is still evident in Wizorak's 2013 Twitter #aufschrei (outcry) campaign in response to everyday forms of feminism. A year later, #YesAllWomen called attention to ubiquitous forms of misogyny via individual stories posted online. The 2016 #ausnahmslos (without exception) campaign to alter Germany's rape laws provides another salient example reminiscent of the 1970's grassroots activism that galvanized women across difference. It is partly the intention of this volume to root out the kinds of simultaneous affinities and differences that complicate an otherwise straightforward generational rubric intent on exposing a mother's or daughter's presumably insufficient knowledge.

This expanded canvas also takes into account an understanding of the adjective "mad" that extends beyond a logical affective response to untenable circumstances—that is, the sentiment behind a hurled tomato. Further along the spectrum we also find more dramatic responses to oppression—embodied, for instance, in the classic mad woman in the attic undone by the extreme privations of a circumscribed life. In this instance, it becomes clear how much perceptions of reality not only respond to oppression but also reveal the unique, sometimes psychologically attenuated perspectives of any given individual. And when a maternal figure stands at the gateway to feminist activism, affective responses can no longer be understood solely as the reverberations of patriarchal culture. Instead, they also speak to the kinds of identifications—as well as what Henry identifies as "disidentifications"—that are foundational to identity.[22] This volume concerns itself with the unpredictable effects of individuals processing overtly political imperatives alongside the deeply subjective elements that characterize particular life circumstances. It pays close attention to the various ways that feminism is embodied and displayed, which extend from the logical to the unpredictable. One witnesses in this process not only the blind spots of, and incompatibilities among, various approaches, but also the full spectrum of human behavior with which political agendas necessarily work. Above all, the singularity of the psychological realm betrays a complicated mix of egotistical and enlightened imperatives that can potentially stymie as much as stoke collective feminist aims.

If generational discourses tend to flatten things out into tired mother-daughter tropes, the results when they seep into literary and filmic representations of women are anything but predictable. In this regard, Claire Hemmings's *Why Stories Matter: The Political Grammar of Feminist Theory* provides a useful reference point, given her examination of the stories that British and American feminists tell about their shared history. She identifies dominant narrative patterns that emphasize not only progress, but also loss (of unified political engagement) and return (to materialist approaches eclipsed by postmodernism). In order to locate alternative visions of a feminist past, present, and future, however, she underscores the need to intervene in these stories and tell them in more ethically accountable and politically transformative ways.[23]

On the one hand, I very much share Hemmings's investment in the utopianism that feminist theories can enable. Yet in activating her attention to "citation tactics" and "textual affect" as starting points for transformation, I often encounter in my literary and filmic protagonists quite the opposite, namely confusion and fragmentation. While this response may implicitly critique conflicting feminist approaches for ameliorating women's circumstances, it also exposes complex psychological structures that process political dogma in their own contradictory ways. Fragmented psyches provide a perennial challenge to feminist approaches, including the possibility of a larger collective identity. This terrain takes us beyond cohesive narratives, like mothers losing touch with new perspectives. It also reveals how deeply subjective needs less amenable to correction can be far more complicated than a third-wave predilection for porn or postfeminist love of pumps. Yet as much as the mother-daughter nexus constitutes its own simplistic narrative, it nonetheless provides a useful touchstone given the complicated nature of initially primal bonds. These combine the sustenance that comes from overlapping selves with the gradual detachments that presage autonomy. They combine strong identification with the kinds of disidentifications that fuel the whole process of individualization. The simultaneity of seemingly antithetical forces not only provides an alternative to cut-and-dried political rhetoric, but also fosters the kinds of enigmatic relations that require art's more nuanced lens. This volume is primarily concerned with examining the complexities of generational tensions among women, often articulated via mother-daughter bonds, and meditating on their larger resonances for feminist discourse.

The significance of identification/disidentification for this bond requires further attention since this polarity will remain key to *Mad Mädchen*. If contrary forces feel like evidence of a bipolar selfhood, Diana Fuss has underscored the psychoanalytically normative nature of these forces in her 1995 work *Identification Papers*. Identification, she writes, is the psychological mechanism that instantiates identity via self-difference—that is, via "the detour through the other that defines a self."[24] She describes it, on the one hand, as an "embarrassingly ordinary process, a routine, habitual compensation for the everyday loss or our love objects," while also emphasizing its incalculable effects and the emotional turmoil that identification can cause. In addition, Fuss emphasizes its "astonishing ability" to reserve and disguise itself, to multiply and contravene previous identifications, and to disappear and reappear in ways that make identity profoundly unstable and perpetually open to radical change. Indeed, Fuss's range of identifications includes various antagonistic binaries: feminine and masculine, maternal and paternal, centrifugal and centripetal, positive and negative.[25] Crucially for my study, however, the identification/disidentification dyad incorporates a "play of difference" *with* "similitude in self-other relations."[26] If the pairings above provide foundational forms of difference, my approach will balance the scales by searching for similarities, however opaque they remain to rebellious daughters.

Significant as well is the notion of identification as both unstable and open to change, which has far-reaching, if contrary, implications for the political uses of this mechanism. Writing in the wake of various seminal works on queer performativity, such as Judith Butler's *Gender Trouble: Feminism and the Subversion of Identity* (1990) and Eve Sedgwick's *Epistomology of the Closet* (1990), Fuss continually emphasizes the challenges that identification provides for a politics of affiliation. For the latter to function, it must fully recognize, Fuss argues, the "sacrifices, reversals, and reparations involved in every imaginary identify formation."[27] By way of example she cites Butler's notion of *dis*identifications that in fact reveal a disavowed identification "that has already been made and denied in the unconscious."[28] This possibility clearly has ramifications for fraught mother-daughter bonds, particularly when identification "operates . . . as an endless process of violent negation, a process of killing off the other in fantasy in order to usurp the other's place, the place where the subject desires to be."[29] More generally it underscores the elastic and mobile nature of identification, which "exceeds the limits of its social, historical, and political determinations."[30]

Fuss cites Douglas Crimp's observation that social movements such as ACT UP and Queer Nation were enabled by previous identifications with political movements such as Black Power, feminism, third world liberation, and the Gay Liberation Front. But she also quotes his insight that "there is no predicting what identifications will be made and which side of an argument anyone might take."[31] This capriciousness bespeaks the role of the unconscious in producing identifications, a realm over which the political subject has no steady or lasting control. Fuss continues: "Given the capacity of identifications continually to evolve and change, to slip and change under the weight of fantasy and ideology, the task of harnessing a complex and protean set of emotional ties for specific ends cannot help but to posit intractable problems for politics."[32]

If, for instance, the politics of young German feminists emerge from an affectively charged disidentification with an older generation, we can recognize the basic operation of instantiating selfhood via differentiation from another. Despite this very "ordinary" and "everyday" process, the attendant emotional affect can extend, as it has in the German context, to anger and contempt as markers of separation. Such colossality would indeed suggest Butler's notion of disidentification covering over an identification already made but subsequently disavowed. At the same time, Fuss's use of the adjective "protean" above suggests that "emotional ties" can take ever-changing forms, influenced not only by ideology but also fantasy, forces that do not necessarily align with each other. It is particularly in the latter realm that identification "exceeds the limits of its social, historical, and political determinations," revealing a deeply personal, idiosyncratic, and egocentric realm potentially at odds with larger collective aims. Yet fantasy need not be solely the result of deeply psychological needs in need of satisfaction. If it taps into the energies of ever-evolving identifications, it can also be the means through which the affiliations that fuel social movements continually reimagine themselves in the face of perpetual differences. In this sense, fantasy and ideology can also work in tandem and in the process create what Hemmings alludes to: alternative visions of a feminist past, present, and future that aim for political transformation. However optimistically humanist this goal appears in the face of fragmented psyches, it provides a potentially powerful antidote to embattled mothers and daughters.[33]

Overview

Chapter 1 looks at German feminism during the first decade of the 2000s, using Anglo/American tensions in second-wave, third-wave, and post-feminisms as point of reference. Concretely, the early years of the new millennium brought the challenges of the "Demography Debate," during which some conservative voices chastised feminism for causing falling birth rates. Curiously, two moments that crystalized generational tensions within German feminism bracketed this debate: the televised debate between Alice Schwarzer and Verona Feldbusch I mentioned above and the appearance of two bestsellers in 2008—Jana Hensel and Elisabeth Raether's *New German Girls* and Meredith Haaf, Susanne Klingner, and Barbara Streidl's *We Alpha-Girls: Why Feminism Makes Life Nicer*.[34] Both of these volumes advocated new forms of feminism that challenged basic tenets their authors associated with Schwarzer. If Feldbusch embodied a vanilla-flavored version of 1990's girl culture, again later revived by the emergent feminists of 2008, its efficacy was never situated directly in relation to the Demography Debate. The centrality that motherhood retains in German culture certainly raised the bar for girl culture performativity borrowed from an Anglo/American context as the means to alter long-entrenched cultural values. Significantly, only Schwarzer and journalist Iris Radisch provided trenchant critiques of the Demography Debate's reactionary and blanket social condemnation of feminism, perhaps providing early evidence of a highly polarizing decade for German feminism.

The profound effect of Judith Butler's groundbreaking work on young feminists in Germany, *Gender Trouble: Feminism and the Subversion of Identity*, certainly contributed to this widening divide. As Mikus and Spiers observe, her text constituted a short-hand reference point for a seismic shift in feminist theory, signaling as well a spatial break with second-wave forbears given Butler's US context.[35] Yet by also examining, in chapter 1, Butler's critique of *Gender Trouble*, which includes its inattention to social context, I also identify two important elements for this study, one conceptual, one concrete. Significantly, both of these elements rely on a binding principle. Butler's self-critique included her initial omission of examining performativity in terms of its psychic and corporeal effects. If one keeps in mind the fragmented nature of selfhood, as I underscored above, it becomes possible to recognize how a psyche that imagines itself empowered can also coexist with bodily effects that communicate the opposite. Some of the literary works I analyze in the first half of this volume provide examples of women who embody feminist tenets in freakish or self-destructive ways. Butler understands bodies and psyches as both incongruous and inseparable, a notion that resonates in relation to the mother-daughter trope and the complexities I will examine in subsequent chapters.

Ironically, though she critiqued the second wave's unified sense of itself, Butler's framework, as she subsequently acknowledged, certainly did not occlude an understanding of solidarity as a kind of self-aware, ever evolving performance. In a similar but journalistic vein, the feminist magazine *EMMA*, which Schwarzer founded in 1977 and continues to edit, reacted to the debates of 2008 with two special issues emphasizing bridge-building among fractured feminists. Similarly, some of the voices who emerged in 2008, evident in Sonja Eismann's volume *Hot Topic: Popfeminism Today*, in fact promoted a hybrid approach that combined second- and third-wave imperatives.[36] What demands further examination, however, is an undercurrent in *We German Girls*, what Katja Kauer has called a "sampling" of earlier forms of feminism, largely unacknowledged, which the volume otherwise expressly rejects.[37] In other words, the volume's overt dichotomies obscure the simultaneous affinities and differences it otherwise displays. As much as I will examine, particularly in the final chapter of this volume, the bridge-building possibilities that *EMMA*'s two special issues and popfeminism open up, I find the psychological complexities of the mad Mädchen—overtly rejecting and tacitly embracing the preceding generation—equally compelling. Again, they point us in the direction of literature, where the warring factions that comprise selfhood can be fully displayed. And indeed, numerous novels dating back to the late 1990s vividly depict the impact of feminism in all its manifold forms.

Chapter 2 analyzes Zöe Jenny's *Das Blütenstaubzimmer* (The pollen room; 1997), Alexa Hennig von Lange's *Relax* (1999), and Elke Naters's *Lügen* (Lies; 1999). All three novels examine deeply conflicted female protagonists, sometimes overtly or subtly situated in relation to feminism. Indeed, we witness profoundly neurotic behavior that creates a funhouse version of basic feminist precepts, as well as clichéd versions of student movement ideals such as escape and experience. What results is not so much a critique of either second- or third-wave feminism, though female grotesques may indeed reveal the underside of individualist approaches and their detachment from larger, collective goals. Instead one senses how some female protagonists perceive feminism not as a web of intersecting voices but as a disjunctive cacophony that further agitates already fragmented selves.

In this sense, all three novels implicitly depict how a socially progressive movement meant to improve women's circumstances can also directly feed into the kinds of psychological distortions that thwart an integrated selfhood. "Striking the pose" for these protagonists becomes tantamount to putting fractured selfhood on full, uninhibited display.[38] Their strategic exhibitionism often betrays a regressive narcissism, with girl culture taking more literal, infantile form. Yet at the same time, this realm adds an entirely new affective response, situated in relation to a lost maternal object otherwise barred from cultural expression. In all three novels, anger and madness exist alongside melancholia for eclipsed bonds of intimacy, in another example of affective dissonance. More important, by tapping into the precultural roots of mother-daughter relations, *Lies* in particular suggests the possibility of individuality and shifting power relations coexisting with deep bonds and solidarity. And in an overtly performative vein, inspiration comes at the very end of the novel when two women are deeply moved by the melodramatic woes of mothers and daughters in Douglas Sirk's *Imitation of Life* (1959).

Analysis of contemporary German feminism as refracted in literature would not be complete without attention to Charlotte Roche. She not only vigorously participated in the debates of 2008 but also penned two novels—*Feuchtgebiete* (Wetlands; 2008) and Schoßgebete (Wrecked; 2011)—with narratives structured around mother-daughter animosities. Just as she accused Alice Schwarzer of forgetting about the human being in the woman, Roche created female characters quite antithetical to a second-wave-style, exemplary femininity that defines itself in opposition to the patriarchy. Yet the young protagonist of *Wetlands* in fact embodies a potent mix of second- and third-wave impulses, literally wearing them on the surface of her body. The vaginal secretions she dabs behind her ears, for instance, recall both the natural body mandated by the second wave and a more contemporary, third-wave pleasure in styling. Similarly, she combines the self-reflexive "Innerlichkeit" (interiority) of German women's novels of the 1970s with an in-your-face "Äußerlichkeit" (outwardness) reminiscent of girl culture's exuberant playfulness. What complicates this seemingly less fraught paradigm of simultaneous affinity and difference, however, is a younger daughter's inability to acknowledge the former. *Wrecked* takes this inability to an extreme, depicting a daughter highly invested in simplistic dichotomies that demonize the mother. Only once does the protagonist wonder whether her perceptions constitute a personality disorder. If both novels embody a younger generation's heady anger towards its maternal forbears, *Wrecked* amplifies and implicitly critiques the irrational psychic structures that feed this emotion.

In chapters 3 and 4, I move into the realm of film, in both mainstream and more experimental form. Access to interiority necessarily shifts here from solely textual form to more varied filmic modes. As such, it becomes less explicit and more enigmatic because it resonates across a range of verbal and visual details. My analysis shifts somewhat as well, concerning itself as much with the influence of feminism on representation as with its impact on individual psyches. This broader vantage point becomes all the more relevant when two iconic and historically controversial women inextricably linked to the legacy of 1968—Ulrike Meinhof in Uli Edel's *Der Baader Meinhof Komplex* (The Baader Meinhof Complex; 2008) and Uschi Obermaier in Achim Bornhak's *Das wilde Leben* (released in English as *Eight Miles High*; 2007)—are the subjects of analysis. One the one hand, their legacies, as I will demonstrate, do indeed reverberate differently through a feminist lens. Yet when representation shifts along politically progressive lines, this approach may not necessarily yield the kinds of insights with which feminism could complicate its notions of collective versus individual aims. Particularly in the realm of mainstream film, signifiers of a feminist trajectory that once prized authentic voices and now celebrate performative agency can quickly devolve into clichés.

In general terms, Edel's film implicitly speaks to an earlier era's sexism, embodied in hysterical media responses to female terrorists as an outgrowth of feminism. By couching *The Baader Meinhof Complex* in terms of Ulrike Meinhof's political awakening, Uli Edel retroactively corrects facile links between female emancipation and unbridled anarchy. In the process, he not only manifests Hollywood's tendency to enlighten spectators along liberal humanist lines, but also creates a conventional narrative of a woman finding her voice, a blueprint otherwise evident in German feminist classics of the 1970s such as Verena Stefan's *Häutungen* (English edition titled *Shedding*; 1975). Bornhak approaches his depiction of Obermaier by tapping into a more contemporary investment in performativity. If her assertive sexuality has been understood historically in terms of an era's hedonistic excesses, Bornhak links it to Obermaier's agency within the arenas of fashion and tabloid journalism. Significantly, his narrative, too, taps into earlier feminist impulses to represent women not only finding their voices, but also some form of authenticity, in Obermaier's case above and beyond the visual realms she so skillfully commands. Yet, if feminist frameworks render historically fraught female figures more sympathetic, they may also flatten out what could have been more artistically enigmatic, such as, for instance, the complexities of fragmented, incongruous selves. Each film gives us the sense of a social movement's overall effects on representation but not on individual psyches and their alternately self-empowering and self-aggrandizing manner of processing political precepts.[39]

What happens, though, when a film combines mainstream and experimental elements tapped into historical approaches intended to complicate the representation of women's lives? Here I am referring specifically to Douglas Sirk's 1950's melodramas, Rainer Werner Fassbinder's female-centered *Bundesrepublik-Trilogie,* and the radical potential of feminist filmmaking imagined by Claire Johnston in 1975. These lineages, I argue in chapter 4, manifest their traces in Christian Petzold's *Die innere Sicherheit* (released in English as *The State I Am In*; 2000) and Fatih Akin's *Auf der anderen Seite* (released in English as *The*

Edge of Heaven; 2007) Given that four of the five names above belong to men, with Edel and Bornhak tipping the gender imbalance even further, my choice of these two films warrants justification. Sirk, of course, sympathetically portrayed female oppression—sometimes across race, as in the film *Imitation of Life*—within a liberal humanist frame that both exposed basic inequities and invited identification. The inspiration that Fassbinder took from Sirk's films manifests itself in melodramatic narratives, though coupled with estranging effects. We partly sympathize with his emotionally complex female characters but also witness the kinds of incongruities that reveal their complicity in the larger social structures that otherwise oppress them. Petzold's and Akin's films partly depict conflicts between mothers and daughters, situated in relation to leftist and humanist ideals within contemporary commodity culture and global capitalism. While their female characters, like Fassbinder's, embody the push and pull of antithetical forces, Petzold and Akin also create various forms of disjuncture that recall Johnson's paradigm, though ultimately to dystopian and utopian effects respectively.

The German title of Petzold's film, *Die innere Sicherheit,* or the inner security/certitude, and the young age of his female protagonist evoke primal needs and individualistic attempts at securing them. As the daughter of former RAF members, she looks to the consumer world around her to forge a separate identity. Nothing girlish or playful characterizes this process; instead what should offer the means to cultivate identity amounts to nothing more than generic t-shirts and shiny plastic bags. Ultimately, the film ends with her pain and injury after a car accident leaves her broken and bloody in a barren field. Here "disjuncture" takes the form of an affective register that puts the lie to neoliberal promises regarding an ever-deferred "good life," to borrow Lauren Berlant's formulation in *Cruel Optimism* (2011).[40] Similarly, there is no securing a "Heim" (home) in an uncanny world where consumerist fantasies eerily overlap with fairytales, fascism, and failed utopian projects. In essence, Petzold exposes how fallacious the whole project of self-realization remains within a larger, neoliberal framework, a dystopian endpoint particularly for forms of feminism invested in mass cultural forms as tools of expression.

Mother-daughter bonds, both in biological and ersatz cross-cultural form, are central to Akin's narrative, which provides its own utopian salve to the logic of exchange that structures the film. Specifically, *The Edge of Heaven* suggests how familial connections, particularly those characterized by deep divides, can nonetheless model solidarity in a manner that has utopian implications for concrete national divides. This scenario resonates even more strongly given some forms of feminism in the 2000s that resolutely distanced themselves from larger global concerns about women's circumstances. As much as the family as metaphorical rubric can manifest difference at its very core, it also necessitates accepting difference in the name of retaining a life-sustaining bond. This structure suggests a utopian alternative to the European Union in its present form since the former is built across differences rather than invested in an Enlightenment-based supremacy. Ultimately Akin positions women, bolstered by humanist and revolutionary ideas as well as psychic mother-daughter bonds that extend beyond a German frame, as contemporary agents of change in the spirit of 1968. In his film, Johnston's concept of "disjuncture" involves attaching melodrama's contrived resolutions to abandoned political utopias that create a salve for contemporary social and cultural divisions.

The final chapter of this volume examines German feminism from 2012 to the present and activism that articulates itself on digital platforms and in globally connected, often highly performative, street-based demonstrations. Now more than in 2008 the undeniably multiple, intersecting, sometimes clashing voices of German feminists no longer lend themselves to bifurcated frames, yet the possibility of solidarity nonetheless remains a topic of discussion. In fact, the fifth anniversary issue of the feminist *Missy Magazine,* founded in part by Sonja Eismann not long after the debates of 2008, consists of feminist voices that partly bemoan the lack of solidarity among feminists. Despite *Missy Magazine's* status as a younger feminist's alternative to *EMMA*, this issue recalls *EMMA's* two special 2008 issues that attempted to build bridges with younger feminists. Implicitly, *Missy's* voices responded to fallout from a Berlin SlutWalk demonstration during which topless activists in blackface protested Islamic misogyny, which stoked tension with Muslim women and other people of color. As I argued above, despite a younger generation's heightened sensitivity to issues of difference, speaking for women inevitably constitutes a simultaneous speaking at women with differing experiences of oppression.

In the face of such continued conflict, I attempt to map out more fully the political possibilities of simultaneous differences and affinities—what my literary and filmic protagonists embody—and their implications for conceptualizing solidarity. In *Feminism Without Borders: Decolonizing Theory, Practicing Solidarity,* Chandra Talpade Mohanty imagines solidarity in the form of "mutuality, accountability, and the recognition of common interests as the basis for relationships among diverse communities. Rather than assuming an enforced commonality of oppression, the practice of solidarity foregrounds communities of people who have chosen to work and fight together."[41] While acknowledging unequal power relations among feminists, she also argues that by recognizing differences in all their particularities, it becomes all the more possible to see connections and commonalities. This outcome reflects the notion that "no border or boundary is ever complete or rigidly determining."[42] Her argument ultimately promotes a cross-cultural rather than hierarchical feminist pedagogy, which has typically favored Euro-American theories and activism over non-Western approaches that are reduced to a supplemental function. What I would like to retain for my purposes, and augment with literary and filmic examples, is first the importance of "recognizing differences in all their particulars." Second, I will demonstrate how delineating a particular form of difference simultaneously sets the parameters for recognizing commonalities.

As my literary examples in particular show, difference can be understood in terms of basic psychic partitioning and conflicting impulses, evident when subjective needs bump up against more exemplary selfhood in feminist terms. Together these forces provide a useful metaphor for the difficulties of a larger solidarity. No matter how expansively progressive feminist agendas aim to be, individual parts of the whole—meaning, the varieties of feminism at a given moment—will always assert their own needs and aims. Political goals will never perfectly align given the uneven effects of power structures on women's lives. If understood in relation to partitioned psyches, conflicting forces exhibit both an inability and an unwillingness to recognize each other. "Unable" underscores the difficulty of recognizing the partly unconscious needs that program behavior, like the narcissistic theatricality I identify in some of my novels as the base for feminist activism. In less psychological terms, being unable to perceive differing feminist imperatives could simply underscore how some women have little to no experience of material constraints beyond their own circumstances. "Unwilling" suggests more of a defensive response in the face of repetitive patterns clearly in need of correction, like when some feminists continually ignore the conditions that different kinds of women need to flourish.

This framework thus views repetitive conflict as normative, not cause for shock or recrimination. Equally important, all factions constitute part of an organic whole, opening up the possibility of ecological metaphors where individual elements infuse as much as impede each other over the course of time. This dialogical relationship consists of past and present forms of feminism not only speaking to each other—however divisively—but also continually altering and ultimately sustaining each other. Topless activism provides a useful example of this interplay. First, it suggests affinities with an earlier moment in German feminist history when topless university students disrupted a lecture by Theodor Adorno. Yet its reactivation in a contemporary context simultaneously reveals a younger generation deeply concerned with cross-cultural forms of misogyny that oppress women beyond German borders, a key difference in a now more globally connected world. Mohanty's argument that recognizing particular kinds of differences simultaneously sets the terms for perceiving commonalities, however, brings additional elements into view. If recent topless activism deeply offended precisely the women it intended to support, the three women who leapt to Adorno's podium and bared their breasts received their own kinds of mixed reception. Not only did the press and public, as Barbara Becker-Cantarino argues, find their actions "shameless, immoral, and reprehensible," their image nonetheless appeared on various magazine covers, no doubt to bolster sales.[43]

The larger insight that emerges alongside these examples of simultaneous differences and affinities is simply that historically connected approaches will necessarily resonate differently over time. Importantly, this perspective runs counter to a more teleological narrative in which succeeding generations always evolve beyond the blind spots of their successors. To embrace this notion is to reject a long, rich history as living substratum. In the best possible scenario, feminism consists not so much of tangled-up voices that stifle each other but rather a thriving ecosystem capable of modifications that ensure its ability to thrive over time. Given that some feminist approaches may be more noxious (toplessness as antidote to the hijab) than salutary in achieving a particularly aim, the focus should be on the suitability of a particular approach at a given moment in time. Thus, solidarity needs to be imagined not as an endpoint in time and space but rather in ways elastic enough to accommodate repetitions of the same, or contrary needs perpetually reasserting themselves, as well as always shifting contexts. Mohanty emphasizes that it is "always an achievement, the result of active struggle to construct the universal on the basis of particulars/differences."[44]

Given this volume's investment in literary and filmic representations and their implications for feminism, it should not surprise that my most utopian example of mother-daughter dynamics, evident in *The Edge of*

Heaven, offers a concrete example of this process. The German mother in this film represents the generation of '68, though her ideals have ossified and her German identity props itself up on a sense of enlightened superiority to Turkey. Despite the Turkish daughter's initial angry response to her—their first encounter culminates with her statement "fuck your European Union"—her globally informed activism ultimately rekindles buried impulses in the German mother. Rather than attempting to combat global forces, however, the mother recognizes and corrects her own authoritarian tendencies, on full display in her interactions with her biological daughter. As much as the Turkish daughter reignites an impulse to change, the mother also alters the Turkish daughter's unmitigated anger towards power structures writ large. Part of their initial encounter includes the mother's observation to her: "maybe you're just someone who likes to fight." What we witness by the end of the film is not so much anger defused, but rather deep bonds that emerge within and across familial—but not necessarily biological—structures as the ur-locus of hierarchy. By tapping into each other's energies and tempering each other's excesses, these two women model a process of transformation whereby mothers and daughters continually reinfuse and sustain each other across difference. This relationship thus models solidarity not as quiescent endpoint but as residing in the continually shifting interstices between difference and affinity, imagined in ways that preserve a larger whole.

Notes

1. Alice Schwarzer, "Die Folgen der falschen Toleranz," AliceSchwarzer.de, 5 January 2016, http://www.aliceschwarzer.de/artikel/das-sind-die-folgen-der-falschen-toleranz-331143.
2. Stefanie Lohaus and Anne Wizorek, "Immigrants Aren't Responsible for Rape Culture in Germany," *Vice*, 8 January 2016, https://www.vice.com/read/rape-culture-germany-cologne-new-years-2016-876.
3. Such challenges were explicitly articulated in the #ausnahmslos campaign, released online on 28 April 2016 in order to influence parliamentary revisions of existing rape laws in Germany. Authored by more than twenty feminists whose names indicate a mix of German and non-German origins, the text critiqued the media's attention to sexual violence only when committed by those perceived as cultural others or against white cis-gendered women. To counter this skewed approach, they cited a range of statistics about the prevalence of sexual violence in European culture, including a 2014 study by the European Union Agency for Fundamental Rights that

one in two women experience sexual harassment. They also cited German police statistics that record 7,300 sexual assaults yearly, which amounts to roughly twenty each day. Equally important to #ausnahmslos was making sexual harassment a crime and revising existing laws that determined whether a rape has occurred based on the victim's behavior, specifically whether she tried to defend herself. The English version of their text can be found at http://ausnahmslos.org/english.

4. See Christiane Hoffmann and René Pfister, "A Feminist View of Cologne: 'The Current Outrage is Very Hypocritical'" (interview with Alice Schwarzer and Anne Wizorek), *Spiegel Online*, 21 January 2016, http://www.spiegel.de/international/germany/german-feminists-debate-cologne-attacks-a-1072806.html. Wizorek observed: "When I see the kinds of people that are now jumping into the debate over women's rights, it also includes, among others, the same politicians who, during the #aufschrei (outcry) debate in 2013, said that women shouldn't be so demanding. Now that men with immigration backgrounds have committed sexual assaults, it is being instrumentalized in order to stigmatize them as a group. I think that is racist."

5. The introductory text continues: "For decades, Schwarzer—as publisher of *EMMA*, the country's highly influential women's magazine—has been at the forefront of women's issues. In more recent years, a younger generation of feminists, led by Wizorek, has sought to challenge Schwarzer's preeminence." See "A Feminist View of Cologne."

6. Astrid Henry, *Not My Mother's Sister: Generational Conflict and Third-Wave Feminism* (Bloomington: Indiana UP, 2004), 2–3. She writes, "In recent years, there has been an increasing tendency to speak of feminism in terms of generations. . . . In its most-often-used form, the phrase 'feminist generations' points to the existence of at least two—if not more—coexisting generations of US feminists: second-wave feminists of the 1970s and a new generation of feminists, who emerged in the 1990s, who are called the third wave. This latter term, the 'third wave,' has frequently been employed as a kind of shorthand for generational difference among feminists."

7. Birgit Mikus and Emily Spiers, eds., "Fractured Legacies: Historical, Cultural and Political Perspectives on German Feminism," *Oxford German Studies* 45.1 (2016), 6. They cite author and early feminist Hedwig Dohm (1831–1919): "In der Frauenfrage, wie in allen großen sozialen Fragen, gilt es nicht, festzustellen, was war und was ist, sondern was sein wird" (Regarding the Women's Question, as with all important social questions, it is not about determining what was and what is, but rather what will be, 9). Her vision also implicitly responded to differing approaches and ideologies within the movement by situating met goals in the future. As Mikus and Spiers argue, it was vitally important to her to create a "systematic structure of thought which can function as an intellectual and cultural legacy for women of future generations, so they can build from there" (11).

8. Ibid., 16.
9. In critiquing some of the younger generation of German feminism, Mikus and Spiers observe that "they generally avoid glossing a domestic feminist tradition before 1968, a phenomenon which contrasts the practices revealed by cognate texts in the Anglophone context." They also argue that younger feminists prefer to cite Anglo-American discourse rather than German or European sources, beyond Simone de Beauvoir and Luce Irigaray (ibid., 16)
10. Henry, *Not My Mother's Sister*, 3.
11. Unless otherwise stipulated, all translations are my own. Miriam Gebhardt, *Alice im Niemandsland. Wie die deutsche Frauenbewegung die Frauen verlor* (Munich: Verlagsgruppe Random House, 2012), 14.
12. This idea is taken from a paper Baer presented at the German Studies Association Conference in 2008.
13. This description appears in the following longer quote: "Das Beschweigen und Nichtwahrnehmen von Rassismus, auch durch 'progressive Linke' und unter frauenbewegten Frauen, empfand ich im Jahr 1990 als beängstigend und schockierend und doch überraschte es mich kaum. Zwar waren seit Mitte der 80er Jahre vermehrte Diskussionen zum Thema 'multikulturelle Bundesrepublik' geführt worden, jedoch nur in Ausnahmefällen mit der Konsequenz, die eigenen Lebens- und politischen Zusammenhänge so zu verändern, das seine kontinuierliche, gleichberechtigte Zusammenarbeit mit ImmigrantInnen und Schwarzen Deutschen zu einer unverzichtbaren Selbstverständlichkeit geworden wäre und die Auseinandersetzung mit Rassismus zu einem permanenten Bemühen" (To be sure, there had been discussions about the "multicultural Federal Republic" since the mid 1980s. But only by accident would these have the effect of adjusting one's own personal and political relations in a way that would render it natural and inevitable to cooperate with immigrants and black Germans on a permanent, equitable basis in order to make the issue of racism an automatic consideration). See Peggy Piesche, ed., *Euer Schweigen schützt euch nicht. Audre Lorde und die Schwarze Frauenbewegung in Deutschland* (Berlin: Orlanda Frauenverlag, 2012), 63.
14. Valerie Renegar and Stacey K. Sowards, "Contradiction as Agency: Self-Determination, Transcendence, and Counter-Imagination in Third Wave Feminism," *Hypatia* 24.2 (Spring 2009), 11.
15. Fatima El Tayeb, *European Others: Queering Ethnicity in Postnational Europe* (Minneapolis: University of Minnesota Press, 2011). She observes, "Anti-Enlightenment migrant fundamentalism . . . places the continent in the position of victim, occupied with defending its values rather than imposing them on others. The imagery of a European culture faced with possible extinction or at least dilution invites a binary rather than an interactive view of

cultural exchange and has become a familiar feature in European discourse in particular on the continent's Muslim population" (xvi).
16. Ibid., xxviii.
17. Ibid., xxix.
18. Madelyn Detloff, "Mean Spirits. The Politics of Contempt Between Feminist Generations," *Hypatia* 12.3 (Summer 1997), 97.
19. As Mikus and Spiers note, by self-identifying as girls, these women distanced themselves linguistically and ideologically from an anachronistic "women's" movement ("Fractured Legacies," 20).
20. Myra Marx Ferree, *Varieties of Feminism: German Gender Politics in Global Perspective* (Stanford: Stanford University Press, 2012), 22.
21. Barbara Becker-Cantarino has tallied the successes of second-wave feminism in Germany: "Compared to the 1960s, women in the 2000s have gained—at least the possibility of—unrestricted access to (higher) education, to all professions and jobs including the military, more control over their own bodies and procreative functions, control of their own finances, protection against sexual and physical abuse by men, better financial report during the childbearing phase and for child-rearing for working parents, equal rights in divorce, guardianship, and a right to equal pay and pensions." See Barbara Becker-Cantarino, "The Politics of Memory and Gender: What Happened to Second-Wave Feminism in Germany?" *German Life and Letters* 67.4 (October 2014), 609.
22. Henry cites early feminist Ann Snitow's fraught relationship with her mother, a sentiment she identifies among other women in the second wave: "Snitow offers an illustrative example of disidentification: she suggests that the desire to escape her mother's life was particularly strong because she could . . . recognize herself in this life and in the female role it mandated. Thus, for many white, middle-class feminists of the second wave, according to Marianne Hirsch, mothers 'became the targets of the process of disidentification and the primary negative models for the daughter'" (*Not My Mother's Sister*, 8). This cycle, of course, then reprised itself with their third wave daughters.
23. Clare Hemmings, *Why Stories Matter: The Political Grammar of Feminist Theory* (Durham: Duke University Press), 1–2.
24. Diana Fuss, *Identification Papers* (New York: Routledge, 1995), 2.
25. Other pairings include primary and secondary, imaginary and symbolic, idiopathic and heteropathic, partial and total, narcissistic and regressive, hysterical and melancholic, multiple and terminal (Ibid., 4).
26. Ibid., 2.
27. Ibid., 7.
28. Ibid., 6–7.
29. Ibid., 9.
30. Ibid., 8.

31. Ibid., 8.
32. Ibid., 9.
33. Drawing on Jasbir Puar's notion of "affirmative becomings," Carrie Smith-Prei and Maria Stehle describe a similar process in their book, *Awkward Politics: Technologies of Popfeminist Activism* (Montreal: McGill-Queen's University Press, 2016), i.e., "the creation of a space of multiplicity and emergence where acknowledgements of difference can become a starting point for developing a sense of political solidarity" (202).
34. See Jana Hensel and Elisabeth Raether, *Neue deutsche Mädchen* (Reinbek bei Hamburg: Rowohlt, 2008); Meredith Haaf, Susanne Klingner, and Barbara Streidl, *Wir Alpha-Mädchen. Warum Feminismus das Leben schöner macht* (Hamburg: Hoffmann und Campe Verlag, 2008).
35. Mikus and Spiers, "Fractured Legacies," 24.
36. See Sonja Eismann, ed., *Hot Topic. Popfeminismus heute* (Mainz: Ventil, 2007).
37. See Katja Kauer, *Popfeminismus! Fragezeichen! Eine Einführung* (Berlin: Frank & Timme Verlag, 2009).
38. The effect bears resemblance to Carrie Smith-Prei and Maria Stehle's notion of "awkwardness," which describes the often contrary meanings that arise in a transnational arena of popfeminist performance art and street and hashtag activism. See Smith-Prei and Stehle, "The Awkward Politics"; and "WiG-Trouble: Awkwardness and Feminist Politics," *Women in German Yearbook* 30 (2014), 209–24.
39. Alternatively, in a film such as Doris Dörrie's *Alles inklusiv* (2014), which examines mother-daughter tensions around the spirit and effects of '68, we do see highly flawed and thus psychologically complex female characters. However, traces of feminism, whether their specific effects on individual characters or as larger shaping influence on the film's representational strategies, seem less evident in the film.
40. See Lauren Berlant, *Cruel Optimism* (Durham: Duke University Press, 2011).
41. Chandra Talpade Mohanty, *Feminism without Borders: Decolonizing Theory, Practicing Solidarity* (Durham: Duke UP, 2003), 7.
42. Mohanty, *Feminism without Borders*, 226.
43. Becker-Cantarino, "The Politics of Memory and Gender," 609. She actually argues that both the "Tomatenwurf" (thrown tomato) and "Busenattentat" (bosom assault) prompted this response given that both events "flew in the face of 'feminine' decency."
44. Mohanty, *Feminism without Borders*, 7.

CHAPTER ONE

German Feminism in the 2000s
Brains, Bodies, and Bridges

A lone medieval tower, stalwart and anomalous, stands among the once dilapidated but now sleekly refurbished port buildings alongside the Rhine River in Cologne, Germany. Waterfront strollers might miss the "Bayenturm" (see Figure 1.1) entirely in the panorama of showcase architecture that emerged around it in the new millennium, including three massive, crane-shaped apartment buildings made of glass. Historically, Cologne's iconic cathedral has dwarfed the tower as well, though foreshortening techniques in Renaissance engravings reversed such optics. Built between 1180 and 1250 as part of the city's original fortification wall, the Bayenturm became the most strategically important of the wall's numerous fortress towers. Over time, it came to be known simply as "die Burg" (castle), and as one historian observed, whoever occupied it, particularly during tumultuous uprisings, had the power.[1] When a thirteenth-century archbishop stationed troops in the tower in an effort to assert his dominance beyond spiritual matters, the city populace stormed its doors. Crying "Kölle Alaaf!" (Onward, Cologne), nowadays the rallying call during yearly Karneval festivities, they ended his ambitious machinations.

If such events accord the Bayenturm a populist, power-to-the-people vibe, it later housed customs officials, then served as a city prison and eventually military garrison, functions that conjure power in more traditional, monolithic form. Yet its links to Karneval underscore the shifting nature of hegemonies and shrink power to a brass ring within reach of the masses. To this day Karneval in Cologne commences in the city hall plaza with women cutting off men's neckties in a playful, performative assault on gender relations. Unlike the renaissance aesthetics that magnified the Bayenturm's contours, Karneval participants create

26 • Mad Mädchen

Figure 1.1. Bayenturm. Source: FrauenMediaTurm Köln

a funhouse mirror of patriarchal structures, staging their own purely symbolic sieges in a repetitive, socially sanctioned ritual. In the process, power becomes a surmountable entity, prey to errant, semiotic acts that mimic more concrete expropriations. Equally important, a severed necktie underscores a more imaginary type of agency stoked by visual display. Whether one needs to literally take back the tower or simply make do with a token necktie depends very much on shifting notions of empowerment.

Since 1994 the Bayenturm has been home to the FrauenMediaTurm (FMT), hailed by its founder, Alice Schwarzer, as the most accessible information center for concerns about women in the German-speaking world. It also houses the editorial offices of *EMMA*, the feminist magazine that Schwarzer, Germany's enduring icon of 1970s feminism, created and has coedited since 1977.[2] In an essay written the same year the FrauenMediaTurm opened its doors, Schwarzer invoked Virginia Woolf's *A Room of One's Own* (1929), a touchstone for many second-wave feminists. In it, she pronounced the FMT "a tower of one's own" and a "beautiful, proud place ... conquered" by women after men made history there.[3] Her use of a militaristic verb alludes to the battles she fought with city politicians to acquire the space, as well as flaunts her possession of the master's house and its transformation into a beachhead of women's history and feminist inquiry.[4] In Woolf's terms, of course, such possession signals not military might but economic advantage, and in this sense Schwarzer triumphed as well in acquiring prime real estate in what would soon become a very posh surround. Equally important, fortified walls ostensibly provide a number of the conditions necessary for a social movement to endure. In calling the FMT a "refuge for the living memories of women," Schwarzer invokes a separate space where women's experiences, both lived and literary, can be uncovered and preserved.[5] Historically, convents and the "Beguine" movement that flourished in Cologne in the twelfth and thirteenth centuries provided an outside space for women to live according to different values.

Figure 1.2. Cologne "Kranhäuser." Source: author's photo

Historian Anna Dünnebier has called the Beguine movement, financed by women of nobility who donated their inheritances to collectives in order to live independently, a forerunner to the women's movement.[6] Against this backdrop, walls that otherwise conjure phallic dominion instead recreate the sequestered conditions under which women were able read, research, and concern themselves with the arts. In a contemporary context, the FMT ideally provides the kind of retreat that ensures critical perspectives on the consumer-driven world beyond its parapet windows and how women stake their place in it. Taking back the tower constitutes a literal power grab and exemplifies the successes of second wave–style feminism in Germany; the extent to which women continue to pursue this ideal, whether in literal or Karneval's more figurative terms, deserves close attention.

The Second Wave, "Pastness," and Postfeminism

In *Interrogating Postfeminism: Gender and the Politics of Popular Culture* (2007), Yvonne Tasker and Diane Negra examine a variety of contemporary postfeminist assumptions in an Anglo-American context that construe feminism in terms of its "pastness."[7] First and foremost, this term evokes an aging, anachronistic entity that contrasts youthful vitality. More pointedly, it suggests feminism's superfluity in the wake of self-evident successes, most obviously female achievement in traditionally male domains. In Germany, not only does Angela Merkel as the country's first female chancellor provide an unassailable example, but also the rising numbers of women in the German Bundestag and the many women's affairs offices in various states charged with advancing women's rights.[8] As of 2016, a "Frauenquote" took effect and mandated that 30 percent of employees in large businesses must be women, which includes management positions. (Currently, only 26 percent of these positions belong to women.) Given these advances, Schwarzer's 1970s-sounding feminism and the FMT's resolutely historical appearance lend themselves easily to the postfeminist trope of "pastness." Cologne's gleaming waterfront facades may very well render retreat and reflection less enticing, particularly among women with enough economic wherewithal to take a room of their own, perhaps in an upscale glass apartment building, for granted. As Tasker and Negra emphasize, women's successes "on the playing field, in the concert arena, or in the boardroom" often underwrite a postfeminist sense of "unfettered material entitlement."[9]

Glass surfaces, too, shift the meaning of reflection away from isolated introspection within fortified walls to underscore instead the mirroring aspect of representation. While the "media" component of the FrauenMediaTurm points to both print and digital means for shoring up historical preservation, its visual aspect complicates the very nature of spatial relations that traditionally sustain power. The master's house, of course, changes shape over time, becoming all the more diffuse and alluring in a global world of omnipresent, proliferating screens. As a consequence it exceeds concrete, spatial parameters that can be acquired, dismantled, and then reconstructed according to the once and future terms of a more egalitarian society. In this regard, Karneval's cyclical nature underscores the need to continually renegotiate power structures in order to undermine their monolithic form.

If severed neckties constitute at best a symbolic sliver of the pie, the performative act itself dramatically confers a heady psychic supremacy stoked by graphic display. Contemporary women have no doubt reaped more concrete material benefits lately than Karneval's gendered reliquaries, rendering heretical acts less imperative. But they nonetheless retain, according to Tasker and Negra, their own kinds of exhilarating fantasies. The makeover that they identify as a favored trope of postfeminism suggests an "empowering desire for transformation, the yearning to achieve perfection in one's physical self and/or domestic environment, and the need to avoid at all costs a politicized understanding of these dynamics."[10] Limited political awareness, of course, underscores less postfeminism's youthful exuberance than the kind of credulity evident in child's play. Unlike sardonic, scissors-bearing women in search of neckties, children lack ironic detachment as they acquire and rehearse the hierarchical structures of selfhood. Instead, toys become an appendage of self, allowing children to assume an exalted position that belies their actual power in the world. Similarly, the makeover melds a beautified surface with an empowered interiority into one cohesive whole. If not possessing the tower, the room, or the necktie preordains a divided, circumspect identity, consumerism stokes a self-affirming doubling whereby idealized cultural forms transform individual lack into successful selfhood.

Playful exultation, it should be noted, may constitute a logical, well-deserved response from women now in a position to attain affluence and conventional attractiveness—that is, the traditional forms of male and female power. More subtly, however, girlish fantasies align with a neoliberal ethos of self-determination and a belief in defining selfhood via a competitive, market-driven meritocracy and what David Harvey identifies as its "lifestyles, modes of expressions, and ... cultural practices."[11] More trenchantly, Christian Marazzi has defined neoliberalism as "the absurd idea of economic government based solely on the market and its ability to self-regulate."[12] And as free-market hegemony expands, social benefits diminish, most evident in Germany's "Hartz IV" labor reforms that significantly reduced unemployment and welfare benefits in the 2000s. Angela McRobbie has critiqued neoliberalism's effects on feminist politics, which guarantee equality via individual achievement, not social provisions: "The young woman is offered a notional form of equality, concretized in education and employment, and through participation in consumer culture and civil society, in place of what a reinvented feminist politics might have to offer."[13] Concretely, the political is reduced to the personal, which in this instance implies that personal problems can be solved via individual achievement. A particularly egregious consequence that resonates for this volume as a whole is the dismantling of collective politics.[14]

It bears repeating that a belief in empowerment through individual choice and achievement alone requires the kind of childlike credulity that belies persistent social injustice and inequities in the larger social field. And as much as fantasy can provide a powerful antidote to oppression for both adults and children, it also makes it possible to cement the erroneous bond between consumer-fed transformation and concrete liberation. In postfeminist terms, Woolf's room becomes the launchpad for further material acquisitions rather than providing the kind of retreat that might spawn critical reflection on the status quo's definition of success. Taking back the tower and transforming it into the FMT, of course, clearly constitutes a feminist gain. Yet the larger question becomes to what extent meritocracy-defined aims, amplified by psychically empowering fantasies, remain too self-interested to alter a larger social field that continues to disadvantage women.

Germany in the 2000s: The Demography Debate

Very heated public media debates in recent years suggest that motherhood retains a centrality in Germany that makes fantasies of girlish exuberance less politically useful than elsewhere. The Demography Debate in particular, which examined the link between career women and falling birthrates, provides a case in point. As Alexandra Merley Hill has observed, "The country seems obsessed with motherhood—less so with fatherhood—as the birth rate declines and the media covers the various steps being taken to counter the trend."[15] Television moderator Eva Hermann's bestselling *The Eva Principle: Towards a New Femininity* (in German, 2006) provided one solution, namely encouraging women to stay home and build a "warm nest" for their families.[16] This domain would also provide the necessary respite for women "exhausted from [a] struggle against men" prompted by feminism.[17]

Newspaper editor and conservative cultural critic Frank Schirrmacher's bestselling book *The Methusalem Plot* (in German, 2004) fanned the flames in equally invidious ways: he linked declining birth rates to a future in which baby boomers, specifically a leftward-leaning, perennially infantile generation affiliated with the student movement of 1968, would control financial and cultural capital.[18] The only solution to avoid warring generations would be for Germans to have more children. More pointedly, he asserted in his subsequent work *Minimum: Regarding the Decay and Resurrection of our Community* (in German, 2006): "When societies find themselves in crisis or species populations at a threatening minimum, nature banks rather resolutely on the eternal feminine."[19] As Carrie Smith-Prei has observed, both Schirrmacher and Hermann call for "the reinstatement of the gender-normative family [as] the only possibility for Germany to survive."[20]

Beyond such polemics and despite the various advances for women cited above, concrete gains in the German work world appear far less egalitarian than postfeminism's upbeat stance would suggest: a June 2010 report from the *Institut für Arbeitsmarkt- und Berufsforschung* revealed that over 70 percent of German businesses are run by men. Across the boards, women's hourly gross earnings are 22 percent less than those of men, in comparison to a European Union–wide difference of 16 percent. Factors such as women being less qualified, relying on more part-time work, and women's difficulty in rising to leading work positions, however, account for only two thirds of the 22 percent difference in pay.[21] More generally, the continued problem of insufficient daycare and the ubiquity of half-day schools in Germany no doubt continue to undermine women's ability to pursue full-fledged careers.[22]

If persistent social inequities and atavistic responses to falling birth rates cast doubt on feminism's redundancy, they also call for a perspective less out of touch with contemporary circumstances than postfeminism's optimistic purview. Indeed, to understand egregiously anachronistic debates requires a comparative frame, one that explains why continued inequities in Germany feel so out of sync with liberal gains made in other western countries.[23] Understanding the efficacy of German women's emancipatory goals also requires attention to their own unique circumstances, which differ from a US trajectory aimed toward equal rights. Equally important, a broader context would also shed light on the extent to which contemporary Anglo-American frames for improving women's circumstances correlate with a concept of female autonomy evolved from a specifically German context.

Historical Forms of Feminism and Female Autonomy

In *Varieties of Feminism: German Gender Politics in Global Perspective*, sociologist Myra Marx Ferree highlights an important and basic cultural difference between Germany and the United States:

> Germany is not a liberal state. Many of the ideas that Americans find obvious, such as the central role of individual rights and equal economic opportunity in allowing women full participation in all the goods society offers, owe their prominence to the dominance of liberal political philosophy. Liberalism has not played as important a role in Germany as in the United States or even Britain. German politics has drawn on both conservative views of patriarchal authority and social democratic ideals of justice to forge a social welfare state that prioritizes family support and the social reproduction of the nation.[24]

Ferree's study charts a struggle for female emancipation that dates back to Louise Otto-Peter and her attempt to make the "woman question" central in the German liberal revolution of 1848. The divisions that hindered the creation of a unified, democratic state were largely class-based, which in turn determined the rhetorical strategies that German women pursued to stake their place in a changing society. Initially, they contended with a "clerical-military-landowner alliance" on the right and a "socialist-democratic-liberal alliance" on the left.[25] Aligning themselves with the latter, whether in the late nineteenth century, during the Weimar Republic, or in the student movement of 1968, always necessitated challenging a social agenda less interested in individual rights than a larger, state-controlled, family-based collective good. Self-determination within this frame became pejoratively "bourgeois" in the nineteenth century, out of sync with the economic crisis of the Weimar Republic, and superfluous to the Marxist agenda during the student movement.

Overall it remained antithetical to the "male breadwinner family" model that was deemed a social good by both sides of the political spectrum. The larger consequence of such prolonged exclusion from male-defined aims, as Ferree argues, was that women became quintessential political outsiders.

Not surprisingly then, the feminism born out of the student movement largely attempted to forge solidarity by defining itself against male notions of the female role. Ferree observes, "Not by ignoring their differences but by deciding that they would not be divisive, women might be able to construct an identity that worked for them as class had for (equally diverse) 'workers.'"[26] Women's strategies included redefining motherhood as a source of female strength, rather than a cause for subordination; challenging patriarchal hierarchies with nonauthoritarian childrearing; opening "Kinderläden," or storefront collectives, for taking care of children so that women could engage in politics; developing "Weiberräte," or Women's Revolutionary Councils, for reconceptualizing Marxist paradigms of women's work in the reproductive sphere; and manifesting loud and clear, often in "Selbsterfahrung" groups inspired by feminist "consciousness-raising" in the United States, that "the personal is political." Over the course of the 1970s and '80s, women's bookstores, cafes, and centers for combatting violence against women, as well as feminist newsletters, magazines, and literature, provided a variety of arenas for cultivating female autonomy.

Many feminists understood this desire for female autonomy as different from and preferable to liberal aims for equal rights. As the editors of the *Frauenjahrbuch* proclaimed in 1976, "Because ... male characteristics fundamentally have more prestige, recognition and above all more power, we easily fall into the trap of rejecting and devaluing all that is female and admiring and emulating all that is considered male.... The battle against the female role must not become the battle for the male role.... The feminist demand, which transcends the claim for equal rights, is the claim for self-determination."[27] What in a US context would have seemed radical—evident in negative responses to Catherine MacKinnon's critique of liberal feminism in *Feminism Unmodified: Discourses on Life and Law* (1987) for instance—became "the mainstream of mobilization" in Germany.[28] Conversely, Ferree points out that a strong antidiscrimination policy still, to this day, seems radical in Germany. Change in recent years often follows larger European Union mandates prompted by more progressive members such as Sweden and Finland and the transnational discourse of "gender mainstreaming" that has reshaped spending priorities. If "radicalism is [thus] relational," providing a specific type of challenge to the politics of a particular time and place, actual progress requires a longer maturation period.[29] In tracing the trajectory of German feminism in the 1970s and '80s, Ferree documents how autonomous feminists organized against domestic violence, sexual assault, and harassment, ultimately making alliances with peace, antinuclear, and environmental activists. In the process, politically efficacious strategies for improving women's lives, often articulated via the Green Party platform, evolved.

The "Butler Boom" and Third Wave in Germany

While the longer history that Ferree traces sheds light on German feminism during the 1970s, it also hovers over its more contemporary incarnations as well. I began this chapter with a polemical opposition between 1970s feminism, embodied by Alice Schwarzer and the FMT, and postfeminists, whose meritocracy-defined gains clearly put back in place patriarchal structures that earlier feminists had hoped to dismantle. In the broadest sense, Karneval aligns with both an anarchical desire to overthrow the powers that be and a playful, psychologically-empowering approach to activism that articulates itself more in semiotic than social form. The latter approach, of course, shares ground with feminist strategies that emerged in the 1990s, what in Anglo-American contexts was termed the third wave.[30] Understanding its reception and effectiveness in Germany over the last twenty-five years requires a variety of frames, including Ferree's historical overview and autonomy as an early feminist modus operandi. Germany's contemporary generational affiliations, which extend beyond feminists to myriad groupings that identify with a particular time or place, provide an important reference point as well.

In a more conceptual vein, Judith Butler's theories of gender, which had a profound impact on German feminism, made it possible to redefine autonomy in relation to a distinctly semiotic realm of speech acts and their consequences. As a social construction, she argued, gender could be subversively performed in ways that opened up the signifying capacities of male and female roles. Conceived as a critique of certain feminist blind spots, Butler's seminal work, *Gender Trouble: Feminism and the Subversion of Identity* (1990), challenged "regimes of truth."[31] These deemed some gendered expressions false or derivative and others true and original, with exclusionary, as well as homophobic consequences. She thus challenged the very boundaries that second wave feminism had constructed in order to create a politically viable identity capable of instigating a social movement.

In the German context, her work shifted attention away from actual, autonomy-aspiring women to a broader, conceptual notion of gender, as well as from collective, grassroots activism to individualistic performances. Even if the latter provided a more effective response to an increasingly dispersed global world, Butler's theories no doubt seemed radical in relation to early German feminism. Lacking the notion that a collective identity itself is a kind of performance, many early German feminists took their boundaries very seriously, evident in women's spaces that literally barred access to men. This exclusionary impulse played out among feminists themselves as well, a perhaps inevitable consequence of when "regimes of truth" dictate discourse. Schwarzer as an emblem of 1970's feminism may work in the public imagination, but in reality German feminists interested in full autonomy rejected her emphasis on "sameness," which meant that no legal justification existed for treating women differently under the law.[32] To many, Schwarzer's position smacked too much of liberal aims to achieve equality. Such tensions within the German movement of course underscore Butler's larger point about the discursive nature of identity, as well as the hierarchical diversions that follow when different versions of selfhood compete against each other.

Strikingly, however, in the preface to the 1999 edition of *Gender Trouble*, Butler critiqued her argument in a number of ways that actually mend bridges with second-wave feminism. She began by underscoring the difference between critique that aims to make a movement more democratic and inclusive versus the kind that would undermine it altogether, emphasizing that *Gender Trouble* belongs in the first category. More importantly, she also retroactively recognized the performative nature of a collective identity itself: "I came to understand how the assertion of universality can be proleptic and performative, conjuring a reality that does not yet exist, and holding out the possibility for a convergence of cultural horizons that have not yet met."[33] Butler also observed how even her own theories could take on precisely the kind of prescriptive coloring she identified in earlier forms of feminism, particularly if readers took her message simply as "subvert gender in the way that I say, and life will be good."[34]

Butler's self-critique becomes all the more precise when she examines the blind spots of her own theoretical paradigms. If *Gender*

Trouble applied a poststructuralist critique to feminism, Butler acknowledges that this paradigm can sometimes remain "aloof from questions of social context and political aims."[35] Social context, of course, matters when feminism operates in different cultural contexts, but more generally it draws attention to the vagaries of reception. If a semiotic field constantly in flux makes it possible to alter the meanings of retrograde forms, it also preordains a variety of responses. There is no guarantee that political aims will be received as intended; indeed, Butler critiques places in *Gender Trouble* that seem to indicate that the "psychic meaning of a gendered presentation can be read directly off its surface."[36]

Even when subversive messages are successfully communicated and received, this act may not necessarily change the social field: "Gender can be rendered ambiguous without disturbing or reorienting normative sexuality at all."[37] In this sense, a radical approach is no guarantee of concrete, progressive gains. Equally important, where commodity culture provides the larger context for performative acts, one needs to keep in mind, as Butler reminds us, that subversion can carry market value. More specifically, "the mobilization of identity categories for the purposes of politicization always remain threatened by the prospect of identity becoming an instrument of the power one opposes."[38]

Butler's most salient critique of *Gender Trouble* comes towards the end of her preface: "This text does not sufficiently explain performativity in terms of its social, psychic, corporeal, and temporal dimensions."[39] Social effects in particular became a point of contention in Butler's reception in Germany. In writing about "Butler boom" after *Gender Trouble*—translated as *Das Unbehagen der Geschlechter*—in 1991, Ferree describes a mostly enthusiastic embrace of her theories. But she also cites critiques from older German feminists suspicious of individual agency, as well as the overall optimistic premises underpinning Butler's theories of gender performance. Female agency manifested in highly idiosyncratic ways appeared to some to undermine a hard-won collective identity. And the poststructuralist premises underpinning such agency also seemed "dangerously individualistic, even *neoliberal*."[40] After nearly two decades making slow but concrete changes to German society, older feminists no doubt wondered what could be gained by playing up the constructed nature of identity, even if their notion of "autonomy" clearly emerged in relation to particular circumstances.

Yet Butler's injunction to understand performativity in terms of its psychic and corporeal effects does, in fact, counter the overall naïve optimism that older German feminists linked to her approach. What gets communicated about the nature of identity may be more than the possibility of turning otherwise sexist social structures to one's advantage. Butler's model is of course very much in tune with a larger cultural-studies model, with its egalitarian emphasis on the semiotic possibilities of the larger social field and the promise of individually salutary and overall subversive effects it proffers. This process aims to correct the wide divide between "haves" with actual power and "have nots," who must improvise an empowering relationship to the social and cultural forms that would otherwise oppress them. While subverting traditional meanings to achieve empowerment clearly remains a desirable goal, it belies the complex nature of subjectivity that might otherwise be communicated in a performative act. More telling and provocative to witness might be something completely contradictory—for instance, a psyche that imagines itself empowered, alongside bodily effects that communicate the opposite.

In her introduction to *Excitable Speech,* Butler cites Shoshana Felman's work, particularly the notion that relations between speech and the body are both incongruous and inseparable.[41] Following Felman she asserts,

> The speech act, as the act of a speaking body, is always to some extent unknowing about what it performs, that it always says something that it does not intend, and that it is not the emblem of mastery and control that it sometimes purports to be.... The body becomes a sign of unknowingness precisely because its actions are never fully consciously directed or volitional ... that unknowing body marks the limit of intentionality in the speech act ... [which] says more, or says differently, than it means to say.[42]

As much as cultural studies provided a necessary correction to the overly pessimistic nature of earlier paradigms such as the Frankfurt School, female subjectivity continues to falter as much as thrive within the arena of commodity culture. Putting such contradiction on display might reveal life experiences less amenable to mapping along an axis of either oppression or subversion. Warring psychic and corporeal factions, too, remind us that performativity is not synonymous with autonomy, even if it conjures an exhilarating sense of control. As Butler asserts, she aimed to open up the "possibility of agency," which is not the same as restoring a sovereign autonomy in speech or replicating conventional notions of mastery.[43] Effects can extend beyond conscious intention when context shapes reception.

Given Butler's profound influence on gender studies, playfulness and performativity—ideally oppositional but sometimes merely affirmative—has become a defining characteristic of contemporary feminist theory. Yet her self-critique and the bridges it builds, I would like to argue, provide an important frame for German feminists, a younger generation of whom fervently embraced her paradigm as initially articulated.[44] And in the last decade in particular, this embrace has led some younger feminists to emphatically burn bridges with the previous generation. If we understand their stance as a performative act, decoding its meanings requires not only theoretical and historical frames, but also familiarity with generational divisions that extend back to the end of World War II. This process also necessitates perceiving more than the empowerment younger feminists strive for, especially where subversive aims slip into neoliberal tendencies that underwrite the status quo. And keeping contradictory messages in mind, it becomes crucial to consider whether younger German feminists articulate something more than rejection of a previous generation, particularly when they draw on older, unacknowledged feminist literary voices.

Ur-Narratives and Generational Divisions within and beyond the German Media

As I briefly alluded to in my introduction, in a 2001 broadcast of the Johannes B. Kerner talk show, Schwarzer sparred for nearly an hour with Verona Feldbusch, a media icon and former Miss Germany. Dubbed "brain versus body," their confrontation served as a harbinger of the impassioned battles that Schwarzer would fight with a younger generation of feminists in the ensuing decade. Prompted by Schwarzer calling Feldbusch a "Barbie doll" and a "slap in the face for women" at an April 2001 lecture in Hannover, the show put on full display the once and future tenets of a then thirty-year-old social movement. A variety of mediating frames, beginning with Koerner's facile binary, raised the stakes by stoking the need to determine a winner, as if one regime were in the process of toppling another. The show began with Schwarzer's and Feldbusch's awkward entrance through a door behind the audience, obliging them to decide who would hold the door for whom. This staging preprogrammed a hierarchical divide, as if only one person could have the power, the other reduced to a position of deference and respect. Schwarzer's simple black dress and sensible, demonstration-ready shoes countered Feldbusch's white, cleavage-exposing pantsuit, amplifying again the show's either/or frame. Equally striking, the then 58-year-old Schwarzer and 33-year-old Feldbusch quite vividly embodied and articulated the "ur-narrative" of generational differences prominent among feminists since the 1990s. This frame facilitates a more nuanced understanding of their encounter than simplistic dualities, though it, too, carries loaded rhetoric that generates high stakes. Equally important, Germany's post–World War II generational affiliations reveal complicated psychological investments with potentially crippling and/or enabling effects.

In *Not My Mother's Sister: Generational Conflict and Third-Wave Feminism,* Astrid Henry examines the mother-daughter relationship as "*the* central trope," or the "matrophor," for "depicting the relationship between the so-called second and third waves of US feminism."[45] This problematic configuration, as she points out, reduces the plural "generations" to a dyadic structure. In the process, one set of possibilities is pitted against another, creating an either/or framework with sharper edges than the looser "wave" metaphor that has defined feminism in the twentieth century.[46] Evoking a biological backdrop of reproductive life cycles that inevitably pass out of existence, this dyad also encompasses the equally forceful psychological need to differentiate from parental forebears in order to articulate an individuated selfhood.

In broad-brush form, Schwarzer embodies many of the elements of second wave feminism in an Anglo-American context. Similar to Gloria Steinem, Schwarzer as journalist has waged her campaigns largely within the media arena. Most notably, she spearheaded a 1971 cover story in the magazine *Stern* in which 374 women, including celebrities, acknowledged having had abortions. In addition, not only did she found *EMMA,* in more recent times Schwarzer has brought hot-button issues, including the controversial rape trial of TV weatherman Jörg Kachelmann, to print venues as varied as the *Frankfurter Allgemeine Zeitung* and the tabloid *Bild Zeitung*.[47] Whether viewed as pragmatic or savvy, Schwarzer's command of the media domain posits an alternative to earlier feminists seeking autonomy, since her goal has clearly been to reach as wide an audience as possible. But as much as the media provides the platform to articulate a particular message, it also creates the conditions for becoming a projection screen. And in this regard, "autonomy" not only gives way before the "Männerpresse" that Schwarzer often critiques, but also an ensuing generation of women eager to situate autonomy in relation to older feminists, not the patriarchy.

Following the mother-daughter rubric, the second wave's hard-won, enlightened vantage point inevitably mutated into rigid precepts for the next generation, who then pursued antithetical aims to assert their own identity. Feldbusch staked her place in the media firmament during the 1990s with an erotic talk show called *peep!* which showcased soft-porn scenarios, as well as celebrity chat about sex and love. In this role, as I will discuss in more detail below, Feldbusch embodied a mild variant of girl culture which flouted second-wave critiques of porn's role in promoting violence towards women. Her link to soft porn not only underscores the contrary impulses that second-wave feminism may have preprogrammed, it also conjures private and hedonistic pleasures.

Significantly, German generational affiliations have historically involved pain as much as pleasure, resulting in mother-daughter tensions that played out with particular force among German feminists. As much as a feminist identity would empower women tout court, Germany's collective identities since World War II have often had far less salutary effects given the persistence of both guilt and trauma. Sigrid Weigel has identified attempts to forestall both of these emotions as early as the "Hitler Youth Generation." This group included postwar literary figures who imagined their identity in terms of a "pure birth from the head [that] cuts the umbilical cord" linking them to war, or as a new beginning unconnected to procreation in the traditional sense.[48] Later generations, like those who came of age during the student movement, created their own sharply defined parameters of selfhood as well by challenging their parents to confront and work through the effects of their fascist past. *Vergangenheitsbewältigung* posits a German identity requiring the hard labor of self-critique and constitutes the flip side of collective empowerment. It requires the kind of arduous internal reprogramming that flies in the face, for example, of a pleasurable external makeover. And as I emphasized in my introduction, subsequent generations have differentiated themselves in various ways from a seeming overarching parentalism that would correct rather than affirm. The demands of *Vergangenheitsbewältigung*, alluded to in Florian Illies's bestselling *Generation Golf* (2000), fade in comparison to the primal pleasures Illies experienced in the consumer artifacts of his coddled, apolitical youth during the 1980s.

Significantly, his work's consumerist component appeared to provide the blue print for a book published two years later, Katja Kullmann's autobiographical *Generation Ally*. In it she posited the American sitcom figure Ally McBeal as emblematic for young professional women like her. Their identification, though, is more complicated than simple pleasurable affirmation via consumer choices, since Ally exudes neurotic discomfort, although not the kind instilled by historical consciousness or prescriptive feminist mothers. Improved circumstances, as McBeal's example shows, can lead women to experience lack in even more acute ways than the previous generation, insofar as societal definitions of female success blend old and new expectations. When Ally bemoans the fact that she anticipated having both financial success and a family by age thirty, she articulates the downside of a meritocracy in which success as a bottom-line value highlights all the more individual failings. Her amusing neurotic tics, however, make it possible to wear lack as a badge of honor. One is simultaneously empowered by the possibility of having it all and comforted by the knowledge that others miss the mark as well.

Feldbusch, Postfeminism, and Girl Culture

In many ways the embodiment of women who have it all—professional success, the kind of idealized looks that set the bar for makeovers, as well as a boyfriend she would later marry and have a child with—Feldbusch may well have fed the Ally McBeal fetish among German women like Kullmann. The apparent lack of discomfort that Feldbusch displayed on the Johannes B. Kerner show suggests that feminist values do, in fact, mesh with a larger meritocracy's definitions of success for women. Her barbed observation to Schwarzer—"I earn my own money"—points back to Woolf's bottom-line economic independence, though the Hamburg condo she referenced could well point to neoliberalism's luxury lifestyling as well. Feldbusch has used the power she acquired in male domains, however, to a variety of ends, not all of them self-interested. In a perhaps implicit acknowledgement of Schwarzer's wider political arena, Feldbusch described arguing before the German Bundestag for the construction of "Veronas Casitas," a village that would support impoverished Bolivian children. Though her political cause clearly shores up the traditional domain of family values, it feels in sync with earlier German feminists' attempts to raise children under more optimal circumstances.[49] Yet her activism also clearly demonstrates how formerly disadvantaged social groups will not necessarily pursue oppositional ends once they gain access to power.[50] And of course the marks of second-class citizenry for women disappear all the more quickly if they are white, well-off, and heterosexual.

At the same time, Feldbusch's success—in moderating *peep!* as well as in a subsequent late night comedy show called *Verona's World,* in commercials for everything from spinach to shampoo, and in developing her own jewelry and lingerie and shoe collections—rests on a youthful, willfully naive persona that invites comparisons with girl culture of the 1990s. Tasker and Negra have underscored the centrality of girls and girlhood for postfeminism and the respite they provide from the difficulties of being a woman, as well as a dreary feminist demeanor.[51] In examining the extent to which 1990's girl culture aimed for more—tapping into a subversive pop art tradition and feminist theory—Katja Kauer, however, set the bar higher. Citing both German and Anglo-American examples such as Spice Girls, Britney Spears, Christina Aguilera, and Germany's most successful girl band No Angels, Kauer finds, however, little more than a traditionally stylized, fetishized femininity, however cheekily performed.[52]

But the Riot Grrrl movement, she argues, which was founded in 1994 by Kathleen Hanna of the punk bank Bikini Kill and included Courtney Love and her band Hole, combined spirited girlishness with more traditional feminist imperatives.[53] These included celebrating sexual autonomy and exposing sexual harassment. Even more double-edged in its effects was Courtney Love's mangy look—her messy blond hair, smeared makeup, and boots suggesting both the effects of sexual violence and an aggressive response to it. Kauer calls this particular form of femininity both castrated and castrating.[54] In this sense, Love exemplified the kind of complex performativity I invoked earlier, one that articulates overdetermined, contradictory, messages that display the uncertain boundaries between individual agency and cultural inscription.[55]

Riot Grrrl culture in the German-speaking world was also quite provocative, with its own variants of music and DIY (do-it-yourself) culture, all documented in *Lips. Tits. Hits. Power? Popkultur und Feminismus,* published in Austria in 1998. Up front, this volume taps into the power of unruly female bodies in a sketch opposite the title page in which a girl proclaims, "So . . . *let* them call you LOUD (good!) let them call you obnoxious (fine) just never let them *excuse* you as a dumb girl!" Editors Anette Baldauf and Katharina Weingartner link this aggressive version of girl culture, its Riot Grrrls, Gangsta Bitches, and Hardcore Dykes, with an activist gay and lesbian culture that had already reclaimed its own negative designations. In engaging in an "irritating game with the associations to which these terms remain tied in a heterosexist and misogynist history," they clearly pursued a semiotic approach to activism.[56]

Equally important, *Lips. Tits. Hits. Power?* aimed to make those who buy into girl culture aware of its feminist aims. If, as Baldauf and Weingartner emphasize, girl culture had transformed the second wave's slogan "the personal is political" into something spectacularly exhibitionistic, girl culture's in-your-face sexuality constituted more than a hedonistic celebration of sexual autonomy. Rather, it reacted against religious and biology-inspired forces that would contain women within a domestic sphere and control their reproductive capacities:

> Against the backdrop of a recent retreat into the private sphere and a growing prudishness, the Girls reacted to a regime that would, in the name of biology and religion, order women back into a domestic sphere, that quotes a femininity which is maternal: the family as the moral anchor of the nation, reducing social benefits for women and children, anti-abortion campaigns, homophobia, new abstinence and prudery, racism and violence, all of this alongside of the rise of an enforced ideal of beauty.[57]

Thus "irritating games" and semiotic sabotage are part of a larger aim to expose or blunt the effects of continued social inequities and oppressive patriarchal forms.

Against this raucous backdrop, Feldbusch appears at best as an innocuous, vanilla-flavored example of girl culture. Yet the manner in which she displayed her own "doll parts" during her encounter with Schwarzer constitutes its own kind of irritating game, though one with ambiguous effects. At one point during the show Feldbusch stripped off her jacket as Schwarzer spoke, thereby diverting attention to a cleavage more fully exposed by a simple V-neck vest. "Body versus brain" could not have been more blatantly displayed, even as agency and cultural inscription came together in complicated ways. Although Feldbusch has cultivated a willfully naïve manner, an article in the *Süddeutsche Zeitung* proclaims "self-irony" is her "strongest weapon."[58] Her unveiling gesture does indeed smack of self-aware detachment, as well as playful performativity as the modus operandi of a younger generation. More compellingly and less ironically, it also recalls Karneval's naked grab for power, but here on reconfigured terrain. In this case, Feldbusch combines talismans of male and female power—financial prosperity and conventional attractiveness—to trump the politics of an older generation. If exemplary of postfeminism's unironic embrace of neoliberal values, Feldbusch again presaged the emergence of many younger feminists, though their approaches and aims are less neatly categorized within

Figure 1.3. Still: Alice Schwarzer and Verona Feldbusch on the Johannes B. Kerner talk show, 2001.

either a postfeminist or girl-culture rubric. In the overview that follows of emergent feminists towards the end of the 2000s, it also becomes clear that teleological accounts of feminism, buttressed by generational binaries and wave-based rubrics articulated within the movement or by the media, belie much more diverse and sometimes overlapping voices.

Alpha/New German Girls and Popfeminism

For better or worse, Butler's performative framework, as well as manifold versions of girl culture, set the terms for the ensuing decade, which crested with vociferous debates among German feminists in the year 2008. Three volumes on feminism that appeared in 2006–07—Thea Dorn's *The New F-Class: How the Future Will Be Made by Women* (2006), Mirja Stöcker's *Das F-Wort: Feminismus ist sexy* (2007), and Sonja Eismann's anthology *Hot Topic: Popfeminismus heute* (2007)—however, seemed less motivated by animus for the preceding generation than that which Feldbusch put on display.[59] Only Dorn, whose work consisted of interviews with eleven professional and/or prominent German women about their relationship to feminism, demonstrably distanced herself from Schwarzer in her introduction by deeming *EMMA* hardly worthy of even cut-and-paste art projects.[60] Stöcker's and Eismann's anthologies, by contrast, pursued a strategy that emphasized women's ability to power up from the domain of popular culture, as well as compatibility among various feminist approaches.

Stöcker's introduction to *Das F-Wort* (The F-word) begins by underscoring the perennially vexed relationship between women and image, particularly when patriarchal mandates determine both a feminine ideal and a negative view of feminism. In this case "image" remains tied to the "collective F-Wort neurosis" that hinders women from identifying with feminist politics. Stöcker cites the familiar clichés of feminists as unsexy, man-hating militants, then turns the "F-Wort" in the direction of "facts" (is the girl gene pink? are feminists lesbians?), "feelings" (women still feel repressed, fat, more stressed than men), "fun" (what feminists want more of), and "future" (a horizon of multitasking for women who want career, family, intellectual challenges, and a husband who does housework). Overall, Stöcker's vaguely neoliberal approach makes one wonder whether other social movements have stalled because their proponents fretted about creating negative images while demanding equal rights. Sadly, this seems to be a particularly female problem. And the forces that create negative clichés in the first place set the agenda insofar as women feel obliged to emphasize a contrary image, evident in Stöcker's final fantasy of a brand of feminism both intelligent and sexy.[61]

Her volume, however, includes a more nuanced approach articulated by Jenny Warnecke. In "Das ist mir zu extrem! Eine Generationen-Studie" (That's too extreme for me: A generational study), she takes a web-inspired approach to the problem of negative images, suggesting a new "product design" that taps into the fluid spatiality of a virtual world and supplants hierarchy with compatibility. Warnecke highlights decentralized approaches to political action, evident in a "Bindestrich" or hyphenated feminism that enacts temporary, strategic alliances to react to problems as soon as they appear. Significantly, her examples—"difference-feminists," "equality-feminists," "radical-feminists," "lipstick-feminists," "media-feminists"—challenge the monolithic, ahistorical view of feminism that a newer generation had conjured for the purposes of differentiation.[62] Theoretically, too, hyphenated feminisms could find common ground with earlier forms of activism to achieve political ends, even as the notion of "collectivity" continually reshapes itself with each alliance.

Her emphasis on "male-compatibility," though, may be less about parity between the sexes than public relations problems, or the need to distance a new, improved feminism from the presumably man-hating tendencies of an earlier generation.[63]

The introduction to Sonja Eismann's edited volume *Hot Topic: Popfeminismus heute* echoes some of the strains evident in Dorn, Stöcker, and Warnecke, specifically an emphasis on fun and the importance of undermining cliché versions of feminism. But instead of obligatory jabs at Alice Schwarzer, Eismann underscores perennial problems, such as the gap between the salaries of men and women. The title of the volume, however, activates pop and consumer culture as the antidote to bluntly sociological disparities: "Hot Topic" is the name of an American chain store that sells rock-inspired clothing and accessories to teens, as well as a song by the group LaTigre intended to inspire feminists to continue the good fight. Eismann intentionally sets up an antagonism here between market wares and utopian ideals to launch a "popfeminism"—a term with which other emerging feminists were subsequently labeled—that adds a coolness quotient to an otherwise unmarketable social movement.[64]

If this approach sounds like another attempt to make feminism sexy, Eismann wants more than a feminism rendered palatable by popular culture. Instead she calls for feminist strategies to perforate pop: "It's not the perpetually fatigued feminine skin that has to be marketed in order to make the surface of pop palatable with an adequately tailored feminine surface of feminist principles. Rather, it should be the other way round, with pop culture being perforated and shook up by feminist strategies."[65] Eismann argues that this approach has been around for years in US media forms such as *Bust*, *Bitch*, and *Venus Zine* and also bemoans the fact that *Lips. Tits. Power?*, which highlighted Zines, girl bands, and other forms of DIY culture by women, had little impact on German feminism when it appeared in 1998.

Significantly, when she invokes third-wave feminism in the United States and its emphasis on identity politics over collective experiences, Eismann underscores her desire to retain the latter category for political ends and for simply being intriguing. Despite her emphasis on the power of pop, Eismann's attention to women's experiences and everyday reality suggests that bridges could exist between older and younger feminists, or what Warnecke calls Alice Schwarzer's "consciousness of political solidarity" and Verona Feldbusch's body-based "self-marketing strategies."[66] Eismann went on to cofound *Missy Magazine*, subtitled

Popkultur für Frauen, the same year. Pop culture notwithstanding, the first issue included an article on genital mutilation, as well as a brief reminiscence by Eismann's mother on the awfulness of wearing high-heeled shoes in her youth. Even though on page one the editorial team deemed *Missy* a new kind of magazine, both topics above could have just as easily appeared in *EMMA*.

Eismann's inclusiveness makes one wonder whether Germany had its own version of the third wave, documented by *Lips. Tits. Hits. Power?* but essentially unheralded as such, or if she and other emerging feminists were on the verge of calling it into being. Hester Baer has argued that the third wave, which complicated second-wave sexual politics surrounding beauty standards and sexual abuse with issues of empowerment, pleasure, and cultural production, did not occur to the same degree in Germany in the 1990s.[67] She cites the country's focus on national identity and reconstruction in the wake of unification, migration, and globalization as contributing factors. At the same time, Baer identities the "contradiction and hybridity" that characterizes the third wave as the binding principle between the second- and third-wave issues that characterize *Das F-Wort* and *Hot Topic*.[68] These include the beauty myth, abortion, birth control, sexual violence, DIY culture, girlzines, drag culture, and feminist-positive pornography. Her formulation suggests not so much a bridge as an equitable coexistence, a circumstance that makes defining metaphors such as waves or generational constructs superfluous.

If comparisons with the Anglo/American third wave in the 1990s underscore a certain belatedness, subsequent feminist voices that emerged in 2008 constitute less a "third wave," which implies overlap, than a "third way" that strives for an entirely new trajectory. Baer cites Stephanie Genz's "Third Way/ve" principle, which taps into neoliberal-style activism in the realm of consumer choices that become the sites for self-expression and agency, as a reference point for Jana Hensel and Elisabeth Raether's 2008 bestseller *Neue deutsche Mädchen* (New German Girls). Specifically, Baer points out that Hensel mirrors Genz's language in her introduction when she proclaims: "It's time to find a new way" that would renew feminist policies and ideas.[69] Unlike the overlap of second- and third-wave aims that Baer identifies in Eismann's and Stöcker's works, Hensel and Raether favor polemical bridge-burning over impartial contemporaneousness among varying feminist approaches.

A freelance journalist and author of the bestselling *Zonenkinder* (2002), which recounts an East German childhood, Hensel begins her introduction to *Neue deutsche Mädchen* lauding the basic pleasures of Starbucks coffee, a glass of wine, and a cigarette. In doing so she conjures a decidedly private domain. She then describes attending a press conference where Alice Schwarzer gave a speech to mark the thirtieth anniversary of *EMMA*. After finding a seat in the back, Hensel purposely tuned out during an introduction that labels Schwarzer a role model for her campaigns against genital mutilation in Africa, eating disorders, and prostitution. Though Schwarzer's feminist politics have long been criticized for collapsing differences among women, for maligning men tout court, and for unequivocally equating porn and prostitution with oppression and violence against women, Hensel articulates a more basic complaint. Bluntly put, these issues have nothing to do with her generation's lives: "What I had just heard, when I started to think about it, had nothing to do with my life. It seemed to me, a thirty-year-old woman in Germany, to lack even the remotest connection to my life."[70]

If exemplary of neoliberal individualism, her statement has less to do with possible "sites of expression" within given patriarchal categories than a more primitive articulation of selfhood. Henry's framework may be the more useful point of reference for highlighting generational differentiation among mothers and daughters as a recurring feminist trope. At the same time, Hensel's observation feels even more primal than postfeminists pursuing aims purposely antithetical to those of their forbears. To proclaim, more or less, "it's all about me!" resembles a teen's initial steps at differentiation, which necessarily lack the life experience that inspires alternate values and a new and politically viable agenda. Her statement also finds support in the most basic form of girlish empowerment: girls banding together to undermine maternal authority. Hensel describes her friendship with Raether in glowing terms—their "love at first sight" and night of drunken revelry at a Paris café—which may resemble a "sisterhood is powerful" brand of female solidarity, but clearly without prescriptive mothers. Not the oppression of women writ large, but rather whatever disturbs their more grounded reality, their pleasure in cigarettes and wine, is the problem.

To be sure, what Hensel calls the "normalcy" that now characterizes women's lives, like enjoying a drink in a bar without being harassed, would not be possible without the combatant tactics of earlier feminists. Though Raether gives Schwarzer more credit than Hensel does for such achievements, she, too, conjures her own comfort zone—writing in sweatpants in a Hamburg apartment—which separates her from the media fracas in Berlin. Yet Raether cannot resist at least one mean-spirited jab at Schwarzer in which she describes witnessing her purchase several outfits in a high-class Hamburg boutique. Not only does Schwarzer thus inhabit the same stylized world as younger women, but also her boutique markedly contrasts Raether and Hensel's less pretentious consumerism at Starbucks.

Wir Alphamädchen (We alpha girls), a second feminist bestseller from 2008 written by Meredith Haaf, Susanne Klingner, and Barbara Streidl, begins very pragmatically with the statement that anyone who believes in equality between the sexes is a feminist. The authors not only claim that label—unlike Hensel who associates it with being a know-it-all—they also profess their anger at the continued sexism they witness in their everyday lives.[71] Their purview thus extends beyond the *Neue deutsche Mädchen*'s problems with failed romances, recalcitrant men, and female insecurities to the kinds of issues that initially politicized second-wave feminists. These include less pay for women, everyday sexism, and reproductive rights. If one senses the possibility of bridge-building, however, the Alpha Girls' affiliations and repudiations require something more like a Venn diagram. While they critique postfeminist, ironic posing, they nonetheless want a sexy, fun feminism. Like Hensel and Raether, they explicitly distance themselves from feminism inflected either by left-wing politics or academic theory, and, in doing so, also attempt to ground themselves in a seemingly more authentic, everyday realm: "None of us had any experience of Gender Studies or a left-wing, alternative scene. Before the publication of this book we were completely unknown in the feminist establishment. Our feminism arises from the everyday and our journalistic critique of societal tendencies and debates."[72]

Had the Alpha or New German Girls, however, sat in on a gender seminar, they might have gained a more nuanced understanding of their otherwise monolithic view of earlier German feminisms.[73] In addition, they might have recognized not only common ground—evident in the Alpha Girls' attention to lower salaries for women, etc.—but also common blind spots. Critiques of the Alpha and New German Girls invariably begin with their use of the first-person plural, a problem of the second wave long recognized within the academic realms the Alpha and New German Girls distance themselves from. While the Alpha and New German Girls' rejection of Schwarzer's collective "we" echoes the rise of identity politics twenty-five years ago, they nonetheless resemble the educated, white women who had alienated minority women.[74] The authors of *Wir Alphamädchen* concede as much in their introductory ruminations: "Some will miss here the specific perspective of lesbians and immigrant women, which of course belong to the topic of 'women and society.' But it is not the intention of this book to unify all points of view."[75]

Ironically, academics such as Katja Kauer actually redeem the Alpha and New German Girls from some of their negative reception—specifically, charges of neoliberal individualism.[76] Invoking the pop literature concept of "sampling," Kauer compares their autobiographical voices to the "neue Innerlichkeit" (new subjectivity) literary movement of the 1970s, which enabled women in particular to voice their alienation from the patriarchy. She argues that Hensel and Raether's autobiographical approach channels feminist works such as Maxi Wander's East German classic, *Guten Morgen, du Schöne* (Good morning, beautiful; 1977). In addition, both pop literature of the 1990s and Germany's earlier feminist autobiographical voices, she argues, cultivate strong identification with their first-person-singular protagonists. Such singularity translates into a feminism that can only be represented in individual, not collective, struggles: "The strategy followed here emphatically separates itself from resignation in the face of societal structures and favors instead a positive, feminine formation of identity that is actually filtered through individual experiences rather than a strongly ideological feminism."[77] Along similar lines, Baer defines popfeminism as "an eclectic, generationally specific and largely individualistic resignification of feminism" that productively translates and adapts third-wave feminism a generation after it first emerged in North America.[78]

The concept of resignification, of course, underscores Judith Butler's influence on gender studies. Keeping her own self-critique in mind, as well as the contradictory messages that can emerge in a performative act, Hensel and Raether's approach warrants more analysis. Significantly, they also appear to "sample" American third-wave feminists Jennifer Baumgardner and Amy Richards. In Richards's introductory comments to their volume *Manifesta: Young Women, Feminism, and the Future* (2005), she describes how she and Baumgardner would "sneak time together every few weeks, sometimes over coffee, but mostly over glasses of wine that would grow into bottles of wine," a scenario which appears to have inspired Hensel and Raether's Starbucks and bar-based solidarity. Ironically, though, Richards and Baumgardner express deep admiration for Gloria Steinem, Alice Schwarzer's obvious American counterpart. (Richards worked as her assistant, and Baumgardner wrote for *Ms.* magazine.) Their more generous long view not only markedly contrasts the New German Girls, it raises the issues of intentionality in the process of resignification. As much as they reject earlier feminist models and voices, Hensel and Raether often unwittingly embrace them, even when "sampling" American third-wave feminists who presumably represent more evolved alternatives. From a psychological standpoint, their stance is actually quite a bit more interesting than an otherwise seemingly straightforward, intentional act of resignification. At the very least, it underscores the limits of theoretical paradigms that ignore the complex, fragmented factions that constitute identity.

As useful as connections to pop literature and East/West German variants of "neue Innerlichkeit" are, they also open up other thorny issues that extend beyond Hensel and Raether's overt antipathies towards and tacit embrace of earlier feminist forms. In her discussion of sampling and the popfeminism that emerged in the wake of Eismann's volume, Kauer cites Moritz Baßler's *Der deutsche Pop-Roman: Die neuen Archivisten* (2002), which examines the manner in which pop novels activate an archiving principle that draws on elements from a larger cultural archive. For Baßler, good pop neither affirms nor challenges the status quo but instead simply immerses itself in the semantic possibilities of a cultural encyclopedia.[79] It perhaps goes without saying that his apolitical approach may not be the most helpful reference point for popfeminist aims. Unlike the smug disdain that male pop protagonists quite consciously cultivate, for many women the status quo is simply not amusing enough for similar snide mockery. The difference, of course, has to do with unresolved issues of power, hierarchy, and emancipation. Strikingly, Baßler's volume and many others that attempt to define pop focus almost exclusively on works by men. If one considers the kinds of gendered variations that often fall outside of official histories, however, it becomes clear that some writers do indeed have larger, distinctly political aims in mind when they use pop culture to tamper with signifying processes. In this regard, invoking a longer history of literary and filmic attempts to make popular culture signify along new and gendered lines becomes important, even if it raises the always difficult-to-determine issue of what constitutes successful subversion.

In *Framed Visions: Popular Culture, Americanization, and the Contemporary German and Austrian Imagination* (1998), Gerd Gemünden examines American pop culture's influence on German and Austrian artists, including writer and Nobel Prize winner Elfriede Jelinek and filmmaker Monika Treut. He highlights both Jelinek's trenchant critique of media forms that perpetuate the patriarchy and Treut's queer utopia as hedge against traditional, identity-shaping polarities. Both artists' attention to porn is particularly relevant given that this arena continues to occupy feminists of all ages in Germany. If Jelinek's novel *Lust* (1989) exposes porn's savagely misogynist effects, Treut's films have documented performance artist Annie Sprinkle's empowering control of porn's mise en scene and staging. For Jelinek, there is no escape from sexist power structures and their incontrovertible damage; Treut, by constrast, underscores the malleability of power relations even within the most basic subject/object divide of porn, which need not continually reprise male dominance.

When performativity displays both sides of an equation, it reveals what Maria Stehle describes as "the tension between inscription and reaction, discipline and authentic rage, chaos and passion," as well as hysteria and neurosis alongside play and pleasure.[80] Her work on journalist, academic, rapper, and fashion designer Lady Bitch Ray deserves mention alongside Treut's and Jelinek's strategies. If her porn-inflected rap music circa 2007–08 provocatively resignified a female identity in a larger Turkish/German context, it also manifested the "prepubescent playfulness of performance art."[81] While less overtly contradictory than the agency/inscription divide, Lady Bitch Ray's performances, as well as those by popfeminist musicians like Peaches or the band Chicks on Speed, ultimately display, Stehle argues, a kind of messy awkwardness. She links this posture to an uncertainty about whether their powers lie "in a feminist reclamation of the body and sexuality or a male fantasy about such a reclamation."[82]

Compared to Jelinek, Treut, and Lady Bitch Ray and their more radical aims, Hensel and Raether's "sampling" of earlier feminist forms feels both unintended and paltry. Yet it, too, compels attention for combining the act of resignification with emphatic bridge-burning. If one senses the developmentally normal impulse towards psychic, but not necessarily substantive, differentiation from parents, its emphatic force again hints at a culturally specific backdrop. By this I mean a historical need to correct rather than affirm fueled by half a century of working through a calamitous history. Likewise one senses the earlier feminist drive for autonomy that Ferree traced over a century and a half manifesting itself, but in a manner that situates autonomy in relation to older feminists, not the patriarchy. And within a larger, global context, such separation reveals the kudzu-like effects of neoliberal individualism spreading into and suffocating an earlier generation's political aims. Regardless of which social, cultural, or historical factors one emphasizes, however, the blatantly contradictory gesture of overt rejection and tacit embrace evident in works such as Hensel and Raether's demands a psychological framework as well.[83] Though totalizing, essentialist psychological paradigms may often be less helpful given the varieties of feminism over time, attention to contradictions in the struggle for an autonomous or salutary selfhood remains an important consideration. Not only could it move us beyond the "success/failure" so often enacted to assess feminist activism, it also situates "reception"—here of feminist aims—in an interior rather than a larger socio/cultural realm. And when literature in particular imagines such internal realms, the forces revealed there open up the parameters of feminist discourse insofar as they resist easy binaries, teleological trajectories, and quiescent endpoints.

The Maternal Position

Schwarzer's various and contradictory responses to the debates of 2008 deserve mention in this regard if one understands quiescent endpoints in terms of solidarity despite differing feminist aims and approaches. She and several *EMMA* journalists have repeatedly asserted that feminism was never a unified field but instead has always been characterized by competing concerns.[84] Despite a (hypothetically) welcoming stance towards new forms of feminism, Schwarzer nonetheless critiqued the mad Mädchen of 2008 in ways that bespeak the psychological complexities of the maternal position, both its magnanimity and need for affirmation and respect. On a purely analytic level, she, too, critiqued the individualist nature of the Alpha and New German Girls' approach, which she termed "wellness feminism." This label conjures a narrower frame that reduces global concerns to struggles around family, work, and relationship problems.[85] A July/August 2008 issue of *EMMA* took a dim view of girl culture, evident in Vera Schröder's "Feminismus light" essay.[86] She argued that German "Girlietum," embodied by singer Luci van Org and VJs Heike Makatsch and Enie van de Meiklokjes, had very little to do with the more critical, politically effective perspectives of the Riot Grrrl movement in the United States.[87]

Schwarzer's strategies also included what seemed like a discursive retrenching. Numerous issues of *EMMA* over the last decade have reprised women's part in the student movement and feminism's subsequent emergence in Germany. An entire 2008 issue included a series of articles on the movement, beginning with an essay by Schwarzer titled "My personal '68" (in German). With its plethora of black and white images—many iconic—the issue resembled the print media's version of a heritage film, or an attempt to reproduce an earlier era both faithfully and nostalgically. And rather than reevaluating the legacy of 1968 for women, the point seemed to be sandbagging feminist aims that countered another era's imperatives. At the same time, *EMMA's* special 2008 issue on 1968 enacted a still crucial, if dated, feminist aim to make women's experiences visible. This impulse seems particularly necessary for women's part in the student movement. With the exception of Ute Kätzel's *Die 68erinnen. Porträt einer rebellischen Frauengeneration,* first published in 2002 and expanded in 2008, few comprehensive historical overviews of this period exist.[88] Barbara Becker-Cantarino has argued that women are largely absent from "personal and collective memorials, critical evaluations, and historical accounts" of this era, which she links to media distortion, unnegotiated gender issues, and myths of traditional femininity.[89]

If *EMMA's* historical spotlighting felt out of sync with a more contemporary feminist belief in women's ability to manipulate the terms of their own visibility, Schwarzer also underscored the difficulties in attaining this goal. Some of the images used up front in her essay—one of topless female students at a demonstration and another of more topless protesters on the cover of a magazine—depict women performatively displaying their bodies to attain political ends. The fact that one of these images landed on a magazine cover, however, demonstrates how quickly a subversive gesture gets marketed. In this case, male editors deeply invested in the link between nipple visibility and the profit margin, as Schwarzer asserts, neutralized an otherwise political act. Similarly, one of Schwarzer's autobiographical asides makes it clear why she focused on more straightforward political discourse. When she appeared at a demonstration sporting the Bonnie Parker look of the moment, her audience yelled "hey Bonnie" and largely ignored the content of her speech. As she observed, "I never again attended a demonstration looking overtly fashionable."[90]

Yet other *EMMA* articles in the first half of 2008 very pointedly grappled with the emergence of a new generation and sometimes magnanimously attempted to build bridges, evident in its May/June special issue. It featured third-wave voices from the United States, as well as an interview between Gloria Steinem and Bikini Kill founder and lead singer Kathleen Hanna. The issue's lead essay, "The Third Wave?," was penned by Lisa Jervis, founder and coeditor of *Bitch. EMMA's* introductory summation underscores how Jervis views the third wave as the logical continuation of the second and that divisions among generations are a powerful weapon against women. Jervis's essay itself argues that such divisions are construed in highly superficial terms: playful, pop culture–obsessed younger women against the hard-core agenda of older women. She points out, though, that playful elements exist in both factions, evident in protests of the Miss America pageant in 1968 and subsequent guerilla theater groups such as Ladies Against Women or the Radical Cheerleaders. And Riot-Grrrl groups, she argues, retained similarities to the consciousness-raising groups of the 1970s. Beyond building cross-generational bridges, Jervis emphasized the crucial role of contradiction for advancing feminist aims: "Feminism has profited from internal debates and differences of opinion and through them has evolved. Our many differences and often oppositional views are what propel us forward, what make our theories more precise, our strategies more refined, in a comprehensive dismantling of the racist, capitalist patriarchy."[91]

As I stated in my introduction to this volume, the German context in fact offers a wide range of novels and films that vividly depict the impact of feminism in all its hybrid forms, and it is precisely this imaginary domain that could add rich dimensions to wearying debates. The stories that women tell themselves about social inequities, as well as about the competing, feminist models for correcting them, are anything but predictable. Many of the works I will examine in this volume depict female protagonists who exhibit the complicated mesh between psychic life and concrete action.[92] In doing so, they reveal a selfhood not always ruled by the autonomy underpinning second-wave selfhood or the playful pleasure principle of more performance-oriented approaches. Attention to mother-daughter constellations in subsequent chapters reveals generational divides that go beyond straightforward, volitional rejection, as well as differentiation that sometimes takes highly idiosyncratic form. The complicated, not always pleasurable role of fantasy often comes into play in this regard, since it reveals not only salutary powers, but also cracks and fissures, or the weight of contradictory cultural forms that sometimes create untenable, delusional subject positions. Alternately, fantasy in some of the works I will analyze becomes an important domain for reconceptualizing feminism along alternative lines. With this goal in mind, *Mad Mädchen* intends to display how the mother/daughter bond, if understood not in terms of biology or simply as a template for recent feminist conflicts but rather as a complex negotiation, provides a metaphorical framework and potential salve for feminist collectives.

Notes

1. See Anne Dünnebier, "Die Stadt, der Turm, die Frauen." *FrauenMediaTurm*, 1994, http://www.frauenmediaturm.de/frauenmediaturm/bayenturm/geschichte/.
2. Journalist and FrauTV moderator Lisa Ortgies served briefly as chief editor of *EMMA* in 2008, after which Schwarzer took over the post again.
3. Alice Schwarzer, "Ein Turm für Frauen alleine." *FrauenMediaTurm*, July 1994. http://www.frauenmediaturm.de/frauenmediaturm/publikationen/ein-turm-fuer-frauen-allein/.
4. In 2008, Northrhine-Westfalia minister president Jürgen Rüttgers (CDU) promised the FMT 210,000 Euros yearly; financial support grew precarious, however, when he was not reelected. Politicians Hannelore Kraft (SPD) and Sylvia Löhrmann (Greens) argued for reducing the yearly funding to 70,000, which would have threatened the continued existence of the FMT. Ironically, CDU politician and Federal Minister for Family Kristina Schröder, whom Schwarzer had pointedly critiqued for lacking empathy towards women and their concerns, came through with the yearly 150,000 Euros to maintain the archive. See Barbara Schmid, "Emanzipation. Unter Frauen," 30 January 2012, http://www.spiegel.de/spiegel/print/d-83774689.html. Schröder explained her unexpected decision in straightforward terms: "I still think a lot of radical feminist ideas are wrong. But state support should never be understood as partisanship. I studied sociology and was very happy that my university had sources on gender theory. The fact that I ultimately couldn't support a lot of its ideas is a whole other question." See "Gleichstellung. 'Ziemlich lässig,'" 27 February 2012, http://www.spiegel.de/spiegel/print/d-84162299.html.. Schröder even penned a recent book titled *Danke, emanzipiert sind wir schon selber! Abschied vom Diktat der Rollenbilder* (Thanks, we're already emancipated: Farewell to dictated role models) (Munich: Piper, 2012). Her funding constitutes one of very few shows of support for Schwarzer and the type of 1970's feminism she is perceived as embodying.
5. Schwarzer, "Ein Turm für Frauen alleine."
6. See Dünnebier, "Die Stadt, der Turm, die Frauen."
7. Yvonne Tasker and Diane Negra, *Interrogating Postfeminism: Gender and the Politics of Popular Culture* (Durham: Duke University Press, 2007).
8. Myra Marx Ferree emphasizes these gains in the first pages of *Varieties of Feminism: German Gender Politics in Global Perspective* (Stanford: Stanford University Press, 2012).
9. Tasker and Negra, *Interrogating Postfeminism*, 7.

10. Ibid., 10.
11. David Harvey, *A Brief History of Neoliberalism* (Oxford: Oxford University Press, 2005), 42. Following Harvey's argument, Hester Baer argues that neoliberal values that enhance corporate wealth, redistribute wealth upward, and dismantle the welfare state gained traction in Germany after the Wall came down, despite strong trade unions and Germany's "longstanding emphasis on social welfare policies" ("German Feminism in the Age of Neoliberalism: Jana Hensel and Elisabeth Raether's *Neue deutsche* Mädchen," *German Studies Review* 35.2 [May 2012], 359. She further cites Raewyn Connell about the negative effects of neoliberalism on the welfare state, which redistributes income from women to men and imposes more unpaid work on women as those who care for the old and the sick (ibid., 359).
12. See Christian Marazzi, "Neoliberalism is Destroying Europe," *The Guardian*, 14 September 2010, https://www.theguardian.com/commentisfree/2010/sep/14/neoliberal-europe-union-austerity-crisis.
13. Angela McRobbie, *The Aftermath of Feminism: Gender, Culture and Social Change* (London: Sage, 2009), 2.
14. Hester Baer provides an excellent overview of McRobbie's and other scholars' critiques of neoliberalism on feminism in "Redoing Feminism Within and Outside the Neoliberal Academy," *Women in German Yearbook* 30 (2014), 197–208.
15. Alexandra Merley Hill, "Motherhood as Performance: (Re) Negotiations of Motherhood in Contemporary German Literature," *Studies in 20th and 21st Century Literature* 35:1 (Winter 2011), 74.
16. See Eva Hermann, *Das Eva Prinzip: Für eine neue Weiblichkeit* (Munich: Goldmann, 2006).
17. Quoted in Christina Scharff, *Repudiating Feminism: Young Women in a Neoliberal World.* (London: Routledge, 2012), 108.
18. See Frank Schirrmacher, *Das Methusalem-Komplott* (Munich: Karl Blessing Verlag, 2004); *Minimum. Vom Vergehen und Neuerstehen unserer Gemeinschaft* (Munich: Karl Blessing, 2006).
19. Shirrmacher, *Minimum*, 142.
20. Carrie Smith-Prei, "Satirizing the Private as Political: 1968 and Postmillennial Family Narratives," *Women in German Yearbook* 25 (2009), 89.
21. Other scholars, such as Hester Baer and Christina Scharff, cite additional statistics that underscore German women's less than optimal circumstances. Baer underscores the fact that German women earn 23 percent less than men for the same labor; they are 47 percent more likely to work part-time rather than full-time; only 2 percent of executive positions are occupied by women; and 14 percent of women with one child, as well as 6 percent of women with two or more children, hold full-time jobs. See "Sex, Death, and Motherhood in the Eurozone," *World Literature Today* 86:3 (May 2012), 59–65. Scharff cites tax benefits in Germany for married, heterosexual cou-

ples with a single earner—the "Ehegattensplitting" model—that discourages dual-earner households (*Repudiating Feminisms,* 18).
22. In an opinion piece titled "Sexism is Germany's Hidden Secret," Kate Brady cited Angela Merkel's nickname "Mutti" and a *Stuttgarter Zeitung* article celebrating her sixtieth birthday with the title "From Kohl's Little Girl to the Nation's Mommy." She recounts that in early 2015, Free Democrats leader Katja Suding appeared on television, and a cameraman made the decision to pan downwards for a shot of her legs, which caused an uproar. Brady also mentioned, among other examples, Ferrero Deutschland's Kinder Surprise eggs, which include a pink one only for girls and others dubbed "World Cup Footballer" egg and "Footballer's Wife" egg. Women Talk Online, 10 February, 2015, http://blogs.dw.com/womentalkonline/2015/02/10/opinion-sexism-is-germanys-hidden-secret/.
23. To be sure, parity between the sexes is still a long way off in other western countries. Rory Dicker and Alison Piepmeier do some mathematical calculations in the introduction to their volume *Catching a Wave: Reclaiming Feminism for the 21st Century* (Boston: Northeastern University Press, 2003). Citing the slow increase of women in top professional positions over the preceding twenty-five years, they quote Susan Estrich's observation that "at the rate we're going, it will be another 270 years before women achieve parity as top managers in corporations and 500 years before we achieve equality in Congress" (4). See also Susan Estrich, *Sex and Power* (New York: Riverhead Books, 2000), 72.
24. Ferree, *Varieties of Feminism,* 5.
25. Ibid., 30.
26. Ibid., 51.
27. Quoted in Ferree, *Varieties of Feminism,* 60–61.
28. Catherine MacKinnon, *Feminism Unmodified: Discourses on Life and Law* (Boston: Harvard University Press, 1987).
29. Ferree, *Varieties of Feminism,* 8.
30. Jo Reger offers a useful overview of the various origins that scholars have identified for the third wave: Lynn Chancer's call for a "third wave" feminism in 1991; Rebecca Walker calling herself the "third wave" in her introduction to the anthology *To Be Real* (1995); the uprising of the Riot Grrrl movement as a reconceptualization of feminism along punk-infused, generational lines; and the challenge women of color articulated towards the second wave for not being racially and ethnically inclusive. See *Different Wavelengths: Studies of the Contemporary Women's Movement* (New York: Routledge, 2005), xxii.
31. Judith Butler, *Gender Trouble: Feminism and the Subversion of Identity* (New York: Routledge, 1999).
32. Schwarzer articulated this position in her seminal work *Der kleine Unterschied und seine großen Folgen* [The small difference and its big conse-

quences] (Frankfurt am Main: Fischer, 1975), which asserted that "compulsory heterosexuality" was not natural but cultural and a product of power relations. Overall she argued for women's autonomy in economic and sexual terms.
33. Butler, *Gender Trouble,* xvii–xviii.
34. Ibid., xxi.
35. Ibid., ix.
36. Ibid., xxv. Along similar lines, Butler argues in *Excitable Speech* that although rebellious speech, which takes the risk of making sexist forms resignify via citation and shifting contexts, potentially forces change, what actually results remains "out of control." *Excitable Speech: A Politics of the Performative* (New York: Routledge, 1997), 15.
37. Butler, *Gender Trouble* (1999), xiv.
38. Ibid., xxvi.
39. Ibid., xxiv.
40. Ferree, *Varieties of Feminism,* 180.
41. Judith Butler, *Excitable Speech: A Politics of the Performative* (New York: Routledge, 1997).
42. Ibid., 10.
43. Ibid., 15.
44. Sabine Hark has traced the reception of *Gender Trouble* among German academic feminists and the anxieties it stoked regarding how to define gender. She argues that what was coded as a conflict between different feminist generations served to displace issues of queerness and their impact on gender studies. See "Disputed Territory: Feminist Studies in Germany and Its Queer Discontents," *Amerikastudien/American Studies* 46.1 (2001), 87–103.
45. Astrid Henry, *Not My Mother's Sister: Generational Conflict and Third-Wave Feminism* (Bloomington: Indiana University Press, 2004), 2.
46. Henry notes that the first wave of feminism covered a long enough period of history and that multiple generations of women participated in it, particularly in prosuffrage families in which grandmothers, mothers, and daughters all strove for this common goal (ibid., 4).
47. Schwarzer's association with *Bild Zeitung,* however, proved to be controversial. Journalist Peter Disch pointedly queried, "But is Schwarzer as renowned feminist allowed to have anything to do with *Bild Zeitung* of all places? Can a woman who once spearheaded a campaign against pornography deal with a rag that presents a naked woman each day on page one? That shows naked videos of Bild-Girls on its Internet site right next to commercial fare from porn sites? That outed celebrities like actress Sibel Kikeli for making sex films? That freely interpreted basic journalistic practices in its headlines regarding Kachelmann?" See "Alice Schwarzer verkauft ihre Seele," *Badische Zeitung,* 5 September 2010, http://www.badische-zeitung.de/debatte-x3x/alice-schwarzer-verkauft-ihre-seele--35085994.html.

48. Sigrid Weigel, "'Generation' as Symbolic Form: On the Genealogical Discourse of Memory since 1945," *Germanic Review* 77:4 (fall 2002), 275.
49. Feldbusch's choice to become "Verona Pooth" when she married a few years later, however, quite clearly embraces tradition, and unlike girl culture's embrace of porn, she also eventually left *peep!* when it became too pornographic for her tastes.
50. Leslie Heywood and Jennifer Drake identify this pitfall in the introduction to *Third Wave Agenda: Being Feminist, Doing Feminism* (Minneapolis: University of Minnesota Press, 1997, 12): "Striving for success and equality with white men that second-wave feminism made possible, white women in particular often became so focused on individual achievement and success that we became wholehearted supporters of the very structures we most want to contest."
51. Tasker and Negra, *Interrogating Postfeminism*, 18. They even cite *Ally McBeal*, among other pop-culture franchises such as *The Princess Diaries* and the television show *Mean Girls*, for highlighting girls and girlhood.
52. She writes: "The female singers and Girl-Band stars never play an active role in their videos. They loll about lasciviously for an imagined male spectator, display themselves in erotic poses and choreography and trill and sob their songs into the camera. This display of femininity as desired object hardly ever varies and can be found in almost every commercial video of pop girl bands or pop singers." Katja Kauer, *Popfeminismus! Fragezeichen! Eine Einführung* (Berlin: Frank & Timme, 2009), 10–11.
53. Maria Stehle cites German versions of Riot Grrrl bands, which include Die Braut, Mobylettes, the Lassie Singers, the Lemonbabies, as well as the mainstream oriented Tic Tac Toe and Lucilectric. She sees a continuation of their innovative and avant-garde approaches in contemporary bands such as Peaches and Chicks on Speed. See "Pop-Feminist Music in Twenty-First Century Germany: Innovations, Provocations, and Failures," *Journal of Popular Music Studies* 25.2 (2013), 222–23.
54. Along similar lines, Christina Mohr has argued that Riot Grrrl bands donned patriarchal trappings of beauty not to support the values of superficial lifestyling, but "rather in order to look like broken Barbie dolls." See "Wie sich's für ein normales Mädchen anfühlt," in *Madonna und wir. Bekenntnisse,"* ed. Kerstin Grether and Sandra Grether (Frankurt am Main: Suhrkamp, 2008), 56.
55. Heywood and Drake also pay particular attention to "Doll Parts" in the introduction to *Third Wave Agenda*, identifying in Love a feminist sensibility that "combines the contradictory aspects of [feminist] discourse[s] in a way that recognizes and makes use of complications that young women working within dominant culture face today" (5–6).
56. See Anette Baldauf and Katharina Weingartner, eds. *Lips. Tits. Hits. Power? Popkultur und Feminismus* (Vienna: Folio, 1998), 18: "[Sie] treiben ihr irritie-

57. Baldauf and Weingartner, *Lips. Tits. Hits. Power?*, 18: "Vor dem Hintergrund eines neuerlichen Rückzug ins Private und einer wachsenden Prüderie reagierten die Girls auf ein Regime, das Frauen im Namen von Religion und Biologie in den häuslichen Bereich zurückbeordert und eine Weiblichkeit zitiert, die Mütterlichkeit heißt: Familie als moralischer Rettungsanker der Nation, Kürzung von Sozialhilfe für Frauen und Kinder, Anti-Abtreibungskampagnen, Homophobie, Neue Abstinenz und Prüderie, Rassismus und Gewalt, all das bei anhaltender Hochkonjunktur zwanghafter Schönheitsideale."
58. See "Meine naive Art ist eine Marktlücke." *Süddeutsche Zeitung*, 22 April 2008, http://www.sueddeutsche.de/leben/verona-pooths-geburtstag-meine-naive-art-ist-eine-marktluecke-1.188488.
59. Thea Dorn, *Die neue F-Klasse. Wie die Zukunft von Frauen gemacht wird* (Hamburg: Piper, 2007); Mirja Stöcker, ed. *Das F-Wort: Feminismus ist sexy* (Königstein/Taunus: Ulrike Helmer Verlag, 2007).
60. A subsequent book by Miriam Gebhardt, *Alice im Niemandsland. Wie die deutsche Frauenbewegung die Frauen verlor* (Munich: Verlagsgruppe Random House, 2012), devoted itself entirely to Schwarzer's part in undermining German feminism's ability to evolve. As she argues at the beginning of her volume: "Today the women's movement is programmatically unimportant, organizationally invisible, and shrunk down to one symbolic figure. Its substantive thinking plays out in academic enclaves and blogs, which remains its reflexive twitch whenever a societal/political challenge always finds the same feminist answer—'die Antwort' by Alice Schwarzer" (9). Though society has become more multivoiced and multifaceted, she argues, the women's movement still hides itself behind a "matriarch" (11).
61. As Butler emphasizes in her 1997 work, *Excitable Speech*, "[The] ambivalent structure at the heart of performativity implies that, within political discourse, the very terms of resistance and insurgency are spawned in part by the powers they oppose" (40).
62. Scharff argues, "The new German feminists offer simplistic, generalizing, and historically inaccurate portrayals of 1970s feminism that is, of course always referred to in the singular." See *Repudiating Feminism*, 121.
63. Kauer cites male compatibility as one of the defining characteristics of emergent feminist forms in Germany—i.e., that men should be made into feminist accomplices, not automatically viewed as agents of the patriarchy. See Katja Kauer, *Popfeminismus! Fragezeichen! Eine Einführung* (Berlin: Frank & Timme Verlag, 2009), 136.
64. In "'Knaller-Sex für alle': Popfeminist Body Politics in Lady Bitch Ray, Charlotte Roche, and Sarah Kuttner," Carrie Smith-Prei links popfeminism to a longer historical, avant-garde aesthetic dating to the 1960s, which reemerged in 1990's pop novels. This approach "recodes signs of popular cul-

ture through quotations, pastiche, and cut-up methods, resignifying and redefining the original subject in a manner that reflects, exposes, and even problematizes superficial aspects of everyday reality." In *Studies in 20th and 21st Century Literature* 35:1 (Winter 2011), 21. In particular, the potentially problematic arenas of porn, fashion, and rap provide third-wave and/or popfeminists enticing opportunities for making pop culture resignify along feminist lines.

65. Sonja Eismann, *Hot Topic: Popfeminismus heute* (Mainz: Ventil Verlag, 2007), 10: "Nicht die viel strapazierte Haut muss wieder zu Markte getragen werden, um der Oberfläche Pop mit einer adäquat zugerichteten femininen Oberfläche das Prinzip Feminismus schmackhaft zu machen, sondern umgekehrt sollte Popkultur durch feministische Strategien perforiert und erschüttert werden."

66. Jenny Warnecke, "Das ist mir zu extrem! Eine Generationen-Studie," in *Das F-Wort. Feminismus ist sexy*, ed. Mirja Stöcker (Königstein/Taunus: Ulrike Helmer Verlag, 2007), 38.

67. Heywood and Drake define third-wave feminism in these terms in the introduction to *Third Wave Agenda*. Unlike postfeminists who distance themselves from the second wave, they view the second and third waves of feminism as "neither incompatible or opposed" (3).

68. Hester Baer, "German Feminism in the Age of Neoliberalism: Jana Hensel and Elisabeth Raether's *Neue deutsche Mädchen*," *German Studies Review* 35.2 (May 2012), 365.

69. Ibid., 371.

70. Jana Hensel and Elizabeth Raether, *Neue deutsche Mädchen* (Reinbek bei Hamburg: Rowohlt, 2008), 14: "Das soeben Gehörte schien, wenn ich nun noch einmal darüber nachdachte, mit meinem Leben nichts zu tun zu haben. Es schien mir, einer dreißigjährigen Frau in Deutschland, nicht einmal mehr ansatzweise etwas zu tun zu haben."

71. Hensel has stated her feelings about the label "feminist": "Honestly I don't like it that much. It sounds like movement, struggle, a bad conscience and being a know-it-all. I avoid it as often as possible." See Susanne Klingner, "Neue deutsche Mädchen im Interview," Mädchenmannschaft, April 2008, http://maedchenmannschaft.net/neue-deutsche-madchen-im-interview/.

72. Meredith Haaf, Susanne Klingner, and Barbara Streidel, *Wir Alphamädchen. Warum Feminismus das Leben schöner macht* (Hamburg: Hoffmann und Campe Verlag, 2008), 9. In 2007 Streidl, Klingner, and Haaf founded the feminist blog Mädchenmannschaft, partly as a continuation of the *Wir Alphamädchen* project and also inspired by the weblog feministing.com. It offers offers daily critical commentary on German politics and media and has been linked by German journalists to feminist bloggers in the United States who have shifted the third wave to digital form. Between 2010 and 2012 all three left the blog, ostensibly because of their collaborators' un-

willingness to work with heterosexual men and critical stance towards perspectives limited to whites. Currently the blog's mission statement cites its desire to write about things that "make us happy or that make the hairs on the back of our necks stand up" and describes the blog itself as both forum and playground for those interested in a better, more just society. Combining anger and playfulness, the blog would seem to straddle second- and third-wave impulses, also evident in both a critique of men and a more postcolonial problematizing of whiteness. The overall tone of the mission statement is one of cheerful, unconflicted hybridity.

73. In separating herself from other feminists, Jana Hensel declares of herself and her coauthor of *Neue deutsche Mädchen,* "Elisabeth and I, like Charlotte Roche, come from life, not the gender seminar." See Klingner, "Neue deutsche Mädchen im Interview."

74. In her introduction to *Different Wavelengths: Studies of the Contemporary Women's Movement,* Jo Reger challenges the notion that women of color were not present in second-wave feminism because of racism. This perspective, she argues, "ignores the (albeit marginalized) contributions of women of color in building organizations, networks, and communities in the 1960s and 1970s" (xix).

75. Streidel, Klingner, and Haaf, *Wir Alphamädchen,* 8: "Manche werden hier vielleicht die spezifischen Perspektiven von lesbischen Frauen oder Migrantinnen vermissen, die selbstverständlich zum Thema 'Frauen und Gesellschaft' gehören. Doch dieses Buch hat nicht den Anspruch, sämtliche Sichtweisen zu vereinbaren." Hester Baer provides a comprehensive critique of their disinterest in issues of race and ethnicity, which enabled a third-wave critique of white feminism during the 1990s. She writes, "Already in their introductory chapters, Hensel and Raether define the feminist subject as white, ethnically German, upper middle class, and heterosexual, and they subscribe to an ethnocentric worldview that at times appears to be racist." See Baer, "German Feminism in the Age of Neoliberalism," 368.

76. Christina Scharff, for instance, observes, "The new German feminists do not reject feminism outright, but often render their analyses and claims less forceful through the uptake of individualist statements. Indeed, on a more general level, [*Neue deutsche Mädchen* and *Wir Alphamädchen*] do not offer much in terms of a new feminist politics" (*Repudiating Feminism,* 117).

77. Kauer, *Popfeminismus!,* 73: "Die Strategie, die hier verfolgt wird, geht ganz klar ab von einer Resignation vor gesellschaftlichen Verhältnissen zugunsten einer neuen und positiven weiblichen Identitätsbildung, die jedoch mehr durch die eigenen Erfahrungen gefiltert sein soll als durch eine stark ideologisch feministische Prägung."

78. Baer, "German Feminism in the Age of Neoliberalism," 357.

79. He writes, "It is not about words but rather the importation and processing of already existing, loaded encyclopedic words, expressions, discursive

connections and ways of imagining in literature." See Moritz Baßler, *Der deutsche Pop-Roman. Die neuen Archivisten* (München: Verlag C. H. Beck, 2002), 186.
80. Stehle, "Pop-Feminist Music," 235.
81. Ibid., 236.
82. Ibid., 235. Lady Bitch Ray's reception clearly underscored the difficulty of escaping cultural inscription. As Stehle argues, journalists were often unable or unwilling to look beyond the Turkish aspect of her identity, which some critiqued for its presumed essentialism. As a result the "racialized and gendered molds and clichés [she] was fighting against kept haunting the conversations about her work and her 'character.'" See Stehle, "Pop, Porn, and Rebellious Speech. Feminist Politics and the Multi-Media Performances of Elfriede Jelinek, Charlotte Roche, and Lady Bitch Ray" *Feminist Media Studies* 12.2 (2012), 243.
83. Scharff ends her study on neoliberalism and feminism with a similar observation: "There seems to be a need for further research that explores how . . . tensions are experienced, negotiated, and lived out on a psychic level. Such research may be conducted from a psychosocial perspective to trace the psychic landscapes which emerge from the imperative to be self-reliant in a context where structural inequities continue to shape the gender order, but tend to be disarticulated and individualized" (*Repudiating Feminism*, 123).
84. See, e.g., Barbara Sichtermann, "Ohne Kampf geht nichts," *EMMA*, September/October 2008, 42–44. She describes feminists of the late 1960s and early 1970s as "ausgesprochen vielstimmig" or very much a diverse group. Sichterman also characterizes them in terms that speak to contemporary feminists' negative perceptions of this early generation—i.e., as "hedonistisch, experimentierfreudig, und hocherotisch" (hedonistic, experimental, and highly erotic) ("Ohne Kampf," 43–44).
85. While receiving the Ludwig-Börne-Preis in 2008, Schwarzer gave a speech in the Paulskirche in which she distanced herself from the new wellness feminism by observing that its proponents think, in the name of feminism, "only about their own needs and these hot men and careers." She added, "It's not my personal circumstances that constitute the world but instead the world constitutes my personal circumstances." See "Wider den Wellness-Feminismus," *Süddeutsche Zeitung*, 17 May 2010.,http://www.sueddeutsche.de/kultur/ludwig-boerne-preis-fuer-alice-schwarzer-wider-den-wellness-feminismus-1.193970.
86. Kauer offers a small hedge against this critique, arguing, "Even if Girlies are not dyed-in-the-wool feminists, they were still a response to the antifeminist backlash of the 1980s that, particularly in the US, rehashed the feminine ideal of the 1950s. This bourgeois feminine ideal manifested itself in coyness, reserve, a moderate relationship to sex, and an innocent, marriage-oriented sexiness. This is precisely what Girlies defended against,

and it is no wonder that the Mädchen concept was developed as a positive alternative to the bourgeois woman." *(Popfeminismus!* 20).
87. Vera Schröder, "Feminismus Light," *EMMA* (July/August 2008), 28.
88. See Uta Kätzel, *Die 68erinnen. Porträt einer rebellischen Frauengeneration* (Berlin: Rowohlt, 2002). Barbara Becker-Cantarino has observed that making women visible in history was a relatively successful project of 1970's feminist historians. Yet Germany's contemporary memory culture appears to have difficulty finding a place for the roots of feminism: "Equality feminism as a social movement promoted and supported mostly by women does not readily fit into the traditional categories of German national history and present memorial culture in Germany." See "The Politics of Memory: What Happened to Second-Wave Feminism in Germany?" *German Life and Letters* 67.4 (October 2014), 614.
89. Becker-Cantarino, "The Politics of Memory," 605.
90. Alice Schwarzer, "Mein persönliches 68." *EMMA*, May/June 2008, 77.
91. Lisa Jervis, "Die dritte Welle?" *EMMA*, May/June 2008, 45. In "Goodbye to Feminism's Generational Divide," the foreword to *We Don't Need Another Wave: Dispatches from the Next Generation of Feminists* (Emeryville, CA: Seal Press, 2006, 17), Melody Berger makes the same argument: "We all want the same thing: To borrow from bell hooks's phrase, we want gender justice. We may not all agree on exactly what it looks like or how to get it. We should never expect to agree. Feminism has always thrived on and grown from internal discussions and disagreements." In a similar vein, Jennifer Baumgardner expressed a desire for solidarity among feminists in her introductory remarks to *Manifesta: Young Women, Feminism, and the Future* (New York: Farrar, Straus and Giroux, 2000), xx: "Although I wish the Girlie feminists in this book would organize as well as they onanize, they have created a joyful culture that makes being an adult woman who calls herself a feminist seem thrilling, sexy, and creative (rather than scary, back-biting, or a one-way ticket to bitterness and the poorhouse)." In addition, Baumgardner and Richards caution women in the prologue to *Grassroots: A Field Guide for Feminist Activism* (New York: Farrar, Straus and Giroux, 2005, xxiii) not to let conflicts prevent action: "We are advocating, quite simply, that if you wait until you are perfect and free of conflicts, you will never change anything in the world."
92. As Butler observes, "Part of what is so oppressive about social forms of gender is the psychic difficulties they produce" (*Gender Trouble*, xxv).

CHAPTER TWO

Lost Objects, Monsters, and Melancholia in Zöe Jenny's *The Pollen Room*, Alexa Hennig von Lange's *Relax*, and Elke Naters's *Lies*

At least a decade before the debates of 2008, numerous female authors associated with the pop-literature movement were writing novels in which feminism, however idiosyncratically understood, colored women's perceptions and uses of mass cultural forms. As I argued in the previous chapter, their works received far less attention than male authors associated with this genre; more often, female authors of the late 1990s were situated in relation to what *Der Spiegel* critic Volker Hage described as the literary phenomenon of the "Fräuleinwunder." Borrowing a dated epithet coined by Americans in the 1950s to describe young, self-confident German women, including two "Miss Germanys" of that era, Hage praised a group of emerging female writers for their "unscrupulous storytelling."[1] Looking closely at works by Karen Duve and Judith Hermann, he also cited the work of Zöe Jenny, Tanja Langer, and Nadine Barth. In particular Hage praised the authors' frank, often sober depictions of sex, particularly in works by Duve and Barth. As was subsequently pointed out, most of these authors were too old for the "Fräulein" label and exhibited quite different writing styles.[2] And in Zöe Jenny's *Das Blütenstaubzimmer* (The pollen room), as well as pop-literature novels such as Alexa Hennig von Lange's *Relax* and Elke Naters's *Lügen* (Lies), female sexuality takes wildly different forms not compatible with either a sober narrative tone or an antiquated "Fräulein" label.³

Hage substantiates his argument by citing a placid but ultimately Thelma-and-Louise-style response to a man's query "you want me to fuck you?" in Duve's *Regenroman*. To this example I would add Jenny's protagonist in *The Pollen Room,* raped twice over if one includes the treatment she receives in the hospital. Hennig von Lange's protagonist in *Relax* masturbates with a vibrator named Harald while fantasizing about the comic book character Vampirella's breasts. The protagonist of *Lies* imagines being fed to a lesbian who sexually dominates her. Both *Relax* and *Lies* also add enigmatic layers to same-sex desire by linking it in places to memories of maternal figures and primal bonding.

Second- and third-wave feminism provide, of course, useful frames for the various forms of sexuality here, from misogyny in criminal form to pop culture–inflected, individual pleasure. As this chapter will explore, sexuality attached to maternal wellsprings adds an element of melancholia, often the obverse of anger for women, to the picture as well. As I will demonstrate, however, anger as both logical response and trigger to madness also aligns with a barred object of desire for whom "monstrousness" provides the only culturally acceptable form of expression. *The Pollen Room* in particular depicts a mother not only as misguided but also at times frighteningly malevolent. Significantly, in all three novels we witness the volatility of not only daughters' but also mothers' psyches. And each in their own way speaks to cultural prohibitions that hinder the representation of mother-daughter relations in all their complex, contradictory permutations.

Several of Hage's examples—Judith Hermann, Karen Duve, Tanja Langer, and Nadine Barth—also fit within the pop-literature rubric, and Elke Naters's works have often been considered pop, both in terms of content and style. She and her husband, pop author Sven Lager, initiated the project *The Buch. Leben am Pool* (2001), bringing together twenty writers, many linked to pop as well, to contribute to the website www.ampool.de. This project exhibited at least one basic characteristic of pop writing—its aim to create the feel of "speed, fleetingness, directness, and an approximation of oral forms that are played out against current forms of literature."⁴ In this vein Naters called for readable texts with a "Verfallsdatum" (date of expiration), while Lager emphasized the possibility of reaching a new public sphere to initiate an open exchange lacking in hierarchies.⁵ Ideally, such aims, as well as the equitable nature of a husband-and-wife team, would preordain a level playing field;

reception of pop novels, however, has tended to put hierarchies, often gendered, back in place.

When surface-level aesthetics combine with narrative structures, convention has a way of reasserting itself. Torsten Liesegang has described pop as a "catchy brand name for a recognizable group of authors and for a fast-written, easy-to-digest commodity, produced for and well received by a young audience."[6] The texts themselves, he observes, often take place in the present and feature a young, first-person narrator lacking stable bonds who "takes an unfocussed position within society, orienting himself [sic] according to attitudes of style and an affirmative response to consumer society."[7] Liesegang's use of a generic "he," however, subtly underscores how scholars and critics have focused primarily on works by men, with the two most often cited examples being Christian Kracht's seminal *Faserland* (1995) and Benjamin von Stuckrad-Barre's *Soloalbum* (1998). Liesegang's prototypical male protagonist may also reflect the boys' club mentality of works such as *Tristesse Royale* (1999). In it Kracht and von Stuckrad-Barre, as well as Joachim Bessing (Hennig von Lange's husband), Eckhard Nickel, and Alexander von Schönburg, gathered at the Hotel Adlon to make dandyish pronouncements about German culture.[8] Despite the fact that women such as Hennig von Lange and Naters, as well as Else Buschheuer, Rebecca Casati, Katrin Röggla, Karen Duve, Kerstin Grether, and Sybille Berg have authored pop novels, many of the scholarly anthologies on pop from the last fifteen years ignore female authors entirely, reduce the topic of gender to one chapter among many, or focus on one or two female authors alone.[9] Hennig von Lange may be the most frequently cited female author, perhaps because like Kracht and von Stuckrad-Barre she began her career in the media arena, though for her this meant work as a Benetton model and moderator of a children's television show. It perhaps goes without saying that neither of these jobs positioned her to make hip, dandyish pronouncements about popular culture. More likely they provided a vantage point from which to meditate on objectification, which her protagonist in *Relax* does, strikingly with a child's naivety.

Unlike the synchronic principle at work in many pop works, critics and scholars have often pursued a more diachronic approach that sustains its own kinds of hierarchies. Reacting to the seeming affirmation of commodity culture in pop works, they often invoked earlier forms of pop, particularly the works of Rolf Dieter Brinkmann and Hubert Fichte, as well as the historical avant-garde. Pop artists of the 1960s and German post–World War II left-wing intelligentsia, of course, made critiquing the status quo their modus operandi. Pop literature has often articulated disdain for the generation that come of age in the wake of the student movement, embodied for many by Gerhard Schröder's red-green coalition (1998–2006), and by depicting '68ers as dreary, superfluous has-beens. With this disdain so clearly displayed, critical response to pop, not surprisingly, has often consisted of a simple refusal to bequeath an older generation's leftist patrimony. Yet the so-called status quo only assumes clear contours if we look closely at the person observing it. Had critics and scholars paid closer attention to pop authors in all their gendered and ethnic permutations they might have registered something more complicated than pleasurable bathing in the well of consumer culture.[10] Instead they would have witnessed an uncomfortable anchoring within the status quo, particularly in its commodity-culture guises, that precludes the kinds of cocky, ironic posturing on display in *Tristesse Royale*.

Less attention to pop works by women, of course, runs the risk of preprogramming gaps across a longer historical frame, particularly if one considers the kinds of gendered variations that have already been occluded by scholars. Early twentieth-century art and 1960s pop forms provide a striking case in point. Only recent feminist scholarship has recognized, for instance, the contributions of Sophie Taeuber-Arp, Sonia Delauney-Terk, and Anni Albers to abstract, experimental, and Bauhaus forms. Likewise, female pop artists of the 1960s, such as Marisol, Pauline Boty, Yayoi Kusama, and Coosje van Bruggen, remain far less familiar than their male counterparts. Presumably lacking the postmodern irony with which male artists have held mass culture at bay, female artists were thought to have always already capitulated to mass culture mandates. Only later artists such as Cindy Sherman and Barbara Kruger, who armed themselves with theory like their male contemporaries, were deemed intellectual enough to achieve critical distance. As German pop author Thomas Meinecke has observed, a woman who writes "is in fact already pop; that's the problem. By writing, she puts herself out there as the object of representation."[11]

Hennig von Lange provides a case in point, given the fact that her freckled face and curly red hair grace several of her novels' covers. Pop authors have often been cited for their marketing prowess, raising the question about the extent to which Hennig von Lange's image belies or undermines her control in this domain. Von Stuckrad-Barre and Kracht provide a useful point of comparison, especially given their decision to model in late 1990's Peek and Cloppenburg department store ads. Von Stuckrad-Barre has asserted that their gig was simply another way to market his works via a stylized challenge to boring book publication events, creating the sense that he very much remained the impresario of his own objectification.[12] The cover of *Relax* could be understood, by contrast, in terms of the ambiguities of female power vis-à-vis image, especially when compared to the Vampirella imagery the novel's protagonist relies on to stoke her self-esteem.

The cover of *Relax* (Figure 2.1) shows Hennig von Lange gazing off to the right, her raised hand clutching a cigarette, an extended thumb

Figure 2.1. Cover of *Relax*. Source: www.rowohlt.de

Lost Objects, Monsters, and Melancholia • 71

grazing her lips. Her face in profile emphasizes all the more the cascading red locks that fall over her shoulder towards a black t-shirt clad torso, which is cropped to hide her breasts. A leopard-spotted print on the bench she leans into adds a vampish touch that invokes Vampirella (Figure 2.2), who also sports her own lioness-like tresses, though her aura clearly ups the power ante. Vampirella's role in *Relax*, as I will demonstrate, underscores the unattainability of commodity culture for women in particular, given her phallic breasts and power over men. By

Figure: 2.2. Vampirella Comic. Source: Dynamite.com

constrast, Hennig von Lange's protagonist, whom critics have described as a "Proll-Flittchen" (prole bimbo), spends a lot of time before the mirror as she waits for a boyfriend who never shows up, making readers painfully aware of the gap between fantasy and reality. Compared to these two extremes, Hennig von Lange's cover image may invoke something more attainable and maybe even progressive. Despite the vampish touches, her profile deflects our gaze, her "lost in thought" pose rendering audience response superfluous. (A head-on gaze, by contrast, would signal some kind of engagement with a male gaze, whether defiant or submissive.) Overall, Hennig von Lange could be either a haughty party girl or an aloof intellectual. Her unruly red hair adds an element of originality to her aura as well, and one is reminded of third-wave aims to negotiate beauty ideals in individual ways. In this regard, Hennig von Lange's sideways gaze evokes an ability to meditate on this process, unlike her less intellectually aware protagonist.

Cultural studies emphasize individually salutary, subversive uses of culture that make it possible to improvise an empowering relationship to mass cultural forms. Critics have emphasized how easily readers can find their footing in pop novels, particularly if "one knows the records," an oblique reference to the Oasis music invoked in *Soloalbum* and the ubiquity of contemporary music in pop novels in general.[13] The ease with which male pop authors appear to meld themselves with pop culture resembles the pleasurable doubling of credulous children before the mirror, where self is synonymous with image. No matter how effete or ironic, a less credulous adult nonetheless finds his identity there as well, simply in more detached fashion. At both ends of the spectrum, one senses identities that anchor themselves in a comforting play of sameness, rather than in more estranging symbolic forms. Vampirella's unattainability as cultural ideal not only points to gendered differences, but also a disturbing alterity, displayed in various ways in the three novels examined here. All of their protagonists remain passive observers, evident in the novels' frequent references to watching films, a comparison which also plays up the gap between self and other. Strikingly as well, each novel depicts various kinds of lying, thus underscoring the false nature of cultural forms, as well as our embrace of them despite this knowledge. In the end one finds few instances where protagonists enjoy some kind of comforting play made possible by the illusion of sameness.

Moritz Baßler's oft-cited *Der deutsche Pop-Roman. Die neuen Archivisten* emphasizes pop's playful aspects, which he considers neither affirmative nor subversive. Instead, "playful" describes the manner in which authors tamper with the semantic possibilities of a larger cultural archive. But by bracketing political and psychological concerns, he reprises structuralism's disinterest in varying subject positions, evident in the fact that the five authors highlighted in Baßler's chapter headings, as I mentioned in my introduction, are all male. His approach also belies the extent to which pop authors may have bigger aims in mind, which again have to do with exposing or blunting the social inequities experienced by marginalized groups. And even the existential travails of more mainstream pop protagonists can take on political resonances if one explores a bit more in the cultural archive.

For instance, Katharina Rutschky has observed how Goethe and Thomas Mann hover over *Faserland* and Goethe and Kafka over *Soloalbum*, which obliquely positions pop in relation to perennial German debates about selfhood, history, and the function of literature.[14] Frank Degler and Ute Paulokat's "Gendertrouble" chapter in *Neue Deutsche Popliteratur* provides a useful supplement to Rutschky's approach. In it they identify Arthur Schnitzler's 1924 novella *Fräulein Else* (Miss Else) as a literary template for *Relax*, with each work depicting a young woman striving for emancipation in the face of patriarchal power.[15] Digging deeper in the cultural sediment, one finds in *Relax* and *Lies* sources as diverse as Judith Butler, Cindy Sherman, Isabella Rossellini, Madonna, and Douglas Sirk melodramas. Unlike the diachronic comparisons that presumably invalidated the subversive potential of 1990s pop, these various presences suggest myriad ways of interacting with culture and their differing effects.

The synchronic nature of standing before the mirror is of course embedded in a longer history of female selfhood vis-à-vis image. "Striking the pose" in Sherman's or Butler's terms may involve a degree of playfulness, but defiance often factors in as well. Sirk's presence, though, adds melancholia to the mix, the roots of which all three novels situate not so much in pop culture's unattainability for women but rather in an eclipsed maternal object of desire. In the broadest sense we find in each novel a dense tapestry that blends pop culture, missing mothers, and fleeting allusions to feminism. And given the psychological distortions of the novels' various protagonists, a tapestry may be the wrong metaphorical reference point, since it implies cohesive material elements, as well as aesthetic coherence. More fitting would be the back of a tapestry, where one witnesses the messiness of cobbled-together but otherwise disjointed components.

Before turning to the novels, reflection on the link between a socially progressive movement meant to improve women's circumstances and stalled selves mired in psychological distortions deserves attention. To even place these two elements side by side in a sentence runs the risk of reprising Frank Schirrmacher's reactionary claims in the Demography Debate. More recently *New York Times* conservative editorialist Ross Douthat titled a piece "I Love Lena" because Lena Dunham's television show *Girls* presumably displays the downside of "expressive individualism," thereby implicitly affirming conservative values.[16] In both instances, feminism, which Dunham emphatically embraces in her autobiographical work *Not that Kind of Girl* (2014), remains a favored, transcultural projection screen for those who would move things back to a far more traditional place. In this regard, examining fictional selves confused by the movement's various aims and approaches is a risky endeavor. Indeed, in all three novels I will examine in this chapter we witness not only profoundly neurotic behavior, but also freakish tendencies that create a funhouse mirror of basic feminist tenets, as well as female grotesques. Ultimately, however, the novels suggest not so much a cause and effect whereby feminism preprograms problematic individualism and disfunctionality, but rather the highly individualistic ways that women process and make sense of often-disjunctive elements. Just as a teleological trajectory of ever-improving feminism remains problematic, so too does the assumption that all women who embrace the women's movement necessarily evolve in salutary ways. Unique histories and their psychological effects will always preordain a broad range of responses to feminism's imperatives, which literature, of all the various art forms, is particularly adept at exposing.

Melancholia for the Mother and Ambivalence towards the Left in *The Pollen Room*

Zöe Jenny's *The Pollen Room* tells the story of Jo, the child of separated parents, and her attempts as a young woman to reestablish contact with her mother, Lucy, who disappeared to an unspecified Italian-speaking city to begin a new life. Over the course of the novel, we witness the mother's egocentrism continually reprising itself, as does that of a young woman whom Jo befriends as Lucy increasingly ignores her, particularly after Lucy's partner's death and likely suicide. Despite Jo's attempts to lure her mother from the partner's art studio—the blossom-filled pollen room the title refers to—she finds herself ultimately shunned as Lucy attaches herself to a new partner. By the end of the novel, Jo returns north to her father, who has remarried and now has children, to discover her superfluity there as well. The story ends with an image of her alone on a bench in a snow-filled park, which invokes not only stasis but also death.

Pop culture appears only sporadically in *The Pollen Room*—in Kurt Cobain lyrics, Kate Moss's image on the side of a bus, and in techno music at an ecstasy-fueled rave. This last element in particular positions an otherwise temporally oblique story within the 1990s, with Jo born sometime roughly twenty years earlier. The novel was often marketed, despite Jenny's objections, as a "A Techno-Generation's Reckoning with '68er Parents."[17] Along similar lines, Volker Hage's "Fräuleinwunder" article, which mentions Jenny only briefly, links her to the medial presence one associates with pop authors, given her ubiquity in newspapers when *The Pollen Room*, her debut novel, was published.[18] Jenny's novel, though, offers little support of a 1990's "Spaßgesellschaft" (fun society) as the antidote to a militant '68er ethos. Likewise, the dogmatism/hedonism binary underpinning generational rifts among feminists hardly factors into her novel. Instead it exposes, via Jo's mother and new friend, a problematic pleasure principle on both ends of the generational spectrum.

Jo's bohemian mother Lucy provides the novel's most obvious example of hedonism as existential guide. Indeed she serves as an emphatic corrective to the notion of emancipation fed by dogmatism and animus towards men since throughout the novel she continually caters to her artist husband's needs. When Jo joins Lucy twelve years after her departure, she befriends Rhea, a street musician who enjoys her parents' swimming pool and takes Jo to her first rave. Overt and canny similarities link two free spirits and transform otherwise exotic qualities into something either comic or brutally alien. Jo describes Rhea, for instance, as being like a cartoon figure, which evokes the two-dimensionality of Lucy's mirror image as she preens. While doubling underscores both women as potential imagoes in Jo's coming of age, Jenny depicts them in thoroughly uncanny form as well; as I will discuss further below, Lucy bears affinities with an insect that appears at the window in Jo's early childhood, and Jo describes Rhea at one point as looking reptilian in her swimsuit. This absolute otherness anticipates irrevocably broken bonds. By the end of the novel, both Lucy and Rhea have abandoned Jo, though Rhea justifies her disappearance by invoking a dying mother whom she has otherwise emphatically ignored. Given the pervasive lack of intimate female bonds throughout, her gesture feels both expedient and hollow.

The Pollen Room centers largely on Jo's nearly two-year stay with her mother, during which she experiences the self-centered underside of alternative lifestyles, as well as their continuity across generations in Rhea's youthful excesses. Metaphorically, Jenny transforms the discursive underpinnings of such lives into a smoke-and-mirrors element literally lacking in substance. Other olfactory and acoustic elements buttress this effect as well: Lucy's pungent perfume and the frequent sounds of buzzing insects reduce Jo's surround to cloying, nonverbal elements that offer nothing in the way of substantive scaffolding for an emerging self. Instead, these more primal elements suggest a child's earliest experiences of the world through the senses rather than language. And it is, of course, linguistic and visual forms that conjure and articulate selfhood as a discrete and separate entity. Not surprisingly, many of the surrounds that Jo finds herself within resemble cocoons, as if she remains stuck in an unevolved state.

The piled up "books that will never be sold" in the apartment where Jo spends her early childhood provide the first example of what might be substantive discourse taking diminished form.[19] The product of her father's small, unsuccessful publishing business, these books could contain a progressive rationale that challenges, for instance, the traditional conventions of marriage and childrearing, which the father may actually do by raising Jo alone. (Early on, Jo sees Lucy only once a week.) Ideally, alternative types of childrearing would counteract a larger exploitative and hierarchical system. Jenny links these books metaphorically, however, to the "countless cigarette butts" that line the edge of the father's desk, as well as his decaying, cobweb-filled apartment.[20] Significantly, his books mostly take a back seat to raucous parties, Mick Jagger music, and infantile girlfriends who come and go. Given these elements, a smoke-filled apartment points as much to a pleasure principle as it does to empty rhetoric. At the same time, it also contributes to Jo's cocoon-like existence—she watches her father from the window each night as he departs to earn money driving a truck—rather than creating the conditions under which a child could learn to think and act independently. Like one of the father's meditating girlfriends, Jo must find her footing "mitten im Nichts" (in the middle of nothing), an aim that provides the visual and acoustic template for her coming of age.[21] Nowhere do we find the kind of primal bond or salutary embrace from which an individuated self could emerge.

Instead, the novel's cloying elements perpetuate a cocooned existence that reproduces itself in Lucy's reaction to her partner's death—that is, her retreat to a pollen-filled room where she shrinks into a fetal ball or "Mutterbündel" (mother lump), as Jo observes.[22] Along similar lines, Rhea lives alone in her parents' resplendent house, walled in within a library of books that, like those at Jo's father's apartment, also remain unread. Jo's various sequestered locales also include a walled-up garden and an underground pedestrian zone where the unearthed skeleton of a child is displayed. Selfhood merging with surround in palliative ways happens only in artificial circumstances, specifically the chemically fuelled rave where Jo becomes "one with one big body machine."[23] If the metaphor of the cocoon primes readers to expect some form of transformation, the novel ends with Jo as a statue-like presence on a park bench with snow falling around her. Her pose reprises a mediating girlfriend who "plays dead" before the young Jo, as well as Lucy's occasional static moments of inscrutability.[24] In the end, the cocoon creates the conditions for a stillbirth, not a radical transformation.

Jo's circumstances and the lacerating critique implicit in *The Pollen Room* contain autobiographical traces that bear mention. Jenny was raised by a father who published books and an artist mother who lived in Basel, Greece, and Switzerland's southernmost, Italian-speaking canton Ticino. In 2013 she wrote an article for *Die Welt* describing her experiences at the Reformpädagogische Freie Schule Basel from 1982 to 1984, or from age eight to ten. Her essay was prompted by revelations that a small faction within the Green Party, eradicated by 1987, had sexually abused children. This circumstance was presumably abetted by leftist notions of children's eroticism and the Green Party's brief approval of a 1985 position paper supporting nonviolent sex between adults and children.[25] Jenny blamed contemporary Green party members such as Jürgen Trittin and Claudia Roth for insufficiently acknowledging sexual abuse, and she delivered a trenchant critique of 1970's and 80's Green communes for endangering, rather than freeing, children. By transforming them into "toys they could do with what they wanted," adults shaped by the sexual revolution above all freed themselves from "their responsibility," their "falsely understood liberal tendencies" sanctioning all kinds of transgressions.[26] At the Freie Schule in Basel, Jenny experienced what one could consider pedagogical transgressions with their own kinds of long-term consequences. She describes, for example, walks in the woods where teachers admonished children to listen closely for twittering birds that would soon be extinct. Excessive attention to the topic of *Waldsterben* (dying forest syndrome) left her with the impression even the trees would disappear by the time she reached adulthood. Ultimately she articulates a sweeping condemnation: "A leftward/Green ideology was hammered into us in a penetrating, indoctrinating way, as if to proclaim: the world is a really shitty place, and if we don't do everything in our power it will just get shittier."

Such polemics do indeed seem to substantiate an understanding of *The Pollen Room* as a "reckoning" of Jenny's generation with the '68ers. But more importantly, uncanny depictions of nature in the novel also appear to tap into the scare tactics of her early teachers, the psychological effects of which are depicted as equally profound. One of Jo's earliest memories involves a frightening insect that crouches outside her window each night and stares at her with an "angry look." She imagines it jumping in her face, its "knotty, pulsing legs" ensnaring her. Repeatedly in the novel, Jo also registers a buzzing sound that recalls this early experience of a brute, alien presence. If nature removes the temporal element of generational conflict circa the late 1990s, it also renders "perversion" more generally as a tampering with convention across a timeless backdrop. The various ways in which Jo is obliged to mother either her father's childlike girlfriends or Lucy during her nervous breakdown provide the novel's most obvious example of perversion, which Jenny underscores with visual links to the uncanny insect at the window.

In an early scene, Jo lifts a bottle of alcohol to a drunk, "screeching" girlfriend's lips, its contents then trickling out the side of her mouth again in fine lines across powdered checks. Both infantile and grotesque, those "fine lines" recall the spider's pulsing, knotty legs and its frightening uncomfortable proximity. At one point Lucy takes Jo to a sequestered woodland oasis of trickling water and stones warmed by the sun, a locale that vaguely evokes the possibility of oceanic oneness. Yet Jo instead registers a "murderous heat," insects besetting her face, a growing nausea prompted by an overpowering fragrance, and Lucy's face examining her own as if Jo were "an enemy." Traditionally, the mother provides a child's first visual and acoustic mirror; this angry look, however, and cloying elements that recall the insect at the window replace affirmation with a threatening presence. Beyond the categorical inscrutability that can trump familial bonds, one is reminded of the animus that adults direct towards children they perceive as circumscribing their lives. Transplanting this interaction to a natural setting renders the "maternal instinct" a distinctly cultural notion given the base struggle for survival that plays out here. (Elsewhere in the novel starving cats appear, struggling to find some form of sustenance in a world of "piss and garbage." By the end of the novel Jo has replaced food with cigarettes.) Ultimately Lucy seems to disappear in the bright sunlight, and, not long after, she abandons Jo again for a wealthy industrialist living on an island. Like Jo during Lucy's nervous breakdown, he tends to her every need. Jo, on the other hand, is left with either an alienating mirror of self or her mother's vacated silhouette, signifying an unbridgeable gap. Human relations across the parent-child-partner spectrum thus consist here of a cloying, dependent closeness or absolute distance.

Overall, *The Pollen Room* depicts a perpetually passive observer who never really abandons her place at the window. Not only does Jo not find herself "mitten im Nichts," she also gives herself over to the nothingness around her, sinking into a melancholy that transforms her into that statue-like presence in the snowy park. Her self-evident sadness throughout the novel functions as the obverse of rage, her stasis as the antithesis of a defiant performative act that could at the very least put her impossible circumstances on display. Ash, pollen, and decaying matter, too, signal the endpoint of all the bodily fluids that could otherwise conjure early bonds between a mother and child. When the maternal figure remains both self-centered and to a large extent alien, when a child is essentially discarded garbage, it becomes clear that Jo will never experience any kind of restorative intimacy with her mother. At best she can only passively observe and recognize the various "lies" around her.

Lucy's preening throughout, for instance, belies a cruel world in which women are mistreated and often cast aside. Beyond an initial sexual encounter in which she is essentially raped, Jo witnesses from her window some young boys spitting on girls who had beat them at a game; in Lucy's southern town, aggressive teenage boys force Jo to buy dead butterflies, another none-too-subtle indication of her fate beyond the cocoon; she and Rhea watch a film in which a husband abuses his wife; and Lucy's artist husband, Jo surmises, may have intentionally abandoned her if his car accident was actually a suicide. Such egregious acts should ideally stoke the political consciousness that Lucy's brand of emancipation so clearly lacks, but the novel's indifferent natural backdrop renders dreams of equality or salutary autonomy hopelessly naïve. In this sense, Jenny undermines both sides of the dogmatism/hedonism binary, and not only by emphasizing how much the latter fuels the former when Green Party platforms seem to sanction pedophilia, or female emancipation the abandonment of children. Rather, human needs themselves can be too primal to tally with enlightened or socially prescribed forms of human behavior, a problem that extends beyond a specific historical timeframe or the wherewithal of culture at any given moment.

In *The Psychic Life of Power*, Judith Butler examines gender as much in terms of loss as empowerment, given events in the earliest phases of life. Drawing on Freud's ideas in his essay "Mourning and Melancholia," she describes a process whereby the ego incorporates the "lost object" of sexual desire—meaning the mother—within itself in order to avert and disavow her complete disappearance. Lacking the means to grieve this privation, the ego subsequently sustains itself with life-long, melancholy-tinged identifications with the heterosexual norm that she embodies. For females, this means that the mother is barred as object of desire, a process solidified by fears of homosexual desire that would presumably make them more like men than proper women and hence "monstrous."[27] For Butler, the larger problem becomes the lack of public recognition or discourse through which this loss could be named and mourned, which creates "a culture of gender melancholy in which masculinity and femininity emerge as the traces of an ungrieved and ungrievable love."[28] Such is the strength of this foreclosure that it remains part of the "opacity of the unconscious"—that is, barred from a performativity that might exteriorize a wounding loss.

This model of course resonates alongside a text in which the protagonist actively tracks down a lost mother, yet one who embodies a heterosexual norm so strong that it trumps any kind of feminist consciousness, despite an acutely misogynistic surround. Equally important, Jo's passivity, silence, and ultimate symbolic demise not only feel deeply melancholic, they also foreclose the possibility of performativity and its potential to articulate as well as reshape the conditions of selfhood. Her cocooned world and its alien/olfactory forms hardly offer the foundations of an individuated self. Nor does she appear to have the visual and linguistic means for performing a damaged selfhood, ideally to salutary effect. At the same time, "monstrousness" in *The Pollen Room*, unlike in Butler's formulation, appears less as a barred desire than what the alien spider at the window signifies. Simply put, it conjures a natural world beyond cultural conventions that presume mothers can forego their own primal needs in order to cater to those of their children. It signals the absolute otherness that mothers may perceive in their children, even in the earliest phases of life. And as symbol of abdicated nurturing, it also explains Jo's subsequent inability to imagine or experience a world not characterized by ubiquitous aggression. Jenny's novel ultimately adds disturbing, uncanny elements to the mother-daughter bond, particularly when mothers rather than daughters exhibit the will to autonomy that requires jettisoning family ties. For the purposes of this volume, she provides the most extreme version of and perhaps challenge to mother-daughter relations as conventionally understood or as instrumentalized for political ends.

Performativity in *Relax* and *Lies*

Before shifting to individual analysis of *Relax* and *Lies*, I would like to emphasize their commonalities, particularly where they depart from *The Pollen Room*'s decaying world of ash and pollen. If Jenny conjures a mother as alien and thus intractably unavailable for an imaginary conjuring of eclipsed bonds, Hennig von Lange's and Naters's novels more closely approximate the notion that early desire for the mother can only be articulated by bringing monsters into the picture. This activation, however problematic and culturally unfair, at the very least moves us in the direction of performativity, the force that Jo was unable to activate in her insular world. Equally important, in both *Relax* and *Lies* freakish tendencies and female grotesques not only tap into the "monstrous" desire for the lost object, this force in turn also assuages the protagonists' pervasive anxieties.

In general terms, the mediated bases of selfhood manifest themselves in Hennig von Lange's and Naters's novels, providing the props of performativity that bolster otherwise riven protagonists. Women in both novels sometimes blatantly conform to cultural mandates and other times enact them in very idiosyncratic ways. Their first-person-singular, interior monologues provide a variant of 1970's "Innerlichkeit" (subjectivity), but one that lays false consciousness bare via cultural forms both exalted and banal. Augusta, the protagonist of *Lies*, meditates on everything under the sun, from Stendhal's *The Red and the Black* (1830) to her close friend Be's hemorrhoids. In *Relax*, a protagonist dubbed "die Kleine" (little girl) by her boyfriend proclaims at one point that her self-esteem depends on the right nail polish. She often repeats the phrase "that's like in films" and "one knows that from films"; *Lies* echoes this phrase and also structures its narrative around the act of watching or being watched. The novel in fact begins with a dream-like sequence where Augusta witnesses her friend Be below her apartment window, wildly agitated and screaming, and is reminded of *Singin' in the Rain* (1952). The protagonists in both novels show us the "lies" at the heart of subjectivity—meaning not only a selfhood firmly anchored in spurious forms, but also in the ability to mindlessly mimic them. Be's spectacle beneath Augusta's window brings mental instability into the equation as well. And if she functions as a split-off part of Augusta's psyche, she may even reveal a psychotic state, perhaps the ultimate form of false consciousness.

Significant as well is that cultural reference points in *Relax* and *Lies* include feminism, raising the question of its overall effect within a larger mix of disparate cultural elements. Ideally, it would at the very least spawn awareness of or detachment from false cultural forms; instead, it ends up inspiring vacuous charades. Die Kleine, for instance, seems like a clueless, postmodern paper doll as she poses before the mirror citing feminist catchphrases such as "the liberation of women, revolution, men are to blame!" ("Befreiung der Frau, Revolution, Männer sind schuld!"), in addition to passages from Vampirella cartoons.[29] Adding to this already-incongruous amalgamation, she dreams throughout of getting married, having children, and living a very conventional life, a fantasy that requires what Yvonne Wolf has called a "paradoxical balancing act between vamp and housewife."[30] Ideally, feminist credos and subversive uses of pop culture would indeed ameliorate her circumstances, whether via concrete emancipation or by turning gendered power hierarchies around to attain the phallic female supremacy that Vampirella embodies. Yet die Kleine, as her name suggests, exhibits at best a child parroting political discourse.

Along other feminist lines, the various porn-inspired and sometimes homoerotic acts in both novels speak to a third-wave investment in sexual pleasure and its empowering effects. Yet lacking a postmodern sense of impunity, evident in the anxieties that both die Kleine and Augusta experience, each woman can at best strike the pose of a fractured self.[31] The sometimes painful and humiliating sexual fantasies displayed, particularly when they take same-sex form, point more towards female power dyads than damage done by the patriarchy. In *Lies*, sexuality clearly echoes Augusta and Be's hurtful rift, providing a sadomasochistic pleasure principle as its salve. Yet *Relax* depicts erotic fantasies alongside maternal memories, conjuring the power of the lost object and that monstrous desire otherwise barred from cultural expression. If same-sex desire on display in *Lies* lacks a maternal subcurrent, it not only provides the means, as I mentioned above, for working through female-female dyads. Most important, it culminates in restored friendships and healing mother-daughter relations.

Relax

Relax is actually split into two sections, each the interior monolog of a prototypical pop protagonist whose life revolves around drugs, masturbating, and clubbing. The first half focuses on Chris as he hangs out with his male friends, culminating in his overdose in a club and possible demise. The second half consists of die Kleine's thoughts as she waits alone in her apartment for Chris to arrive, which include memories of encounters with her friend Barb and her mother. Her story culminates in fantasies of saving Chris by escaping with him to the Amazon where they can both finally relax and be with each other. Degler and Paulokat, among other scholars, have praised the novel's successful depiction of the chasm between male and female perspectives, deeming *Relax* the "most relevant pop text" for questions of gender.[32] In the broadest sense, die Kleine and her boyfriend Chris are equally childish, egotistical, and unsympathetic.

While her psychic life gives pride of place to a comic-book character, he repeatedly proclaims himself to be a rock star. Chris also peppers his observations about the world around him with the laconic proclamation "original," even if pop novels' worlds are anything but that and Chris's dream of becoming a rock star a blatant cliché. The stream of consciousness perceptions in both sections also align with pop's attempts to create the feel of the present, its fleetingness and directness. For Chris, life consists mostly of jangled nerves and getting stoned, with the occasional fond memory of sitting in a child's car seat as his parents ferry him around. For all the pleasurable elements in both his and die Kleine's world, the novel's title serves as an injunction with which neither is able to comply, a circumstance which renders him sexually impotent.[33] This fundamental sexual dysfunction, of course, undermines his masculine bravura, as well as die Kleine's gendered notion of the world and her role in it. It also points to the underside of pop novels with male protagonists. Despite material trappings, Kracht's protagonist in *Faserland* spends a lot of time throwing up and passing out.[34] (When Chris overdoses at the end of his section, his fate in the balance, he recalls Kracht's protagonist pushing off onto a Swiss lake, where he may or may not drown.) Von Stuckrad-Barre's opening scene in *Soloalbum* depicts its protagonist in bed as an alien presence bangs on his door in the middle of the night, whom he imagines violating his body with a drill.

By comparison, the lot of women like die Kleine, as pitiful as it seems, may at least offer the possibility of a better outcome.[35] Like Chris, die

Kleine often suffers from anxiety; in fact the word "angst" appears in the very first sentence of her section and the word "paranoia" at the beginning of the second paragraph. But instead of getting stoned, die Kleine pulls out a Vampirella comic, whose text and images provide an antidote to her otherwise dull, circumscribed existence as she waits for Chris. Most obviously, Vampirella turns around traditional gendered hierarchies insofar as her sadistic mien literally brings men to their knees. In a passage that mixes die Kleine's voice with Vampirella's action-hero-style revenge, die Kleine imagines, "Vampirella is slowly getting angry. . . . My rage is unending, and I look terrifying. My bosom trembles, and I inhale deeply. Suddenly everything is completely quiet. The glasses stand untouched on the bar, cigarettes fall out of the corners of mouths. Vampirella swings her whip. Thwack, thwack, thwack. This idiot's shirt is slit, on his naked chest there's a huge, bloody "V." He's marked for the rest of his life."[36] The power reversal here could hardly be described as feminist if defined as the dream of parity and mutual respect between the sexes, though it does feel like a fitting response to a boyfriend who treats die Kleine badly. In this regard, Vampirella's stance bears general affinities with stereotypes of second-wave militant tendencies, whether perceived as emancipatory or simply man-hating. Vampirella proclaims, for example, "I'm an emancipated woman and can sleep with whomever I want."[37] Even more important, die Kleine's fantasies play out, in amplified form, the hierarchical conditions at the base of human relations—what one could call the *Realpolitik* missing in the liberal humanist vantage point underpinning second-wave feminism and its optimistic goal of equality.

Yet Vampirella's vampish allure also complicates power hierarchies if one considers how die Kleine enacts it. Proclaiming that all women want to be vamps with men at their feet sucking their toes, she argues that women should thus "conscientiously paint their toenails."[38] One is reminded of her statement elsewhere about her self-esteem depending on wearing the right nail polish. While Vampirella provides an unmistakable example of empowerment through phallic posturing and sexual pleasure, die Kleine shifts the dynamic along postfeminist lines by bringing self-objectification into the equation.[39] Suffice it to say, power remains a moving target in die Kleine's confused fantasies. To wit: she pictures herself at one point as a pole-dancer before a male audience that wonders "Who's this sexy chick? Man, I'd like to fuck her!"[40]

Given how Vampirella provides a potent antidote to die Kleine's insular existence, one wonders why she nonetheless suffers from anxiety and paranoia. At one point she even lies in bed and tries to imagine what it would be like to be paralyzed, a physical state that suggests how immobilizing contradictions can be. As much as Vampirella speaks to female agency, she also quite clearly embodies impossible standards of beauty. (Chris emphasizes at one point that die Kleine has almost no breasts at all.) And though die Kleine mimics Vampirella's statement about emancipated women sleeping with whomever they want, elsewhere she proclaims that "men hate women's libbers." Perhaps not surprisingly, her attempts to forge a political consciousness merge antithetical elements, specifically revolution and self-destruction. Imagining both she and her friend Barb jumping out a window, their squished bodies lying on the asphalt, die Kleine proclaims, "Everybody knows that the men are to blame. I mean Barb and I wouldn't just jump out a window. I mean it's political suicide, right? It's about helping the oppressed women of the 1990s. Hundreds will follow us to their deaths. No, really. It will be a real revolution!"[41] Their "peace with suicide" mission, like die Kleine's alternately sadistic and masochistic fantasies, suggests the unlikelihood of her ever achieving some kind of integrated selfhood. And when self-objectification equals empowerment and emancipation equals suicide, one senses feminism's ultimately untenable status when enacted by a clueless younger generation.

Yet to the extent that a phallic woman like Vampirella feels vaguely grotesque and monstrous in a patriarchal culture, she may also speak to other kinds of political possibilities that die Kleine, with her limited awareness, hardly perceives consciously. In this regard Barb provides a useful point of comparison. On the one hand, she appears to embody her own kind of tortured splitting. Her name, for instance, recalls the big-haired, large-breasted, plastic-doll incarnation of femininity. Barb, however, collects plastic monsters, which she states will appreciate in value, not unlike iconic toys of yesteryear. At first glance, her relationship to them seems to reproduce the distance between reality and fantasy. When die Kleine makes fun of Barb's expensive glasses for making her look like an alien, Barb "runs amok" and throws the monsters around her apartment. Falling short of chic stylishness may be cause for anger, but Barb's uses of monsters elsewhere suggest a protective function. She always carries a monster with her, she tells die Kleine, in case a man rubs up against her too closely. Subsequently, die Kleine cooks up her own vigilante-style fantasy far more frightening than Vampirella's whippings: "I dream of Barb's plastic monsters, who castrate all the guys. One after the other. Balls gone."[42] There's nothing vampish at all going on here—nothing that feeds into heterosexual desire via objectified or phallic femininity. Instead one is reminded of Mikhail Bakhtin's carnivalesque femininity, specifically the laughing grotesque crones that Mary Russo associates with female transgression as public spectacle.[43] As I mentioned in the introduction to this volume, Karneval in the city of Cologne begins each year with women cutting off men's neckties in the square next to the Rathaus, in a socially sanctioned approximation of the ultimate female transgression.

Elsewhere, Barb's example takes things to a more complicated place. At one point die Kleine tries to put her in a relaxed-enough state for early childhood memories to emerge. Barb obliges, moving back in time to a kitchen scene at age five when she made her first sandwich, though sadly her mother refused to believe her. One small step towards autonomy resounds in a novel full of childlike adults tapped into primal needs, evident in Chris's memories of the car seat and die Kleine's effusive descriptions of her "Schnuffi," a blanket that reminds her of being in her mother's lap. Barb deals with this early "trauma" head on: she calls her mother on the phone, who tells her that she knew all along about a sandwich that her father secretly ate. Die Kleine, by contrast, remains in a place of ambiguous parent-child-partner relations, with the mother's role in her fantasies highly evocative of a lost primal bond.

Initially, die Kleine's relationship to Vampirella, which she describes as "better than any porn," appears to fulfill a third-wave aim to locate a pleasurable porn-alternative for women. Her fantasies, however, clearly channel a same-sex desire that deserves closer attention: "Reading a Vampirella comic, letting time pass, looking at Vampirella's huge tits and getting horny. No, really. Vampirella makes me incredibly horny."[44] Strikingly, die Kleine links her pleasurable fantasies about Vampirella to early memories of her mother: "Somehow Vampirella always reminds me of my mother. I mean not because she slept around a lot but because there's a photo of my mother lying naked on the beach, and she really looks like Vampirella. That's why on page eight I'm always painfully touched because on the one hand I find the picture pretty hot and on the other I always have the feeling that my mother is lying there and making me horny. It's really crazy."[45] On the most obvious level, die Kleine's mother represents here something more complex than the caring, nurturing ethic with which mothers have been traditionally associated, which in the 1970s included a kind of gender-based moral superiority. If one considers how nurturing involves the giving and taking of pleasure, a hierarchically tinged eroticism becomes part of the baseline for human interactions. Significantly, die Kleine's otherwise confused fantasies about her mother and Vampirella end up blending in a salutary manner, providing one of the novel's few examples of deeply pleasurable intimacy.

Towards the end of the novel, die Kleine dances in a bar and feels a presence behind her, breath on her neck, hands on her waist, then a pleasant embrace. Though her pronouns identify this person as male, more often she uses gender-neutral formulations such as "someone is holding me tight," "there are hands on my waist," and "the embrace is getting stronger." As in the earlier passage cited where her anger mixes with Vampirella's, she conjures her alter ego with phrases such as "Vampirella's head on his shoulder" and "Vampirella feels good." Eroticism thus combines with a deep sense of security, die Kleine's "goosebumps" with the sensation "I'm being protected" and "I'm in mom's lap."[46] Tapping into the primal roots of adult sexuality, die Kleine finally experiences the satisfaction of psychosexual needs writ large.

Elsewhere in the novel, her childlike perspective gives us a self so stretched between nonsensical extremes that it remains stuck in time, unable to progress towards some form of integrated, enlightened, selfhood. "Girl culture" in this case takes quite literal and infantile form. Clearly it takes an adult to understand the conceptual complexities of identity politics, and at best die Kleine can only mimic feminist catch phrases and strategic exhibitionism. Yet her fantasy here achieves something more elemental and restorative. If female sexuality itself is less fixed and thus more in line with the text's other forms of labile identification, this scene nonetheless displays a kind of integrated sexuality, connected to its earliest manifestations in a manner than ensures adult satisfactions. Vampirella may in the end provide the "monstrous" alibi for acknowledging the mother's part in this outcome. The maternal element here also redefines a third-wave investment in individual needs as something more universal than the circumstances of women at a given moment in time. Though this impulse hardly moves things forward toward some kind of collective empowerment, *Lies* will offer its own kinds of fantasies that serve this end.

Lies

Elke Naters's rendering of complex female bonds plays out by and large between her two protagonists, primarily Augusta, whose interiority the novel reproduces, and her quixotic friend, Be, whose antics structure the novel. Like the mother in *The Pollen Room*, Be is a thoroughly self-centered character; similar to die Kleine, she also quotes various feminist phrases, while attempting to live them out in some fashion. After becoming increasingly alienated from Be, Augusta retreats to her apartment and focuses on writing an academic thesis. When Be's mother dies, Be seeks out Augusta again, and as I mentioned in my introduction, the novel ends with the two of them watching Douglas Sirk's *Imitation of Life*. Most important of all, Augusta ultimately experiences a sense of peace with herself and within her closest relationships, including with Be.

The novel begins with Augusta watching an agitated Be on the street below her window, her histrionics expressed in overtly spatial and theatrical terms:

> The moon shines in my face. Bright like a lamp. I hear screams and get up and see Be standing down on the street and screaming. She wears a yellow coat that I've never seen before. She stands under a streetlight that shines on her like a spotlight and screams and runs around like a crazy person. The water shoots up from the puddles. The street is wet and reflects the light. The light of the moon and the streetlight. It looks like a film. Like *Singing in the Rain*, where Fred Astaire dances in the puddles. She's alone. I can't understand what she's screaming. I shut the curtains, get back in bed, and go back to sleep.[47]

Spatiality as indicator of power relations deserves close attention in this passage. As is the case here, Augusta and Be often inhabit vertical spaces in the novel, most evident in the fact that Augusta's apartment is one floor above Be's. More tellingly, Augusta remembers a girlhood scene when she and Be spit on another girl from a second-floor window. The word "Müll" or garbage often appears in the text, revealing a psychological viewpoint that justifies spitting on others and shutting the curtains on a screaming friend. It goes without saying that anachronistic notions of sisterhood quite emphatically break down in these examples. In fact, Be even uses feminism to stoke her own sense of superiority, telling Augusta to read some books when she fails to understand the various consciousness-raising strategies to which Be pays lip service.

Augusta's operatic vision also provides a wealth of other important textual detail. Its theatrical components—streetlights as spotlights, Hollywood-inspired staging, and the closing of curtains—also include wet asphalt as mirroring element. Such theatricality points, on the one hand, to the lies and narcissism and self-aggrandizement at the heart of selfhood. On the other, the street's reflective surface suggests that Be may be a piece of Augusta's psyche. The moon, of course, has traditionally been tied to lunatic states. Antithetical extremes of singing/screaming even point to a bipolar state, which, however, is not necessarily Be's. The fact that Augusta confuses Fred Astaire with the actual protagonist of *Singing in the Rain*—Gene Kelly—tips us off to her unreliability as narrator. Elsewhere in the novel Augusta describes Be as egotistical and unreliable but later as a good mother. Most telling, at one point Augusta pronounces, "I know Be better than she knows herself."[48] This intimacy brings antithetical parts, such as verbal interiority and superficial, theatrical actions, together into a consolidated whole. If Be is indeed simply a projection, a double, what specifically does Augusta work through in allowing this piece of her psyche to run free and act out?

In most general terms Augusta as apartment shut-in makes herself into a passive observer as Be the street performer plays out the highlights of feminism over the last forty years. Beginning with a vaguely Bohemian aim to articulate her momentary "Lebensgefühl" (sentiment), for example, Be goes blonde and describes the experience as an "*unbelievable experience*" (text's emphasis). Her words provide a confused concoction of pop, with its superficial lifestyles, with lingering 1968-inspired lingo. Augusta underscores potentially progressive aims, however, when she describes Be's need to continually change her appearance in order to "irritate" her surrounding world and its static images of women:

> Ever since she cut her hair Be has developed a flair for feminism. She reads piles of books about feminism and gender and speaks of postfeminism and that it's no longer about fighting against women's oppression. Today it's much more about knowing the differences between the sexes and using this knowledge strategically and as a weapon. Just like Madonna or Cindy Sherman she says. But I don't know what Be's hair has to do with Madonna. I tell her that. But she just shrugs and says I didn't understand a thing and gives me a pile of books to read.[49]

Using differences "strategically and as a weapon" smacks more of old-fashioned feminine coquetry and wiles, not a theoretically informed feminist goal. In this manner, collapsing Cindy Sherman with Madonna also suggests how a postmodern aesthetic can trickle down into the realm of popular culture, its radical potential denuded in the process.[50] If Be, as Augusta claims, has always changed her appearance over the course of her life, feminist theory offers the political rationale to continue the charade, with Be transforming a feminist gesture into one more venue for regressive narcissism.

Oddly, Be's feminist impulses also appear to move backward in time, creating an anachronistic scenario that could have been borrowed from a 1970's feminist text. Midway through the novel she moves into a "besetztes Haus" (house for squatters) with a lesbian lover, as if to strive for a more authentic, less culturally inscribed life. Yet following on the heels of her pseudo-postmodern approach to feminism, this phase feel like just another empty pose, but under the sign of "shedding." Augusta's observations both recapitulate and subtly mock Be's dated discourse: "Her whole previous life, all the men, etc., was just the path she had to take to recognize what she really wanted. Everything that I thought was Be was exactly what she wasn't and never wanted to but had to be in order to recognize it wasn't her. She hid from herself and everyone else. Or something like that."[51] That final sentence fragment—"or something like that"—undermines Be's attempt to reanimate early feminist rhetoric by countering earnestness with a dismissive tone. In reality, her "besetztes Haus" is a conventional, even comfortable abode, hardly an outside space in concrete or cultural terms. And the dream of female solidarity one assumes would be powerfully felt in a lesbian relationship soon gives way to the *Realpolitik* of human relations I referenced earlier. After Be cultivates a relationship with her lover's brother, Augusta asserts that all relationships consist of torturers and torturees.

Her simplistic binary, however, belies the complex power dyads that emerge in Augusta's sexual fantasies. Early in the novel, she has a "horrid" dream that anticipates and perhaps even sanctions Be's relationship with her lesbian girlfriend, if Be is indeed a figment of her psyche. In it, Augusta sees herself having sex with a "fat, mean lesbian." A later passage, however, adds a hierarchical pleasure principle: "I'm supposed to be bait for the lesbian. They bring me to her so that she releases Be and takes advantage of me. My dream is coming true!"[52] On the one hand, lesbian desire, alternately embraced or rejected and pleasurable or debasing, allows her to work through a shifting power dynamic with Be, or perhaps simply her own unacknowledged same-sex desires. On the other, sometimes a maternal presence stokes her same-sex fantasies, for example when Be tucks her in like a child and strokes her head, which inspires Augusta's fantasy of the fat lesbian accosting her all over with dildos. This example combines traditional nurturing with an overpowering sexual presence.

In a less unsettling way, Augusta locates a pop-culture persona to work through her sexuality's maternal component. At one point she meditates on Isabella Rossellini, including her naked walk through a suburb in the film *Blue Velvet* (1986).[53] This scene opens up a variety of uncomfortable associations, beginning with the humiliating exposure also evident in Augusta's fantasies. Rossellini, however, plays her role in this scene in a more beseeching manner, as if she were exposing something otherwise hidden in her wholesome surround. On talk shows she has emphasized how she displayed her body as is—specifically bearing its post-pregnancy blemishes—rather than working out beforehand to achieve more toned Hollywood contours. Augusta, in fact, notes this aspect of Rossellini's physical appearance when she describes her "not flawless body."[54] The overall effect feels like an aberration, and maybe even a female grotesque given how rarely everyday female bodies appear on screen.

Augusta's fantasies about her, though, bring in a maternal element that takes a less disturbing form. Even if, as she points out, Rossellini is known for cosmetics advertising, Augusta associates her more with a newspaper article in which she gives tips on washing dishes like her mother, Ingrid Bergman. The fact that Rossellini and Bergman, two iconic stars of the twentieth century, are stripped of their allure via dishwashing tips and jarring nakedness is telling, especially in a pop novel. Augusta's anecdote thus conjures a highly dichotomous world where female pop-culture icons simultaneously inhabit an everyday underworld in which they bear children and clean kitchens. David Lynch, of course, plays up this gap in uncanny, unsettling ways when Dennis Hopper's character calls Rossellini "mommy" and tells her to spread her legs. Desire for the lost object is thus monstrous, a notion underwritten by all manner of cultural reference points, from Oedipus to Norman Bates. The possibility of mourning the lost object seems remote given this representational lineage, which emphasizes a forbidden, incestuous sexuality alone, not the reproductive role that Rossellini's body evokes as well. If Rossellini and Bergman in *Lies* at the very least conjure unbroken mother-daughter ties and thus a pipeline back through time to the lost object, Augusta benefits in ways that go beyond the domestic legacy implied by dishwashing tips. Since she, too, like die Kleine, suffers from perpetual anxiety, the lost object proffers as much the possibility of primal nurturing as the ur-example of same-sex desire. As much as these two elements remain complexly tangled in Augusta's sexual fantasies, her utter immobility throughout the novel suggests the need for basic nurturing triage before she can determine the shape of her sexuality.

Unlike die Kleine's moment of psycho *and* sexual satisfaction as she dances in the bar, however, Augusta never experiences the same, perhaps because her character is meant to convey a fragmented interior space incapable of concrete action. Be as a possible projection of Augusta's psyche fulfills this latter function on many levels, some of which have to do with fraught mother-daughter relations. (Augusta rarely mentions her own mother, and when she does she recalls how her mother always invaded her privacy.) The fact that Be has two children whom she alternately nurtures and neglects is telling and may contribute to Augusta's anxieties. On the macro level, however, the manner in which Be blends the maternal role with feminist aims anticipates young German women in the 2000s who both strove for improved conditions and kept conventional roles front and center. Be brings all of that together into one complicated, contradictory package, from her overt sexuality to her bourgeois tendencies. It remains for Augusta the introvert to make sense of it all before she can emerge from her secluded space and progress to some kind of integrated, contented autonomy.

Perhaps not surprisingly for a pop novel, the balm for a troubled friendship comes in the form of a film—Douglas Sirk's *Imitation of Life*. The film's title ostensibly shifts things away from interiority to a more artificial place, especially since Sirk's melodramas so strongly evoke lush strings and color-coded representations of repressed emotion. Yet this film depicts deeply troubled relationships between two sets of mothers and daughters, one of which exposes a daughter's cold and heartless treatment of a mother who eventually dies. *Imitation of Life* also spotlights various kinds of lies: a daughter who pretends to be white, an actress who does everything necessary to attain fame, and a housekeeper who wants a bombastic funeral that belies her modest life circumstances. As Augusta emphasizes when they watch the film at the end of *Lies*, all of its characters indulge in the act of "vormachen" (imitation).

Curiously, though, this fake medium enables Augusta and Be to mourn deeply—for both Be's recently deceased mother and for their broken friendship. Conventional film genres like melodrama are structured, of course, to foster identification, which Augusta and Be demonstrate via a mimetic act: as they watch the weeping women on screen, they, too, shed their own tears. More important, they also internalize the film's implicit message about the tragedy of broken bonds among women. Here imitation leads to potential transformation, defined in the novel's final words when Augusta imagines her future friendship with Be, her lesbian lover, and the latter's brother, with whom she has begun a relationship: "Then I could have a boyfriend and two girlfriends, and we'd have a whole lot of fun and lots to laugh about for the rest of our lives. That would really be nice."[55] The novel's final fantasy, evident in subjunctive phrasing throughout and a self-conscious rendering of a Hollywood-style happy ending, proffers the possibility of parity among individuals, whether male or female. Caring relations remain a fiction, but one worth imitating and truly internalizing, which counters the surface theatrics and narcissistic exhibitionism that otherwise characterize the novel. Sirk's film as a form representation constitutes a lie that paradoxically heals. If the false mirror traditionally offered by Hollywood brings resolution to Augusta and Be, it retroactively supplements all the various kinds of lies that permeate the text. As much as lies do damage, they also have the potential to put a salutary selfhood in place.

Conclusion

For '68ers in Germany, fantasy proffered utopian possibilities for changing the world. If we understand the mother-daughter bond as one of feminism's central imaginary constructs, its use in all three novels suggests something more complicated than succeeding generations moving ever closer to an improved world. Rather, as in *The Pollen Room,* what mothers and daughters imagine about each other may never extend beyond the very private realm of primal needs, a sphere often inimical to change. In this regard the kind of satisfying closure that heals melodramatically estranged relations remains unattainable. Though "monstrous" in culture's, not Butler's terms, unmaternal mothers like Lucy are so ruled by basic needs that they resist both traditional norms, such as mothers nurturing children, and progressive aims, such as women no longer defining themselves through heterosexual relationships. The biological imperatives underpinning mother-daughter tropes—in terms of life spans that inevitably pass out of existence—turn into something more brutally survival-based. Conversely, *The Pollen Room* also suggests that biology as foundational to strong familial ties may indeed be altogether false.

If Jo's cocooned self never discovers the external means through which she could articulate her impossible circumstances, characters such as die Kleine and Be at the very least achieve this end via performativity, however infantile or misguided. And if *Relax* and *Lies* offer any kind of foundational truths, along similarly incongruous lines they reveal the fake and psychologically fragmented nature of identity. Does this poststructuralist maxim thus hinder the kinds of utopian but sometimes nonetheless attainable dreams imagined by the '68ers? Strikingly, die Kleine's, Be's, and Augusta's fantasies consist of antithetical parts: some '68er fantasies of more authenticity alongside porn stars and other bald-faced examples of cultural inscription. Despite glaring incongruities, feminism has engaged with these various elements over time as it has continually reinvented itself. On the one hand, the effect could rightly inspire Be's agitated screaming in the rain on a deserted street or the other forms of neurosis that characterize both texts. Yet the ending of *Lies* suggests that for feminism to move forward, it needs fantasies that extend outward and foster collective identification, however optimistically humanist that goal sounds. Excessive interiority or strategic theatrics alone are not enough. Given the quirky individuality of Augusta, Be, and die Kleine, we should, on the one hand, relinquish hope for a unified "we" among women. But we should also meditate on the possibility that *Lies* proffers—that individuality and shifting power relations can coexist with deep bonds and solidarity. It just takes the right imaginary constructs, including dated weepies for women, to conjure this end.

Notes

1. Volker Hage, "Die Enkel kommen," *Der Spiegel* 41 (1999), 244. Daniela Strigl associates the Fräuleinwunder with actresses such as Marlene Dietrich, Lilo Pulver, and Hildegard Knef, though Dietrich would have been in her fifties after the war. Like movie stars, though, the young female authors that Hage cites became media phenomena whose looks were assessed as much as their literary works. Strigl quotes Ulrike Tanzer's observation that "Judith Hermann's clothes and Zöe Jenny's lifestyle are sometimes given just as much or more space than their texts." Daniela Strigl, "Fräulein- und andere Wunder. Galvagni, Röggla, & Co," in *Geschlechter: Essays zur Gegenwartsliteratur*, ed. Friedbert Aspetsberger and Konstanze Fliedl (Innsbruck: Studienverlag, 2001), 132-33.
2. Peter J. Graves critiques the same blind spots in his essay "Karen Duve, Kathrin Schmidt, Judith Hermann: 'Ein literarisches Fräulenwunder'?" *German Life and Letters* 55.2 (April 2002), 196-207.
3. Alexa Hennig von Lange, *Relax* (Hamburg: Rowohlt Verlag, 1999); Zöe Jenny, *Das Blütenstaubzimmer* (Munich: btb Verlag, 1999); Elke Naters, *Lügen* (Munich: List Taschenbuch, 1999).

4. Eckhard Schumacher, *Gerade Eben Jetzt. Schreibweisen der Gegenwart* (Frankfurt am Main: Suhrkamp, 2003), 45.
5. The original German reads, "Neue Öffentlichkeit zu entdecken und nutzbar zu machen für einen offenen Austausch ohne herkömmliche Hierarchien." See Schumacher, *Gerade Eben Jetzt,* 46.
6. Torsten Liesegang, "'New German Pop Literatur': Difference, Identity, and the Redefinition of Pop Literature after Postmodernism," *Seminar* 40.3 (September 2004), 262.
7. Ibid.
8. I borrow this epithet from chapter 6, "Gendertrouble: Männlichkeit, Weiblichkeit und das Dazwischen," of Frank Degler and Ute Paulokat's volume *Neue deutsche Popliteratur* (Padeborn: Fink, 2008). They write: "The new German pop literature has been perceived by the critical establishment often on the one hand as a male-dominated product from a gentleman's club that is pretty much synonymous with the protagonists of *Tristesse Royale*" (74).
9. Thomas Ernst's *Popliteratur* (Hamburg: Europäische Verlagsanstalt, [2002] 2005), the first volume on pop to appear in Germany after the pop boom of the 1990s, makes only sporadic mention of Naters, Hennig von Lange, and Judith Hermann. Eckhard Schumacher's *Gerade Eben Jetzt. Schreibweisen der Gegenwart* (2003) structures its chapters around Rolf Dieter Brinkmann and Rainald Goetz. In *Pop Pop Populär. Popliteratur und Jungendkultur* (Bremen: Universitätsverlag Aschenbeck & Isenee, 2004), edited by Johannes G. Pankau, only one chapter of sixteen deals with a gender-related issue, namely motherhood. The authors cited within Stefan Neuhaus's chapter "Was ist mit den Müttern? Was geht hier ab? Popliteratur und Familie" are by and large male: Nick Hornby, Christian Kracht, Benjamin von Stuckrad-Barre, and Benjamin Lebert. Alexa Hennig von Lange is the only exception. Sandra Mehrfort achieves more balance in her work *Popliteratur. Zum literarischen Stellenwert eines Phänomens der 1990er* (Karlsruhe: Lindemanns Bibliothek, 2008) by devoting individual chapters not only to Kracht and von Stuckrad-Barre but also Hennig von Lange. Kerstin Gleba and Eckhard Schumacher's *Pop seit 1964* (Cologne: Kiepenheuer & Witsch, 2007) features the widest array of female pop authors, including Elfriede Jelinek, Clara Drechsler, Sibylle Berg, Hennig von Lange, Naters, Rebecca Casati, Katrin Röggla, and Kersin Grether.
10. Two obvious examples of non-mainstream, pop-affiliated works would be Feridun Zaimoglus's book *Kanak Sprak—24 Mißtöne vom Rande der Gesellschaft,* 6th edn. (Hamburg: Rotbuch, 2004) and Wladimer Kaminer's *Russendisko* (Munich: Goldmann Verlag, 2000).
11. This quote appears in a conversation Thomas Meinecke had with Benjamin von Stuckrad-Barre. In Gleba and Schumacher. *Pop seit 1964,* 366.

12. See "Wir tragen Größe 46," *Zeit Online*, 9 September 1999, http://www.zeit.de/1999/37/199937.reden_stuckrad_k.xml.
13. See Jörg Sundermeier, "Neue deutsche Vague: Pop-Romane sind da, wo eine Heimat ist," *Jungle World* 19 (3 May 2000), http://jungle-world.com/artikel/2000/18/27872.html.
14. Katharina Rutschky, "Der Poproman-Merkmale eines unerkannten Genres," *Merkur: Deutsche Zeitschtift für europäisches Denken* 57.2 (February 2003), 106–17.
15. See Degler and Paulokat, *Neue deutsche Popliteratur*, 74–84. Ansgar Warner has argued that *Relax* provides a deteriorated version of "marriage and family" novels dating back to the nineteenth century, including *Effi Briest*. He writes, "*Relax* is thus not only in content but also form the most deteriorated version of the traditional, bourgeois marriage and family novel in contemporary German literature. If a novel like *Effi Briest* counts as a 'prototypical example' of this genre in the late nineteenth century, then *Relax* would be its obverse in the twentieth century" (in Degler and Paulokat, *Neue deutsche Popliteratur*, 75).
16. Ross Douthat, "I Love Lena," *New York Times*, 4 October 2014, http://www.nytimes.com/2014/10/05/opinion/sunday/ross-douthat-i-love-lena.html?_r=0.
17. See Inwon Park's observation in, "Liebesdiskurse in deutschsprachigen und koreanischen Texten," in *Parodoxie des Begehrens*. ed. Anne-Kathrin Reulecke, Ulrike Vedder, Inge Stephan and Sigrid Weigel (Cologne: Böhlau Verlag, 2010), 249.
18. He says nothing about critical praise for her work, a bestseller that eventually won the Aspekte-Literaturpreis, the Literaturpreis der Jürgen Ponto Stiftung, and was translated into twenty-seven languages. Günther Stocker, by contrast, carefully details the novel's highly successful reception, including the fact that in the first nine months after *Das Blütenstaubzimmer* appeared, it sold 70,000 copies. See "Traumen des Aufwachsens. Drei Variationen aus der Schweizer Literatur der neunziger Jahre," *Weimarer Beiträge* 48.3 (2002), 382.
19. Jenny, *Das Blütenstaubzimmer*, 5.
20. Ibid, 5.
21. Ibid, 12.
22. Ibid, 24.
23. Ibid, 93.
24. Elsewhere in the novel, Lucy's facial mask reminds Jo of an "auseinanderbröckelnde Statue" (crumbling statue; 27).
25. For more information on this controversy, see Palash Ghosh, "German Left-Wing Greens. The Party of Pedophiles?" *International Business Times* 15 May 2013, http://www.ibtimes.com/germanys-left-wing-greens-party-pedophiles-1260787.

26. See Zöe Jenny, "Meine Lehrer waren pädophile Weltverbesserer," *Welt*, 14 October 2013, http://www.welt.de/kultur/literarischewelt/article120887193/Meine-Lehrer-waren-paedophile-Weltverbesserer.html.
27. Judith Butler, *The Psychic Life of Power: Theories in Subjection* (Stanford: Stanford University Press, 1997), 136.
28. Ibid., 140.
29. Hennig von Lange, *Relax*, 272. The first Vampirella comic appeared in 1969. A Warren Publishing series created by Forrest J. Ackerman and costume designer Trina Robbins, it ran until 1983. Vampirella inhabited the planet Drakulon, together with a race of vampires, but eventually escaped to earth to prey upon evil beings whose blood would save her dying planet. Always scantily clad, she possessed a seductive voice and gaze, and her presence alone was enough to sexually arouse men.
30. See Yvonne Wolf, "Alexa Hennig von Lange," in *Fräuleinwunder literarisch. Literatur zu Beginn des 21. Jahrhunderts.* ed. Christiane Caemmerer, Walter Delabar, and Helga Meise (Frankfurt am Main: Peter Lang, 2005), 97: "The image of women presented here, with its paradoxical split between vamp and housewife, corresponds with the paradoxical stance of magazines like *Bravo*, which on the one hand try and satisfy youthful dreams of sex and hip culture and on the other are a mass culture product meant to preserve the boundaries of societal conventions."
31. For instance, she often repeats the same word three times, a verbal tick that keeps coming back in her section of the novel.
32. The original German reads, "Damit ist *Relax* der für Gender-Fragen wohl einschlägigste Text der Neuen Deutschen Popliteratur, der insbesondere durch das geglückte literarische Experiment eines männlich-weiblichen Chiasmus der Erzählperspektiven besticht." See Degler and Paulokat, *Neue deutsche Popliteratur*, 77.
33. Sandra Mehrfort also understands the title as an imperative verb form, with Chris permanently striving to relax with his "enormous consumption of alcohol and hard drugs" (*Popliteratur*, 120).
34. *Faserland* and *Relax* depict a range of abject bodily substances. One childhood memory in Kracht's novel involves the protagonist getting sick during a sleepover and waking up in a puddle of diarrhea. The protagonist imagines the following scenario: "If you go straight and dare to look right or left, then bam, you've got a real mess. Right into the shit. It's completely disgusting. Such a stomped on pile really stinks and everything sticks to the bottom of your shoe. You can't just scrape it off on the curb. You have to go home with this stinking shit on your shoe and wash it off in the sink. Then your bathroom stinks and suddenly everything stinks and all you want to do is puke" (Wenn du wagst, geradeaus, rechts oder links zu gucken, zack hast du den Salat. Voll in die Scheiße getreten. Das ist komplett eklig. So ein zertretener Haufen stinkt ja richtig und alles klebt an deiner Profilsohle. Das

kannst du nicht einfach am Bürgersteig abkratzen. Das musst du mit der stinkenden Scheiße am Schuh nach Hause laufen und im Waschbecken abwaschen. Dann stinkt dein Bad und plötzlich stinkt alles und am liebsten möchtest du nur kotzen; Christian Kracht, *Faserland* (Cologne: Kiepenheuer & Witsch, 1995), 72.

35. And as Degler and Paulokat argue, by positioning die Kleine's text second, Hennig von Lange gives her the final word (*Neue deutsche Popliteratur*, 78).
36. The original German reads, "Vampirella wird langsam böse . . . . Meine Wut ist unendlich, und ich sehe furchterregend schön aus. Meine Brust bebt, und ich atme tief. Plötzlich ist alles ganz still. Die Gläser stehen unberührt auf dem Tresen, Kippen fallen aus den Munkwindeln. Vampirella ist da. Schwingt ihre Peitsche. Zack, zack, zack. Das Hemd von diesem Idioten ist durschschnitten, auf seiner nackten Brust steht blutig ein riesengroßes 'V.' Jetzt ist er gebrandtmarkt für den Rest seines Lebens" (179).
37. Hennig von Lange, *Relax*, 179. The original German reads, "Ich bin eine emanzipierte Frau, und ich kann schlafen, mit wem ich will."
38. Ibid., 152.
39. In *Female Chauvinest Pigs: Women and the Rise of Raunch Culture* (New York: Free Press, 2005), Ariel Levy critiques a young generation of women for whom "raunchy" and "liberated" have become synonymous, who make sex objects of other women and themselves in more egregious ways than men do.
40. Hennig von Lange, *Relax*, 233.
41. The original German reads, "Jeder weiß, dass die Männer schuld sind. Ich meine, Barb und ich springen ja nicht einfach so aus dem Fenster. Ich meine, das ist ein politischer Selbstmord, oder?! Das geschieht zum Wohl der unterdrückten Frau der 90er Jahre. Hunderte werden uns in den Tod folgen. Nee, echt. Das wird eine richtige Revolution!" (ibid., 264).
42. Ibid., 213.
43. See Mary Russo. "Female Grotesques: Carnival and Theory," in *Feminist Studies: Critical Studies*, ed. Teresa de Lauretis (Indiana: Indiana University Press, 1986), 213–229. She finds these women in Bakhtin's description of the Kerch terracotta figurines. Both senile and pregnant, they combine antithetical but abject female states.
44. Hennig von Lange, *Relax*, 139.
45. The original German reads, "Irgendwie erinnert Vampirella mich immer an meine Mutter. Ich meine, nicht weil sie mit jedem Typen pennt, sondern weil es so ein Foto von meiner Mutter gibt, wo sie nackt am Strand liegt, und da sieht sie echt aus wie Vampirella. Auf Seite 8 bin ich deshalb immer so ein bisschen peinlich berührt, weil ich das Bild einerseits ja ziemlich scharf finde, und auf der anderen Seite habe ich immer das Gefühl, meine Mutter liegt da und macht mich scharf. Das ist schon verrückt" (ibid., 40).

46. Ibid., 300–1.
47. Naters, *Lügen,* 9. The original German reads, "Der Mond scheint mir ins Gesicht. Hell wie eine Lampe. Ich höre Geschrei und stehe auf und sehe unten auf der Straße Be stehen und herumschreien. Sie trägt einen gelben Mantel, den ich noch nie an ihr gesehen habe. Sie steht unter der Straßenlaterne, die die beleuchtet wie ein Scheinwerfer und schreit und rennt wie irre hin und her. Das Wasser spritzt aus den Pfützen. Die Straße ist naß und spiegelt das Licht wider. Das Mondlicht und das der Straßenlaterne. Das sieht aus wie ein Film. Wie *Singing in the Rain,* wo Fred Astaire durch die Pfützen tanzt. Sie ist alleine. Ich kann nicht verstehen, was sie schreit. Ich ziehe die Vorhänge zu und lege mich wieder ins Bett und schlafe weiter."
48. Ibid., 30.
49. Ibid., 31–32. The original German reads, "Be, die sich nie um so was gekümmert hat, entwickelt, seitdem sie kurzhaarig ist, eine feministische Ader. Sie liest haufenweise Bücher über Feminismus und *gender* und spricht vom *Postfeminismus* und dass es nicht mehr darum geht, die Weiblichkeit und die Unterdrückung der Frauen anzukämpfen. Vielmehr ginge es heute darum, um den Unterschied der Geschlechter zu wissen und dieses Wissen gezielt einzusetzen und als Waffe zu gebrauchen. So wie Madonna oder Cindy Sherman, sagt sie. Wobei ich nicht ganz verstehe, was Bes Haare mit Madonna zu tun haben sollen. Das sage ich zu Be. Da verdreht die nur die Augen und sagt, ich hätte gar nichts kapiert, und gibt mir einen Stapel Bücher zu lesen."
50. Sonia Mikich has written about Madonna's various incarnations as seismograph for questions of gender. Though impressed by her ability to import and export signs and moods from minorities and subcultures and make them into mass phenomena, Mikich finds little to admire in Madonna's most recent guise as super-toned dominatrix. She writes, "Hello, there she is again, this time as a half century old dominatrix. Legs spread, hips pressed forward, cat-like eyes. Black lingerie, fishnets, boots, open mouth—oh well, it's all right out of the moth-eaten trunk of male fantasies, very 80s, and somehow conventional. I feel sorry for whoever confuses these steel muscles and hard flesh with sexual satisfaction. Let's simply congratulate a fifty-year-old about her good heath" (Sonia Mikich, "Triumph des Willens," *EMMA* [July/August 2008], 20).
51. Naters, *Lügen,* 73. The original German reads, "Ihr ganzes bisheriges Leben, mit den Männern und allem, das wäre nur der Weg gewesen, den sie gehen musste, um zu erkennen, was sie wirklich will. All das, was sie und ich bisher für Be hielten, war genau das, was sie nicht war und nie sein wollte, aber sie sein musste, um zu erkennen, dass sie das nicht ist. Sie hätte sich vor sich selbst und allen versteckt. Oder so ähnlich."
52. Ibid., 77.

53. Strikingly, Isabella Rossellini also becomes a fantasy object for the protagonist of Kracht's *Faserland,* who imagines one day having children with her. See 52–53.
54. Naters, *Lügen,* 51.
55. Ibid., 192.

CHAPTER 3

Dialogical and Borderline Selfhood in Charlotte Roche's *Wetlands* (2008) and *Wrecked* (2011)

In 2001, the twenty-two-year-old *Viva* video jockey Charlotte Roche appeared on the cover of *EMMA*'s May/June issue, her piercings-dotted face captured in close-up, eyes and mouth wide open in what looks like a primal scream. "Charlotte and Sisters Celebrate 30 Years of the Women's Movement" proclaimed the text beneath her image. On the left was a column of three smaller pictures—Glenn Close making the Vagina Day two-fingered salute, Franco-German politician and former student movement leader Daniel Cohn-Bendit, and a young woman dancing ecstatically—above the text "The Women's Movement: How it all Began." Roche was thus unambiguously tied to a longer history of uppity women, with her silent scream channeling all their energy. The cover layout also signalled *EMMA*'s penchant for situating contemporary German feminism in relation to its origins, a strategy that would often be reprised in the decade to come.[1]

From a vantage point fifteen years later, after the publication of her two novels *Feuchtgebiete* (Wetlands; 2008) and *Schoßgebete* (Wrecked; 2011), Roche's wayward expression also appeared to anticipate the anger evident in both novels, as well as the heady sexual pleasures of *Wetlands*' protagonist in particular.[2] This latter realm, of course, recalls the exhibitionist brands of girl culture that I highlighted in chapter 1, drawing examples from the volume *Lips. Tits. Hits. Power. Popkultur und*

Feminismus. And as I will demonstrate in this chapter, *Wetlands*' protagonist implicitly revamps pop literature strategies, giving them paradoxically fleshly form. Yet the ambiguity of Roche's facial expression on the cover of *EMMA* also invokes what I referred to in my introduction as

Figure: 3.1. *EMMA*, May/June 2001. Source: www.emma.de

the "affective dissonance" of 2008's angry young feminists nonetheless identifying with girl culture's raucous pleasures. If Roche's expression blends otherwise antithetical emotions, it also lures us into the psychological realm that, as I asserted up front, requires more attention. Particularly when the body factors so powerfully into speech acts, it marks the limits of intentionality insofar as it remains "unknowing," its actions never "fully consciously directed or volitional."[3] The meanings that emerge around Roche's female protagonists in word and deed offer something more complex than Alpha and New German Girls rejecting but unknowingly tapping into earlier feminist strategies. As much as this inconsistency invites critique, Roche's novels display a subjective realm where imaginary rationales, as I will demonstrate, make their own kind of sense for being so closely aligned with the psychological particulars of each protagonist's circumstances.

Significantly, within the complexly rendered, richly contrary landscape that characterizes the inner and outer lives of Roche's protagonists, we find not only a manifest rejection of feminist mothers and a tacit embrace of some of their tactics, but also an overt celebration, and at times implicit critique, of the individualist energies that characterize younger feminists. Most important, the young protagonist of *Wetlands* blends hybrid traces of the second and third wave on the surface of her body, which thus signifies the possibility of cohesion rather than conflict. To be sure, Roche's protagonists consciously perceive and vigorously articulate a rejection of their mothers, defining themselves as defiantly stand-alone beings. Yet, at the same time, *Wetlands'* protagonist recalls some of the examples of bridge-building that I highlighted in chapter 1. These include Jenny Warneke's concept of "Bindestrich" or hyphenated feminism, and the range of second- and third-wave feminist approaches articulated in Sonia Eismann's volume, *Hot Topic. Popfeminismus heute.* For these various reasons, *Wetland* and *Wrecked* are indispensible components in German feminism's generational constructs and the conflicts they articulate.

Feminist/Literary Mothers and Daughters

However ambiguous, Roche's roar belied the congenial feel of an interview she had previously conducted with Alice Schwarzer for *Viva*, deemed successful enough for a second airing. Schwarzer's interview with Roche in this issue reprised the affable feel of their *VIVA* encounter, which was not difficult given all the common ground they discovered in both political and personal terms. As quoted in the issue's "Dear Readers" rubric up front in the issue, Roche critiqued her young contemporaries for both distancing themselves from feminism and using sexist names like "bitch" and "cunt" for each other. The introductory text of Schwarzer's interview—which, strikingly, included Roche's mother, Liz—emphasized innocuous affinities: "Both have more in common that one would imagine. For example, they're both crazy about Elvis Presley."[4] In this manner Roche distanced herself from her generation's ironic playfulness, while Schwarzer tapped into the pop-culture pleasures associated with the third wave.[5] The interview that followed focused primarily on mother/daughter stories about fathers, husbands, and boyfriends, as well as Roche's career success, with occasional nods to feminism's influence on their lives. In fact, Roche's mother even gave her a subscription to *EMMA* when she turned fourteen. If this gift signaled a mother's attempts to initiate a progressive coming of age in line with her own politics, Roche's subsequent trajectory emphasized very pronounced antipathies over affinities.

Roche then went on to describe the "fury" that characterized her entry into puberty, which led her to "blame her mother for everything." She observed, "I was always a big fan of yours, Mom. I thought the other mothers were dumb; they were all housewives or something. But mine was political. And nonetheless I still turned into such a tornado who wanted to destroy everything and could do it, too. It was terrible."[6] She ended her interview, however, with very pointed words of reconciliation towards her mother: "But I have my strength from you, Mom. Without you I wouldn't be who I am today." The public acrimony she directed towards Schwarzer in 2008 and distilled in literary form, however, appears to reprise Roche's adolescent ire towards her mother. *Wrecked* even conflates the protagonist's mother with Schwarzer, each of whom serves as the mouthpiece of militant, antisex dogma. In retrospect, Roche's early bonding with Schwarzer provides the most wanton example of generational bridge-burning among emergent feminists, with no subsequent gestures of public or literary reconciliation. Neither *Wetlands* nor *Wrecked* depict any kind of face-to-face interaction between mothers and daughters; at best the provocative acts of *Wetlands*' young protagonist could be understood as a self-contained yet performative form of communication directed towards her mother. In both works, mothers remain at best shadowy, imagined figures and are ultimately purged entirely from the narrative, making it possible for Roche's protagonists to finally achieve large or small forms of autonomy on their own terms.[7]

Wetlands tells a story partly inspired by the autobiography of Roche's mother, who revealed in her interview with Schwarzer that her own mother had tried to commit suicide, as well as take the life of her young son, before a gas oven. This scenario plays out in the life of Roche's eighteen-year-old protagonist, Helen Memmel, though it remains a mostly unexamined backdrop to a story as much focused on the physically as on psychologically incendiary life events. And it was the former that called attention to itself, particularly given Helen's pleasure in smearing her body with its own effluvia, including vaginal secretions, as well as marking the walls of very public places with menstrual blood. In a less overtly brash manner, she describes herself as her own "garbage swallower" and "recycler of bodily secretions," which include "Popel" (boogers), earwax, pus, and vomit.[8]

In a more communal vein, Helen shares bodily substances with those around her, both by rubbing her genitals across the surface of public toilet seats and by switching tampons with girlfriends. Yet a far more mundane than insolent act is what initiates the plot: while performing an intimate shave, Helen accidentally cuts open one of the hemorrhoids that perpetually plague her, which prompts a trip to the hospital to have it removed. Her body thus becomes complicated terrain, not only smeared over in its own substances but also denuded of pubic hair and abject protrusions, making it both anarchical and conventional, as well as medically normalized. In this sense the manifold meanings that emerge around Helen's body over the course of the novel exceed her invidious intentions.

This chapter will examine how its signifying capacities overall speak to third-wave dreams of charting new semiotic terrain, which ultimately, however, remains perpetually entangled with maternal legacies, whether that of the actual mother or of a preceding generation of feminists. "Striking the pose" becomes as much a performative reaction to the mother as a semiotic resignification with political import. Equally important, the way Helen's personal metaphors blend with larger political discourse suggests a third-wave selfhood both overtly angry at maternal figures and tacitly unconflicted in its patchwork uses of second- and third-wave forms. She thus points in the direction of a dialogical mother-daughter bond, where difference and affiliation coexist, even if Helen appears to perceive and enact separation alone. As I will demonstrate in my reading of *Wrecked,* however, when separation becomes performative to the point of eclipsing the real mother entirely, it takes on the characteristics of a personality disorder. Dyadic thinking, evident in the "persistent twoness" of generational constructs that Astrid Henry critiques and in the East/West binaries I cited in my introduction, informs this process, which enacts extreme and artificially constructed categories. As much as this novel appears to embody a younger generation's heady anger towards its maternal forbears, on a more subtle level it amplifies and critiques the psychic structures that feed this emotion. While *Wetlands* literally embodies feminism in new and uniquely blended ways, *Wrecked* provides a metacommentary on the difficulties of achieving this end for a younger generation in particular.

Outward/Inward Ambiguities and the Maternal Legacy

Critical response to *Wetlands* centered largely on Helen's fascination with the physical rather than examining the psychological underpinnings of seemingly aberrant behavior. In this sense, critics, as well as the vast audience that made *Wetlands* a bestseller, may have simply succumbed to the provocations of an eighteen-year-old, a scenario the novel itself displays in literary form. Helen obliges, for instance, her male nurse to photograph her wound; in a similar manner, the novel forces its readers to meditate on it as well via graphic descriptions that unfold over the course of more than two hundred pages. Regardless of their assessment regarding the novel's aesthetic merits, critics often uninhibitedly mirrored its playfully base language and metaphors, thus indulging in the performative pleasures of adolescent impertinence. *Die Zeit* critic Susanne Mayers deemed Roche the author of "rectal fixated prose" and peppered her review with breathless exclamation points, as if to mock the novel's provocations and the media's response to them.[9] Andrea Ritter of *Stern* claimed that the novel had "sprinkled a pubic hair into the beauty industry's soup" and in Helen created a "Super Girl from Pipi-Kaka-Land" (literally "pee-poop land," but also a nod to Pippi Longstocking's "Taka-Tuka-Land").[10] In reviewing an early staging of the book, *Süddeutsche Zeitung* referred to Roche's "overflowing masturbation postulate," which *taz* critic Jenni Zylka deemed Roche's "hemorrhoidal page-turner."[11] Sallie Tisdale, in her *New York Times* review, mostly took the high road, claiming that Roche's novel had as much nuance as and less wit than *Mad Magazine,* then invoked the *Times*' decorum as the reason for not quoting the novel.[12]

Helen's highly graphic "Äußerlichkeit" (outwardness), however, comes together with the "Innerlichkeit" (interiority) of a first-person-singular voice who articulates her story via memory and fantasy. At one point Helen even concedes her status as unreliable narrator, which creates the conditions for unbridled provocations. Certainly Roche herself fed this impulse by stating that 70 percent of the novel was autobiographical, and in doing so blurred the line between actual life experience and unchecked fabulation. Her tongue-in-cheek tone during public readings of the text no doubt added acoustic bravado to the mix. Surface theatrics, however, deflect attention from internal motivations, and Roche in fact tried to close down analysis of this realm by claiming that her protagonist's eccentric behavior should not be explained in relation to family trauma. This stance does indeed make sense if it prevents readers and critics from understanding Helen's actions throughout as a type of pathology.[13] Yet it also belies the novel's final image, which Helen carefully crafts with found objects on her hospital bed: the form of a mother and son, with a drawing of an open stove door on the wall above them. Deeming this site her "farewell letter," Helen reveals the reason why she intends to abandon her parents: "das Schweigen" (the silence). This image, of course, makes it difficult to understand her delinquent theatricality throughout as anything other than a vehement antidote to a suicidal legacy that otherwise remains hidden and unspoken.[14]

Along similar lines Helen's bodily pleasures resemble the attention-getting tactics of small children, and at this end of the identity spectrum provocations speak to psychological needs that inevitably bring the mother into the picture. Throughout *Wetlands,* Helen grapples with a maternal legacy that exerts extreme and possibly even criminal control over her body, if we believe a story about the mother cutting off not only a ponytail but also her eyelashes. The act of cutting amplifies the overall zealous hygiene with which the mother tended to Helen's body, particularly her genital region. Helen both magnifies and condemns this power, however, by labeling sanitizing sprays in public restrooms as the "the ultimate rape by hygiene fanatics."[15] In contrast, she asserts, "Hygiene is not important to me," thus defining her identity in opposition to her mother.[16]

Wetlands manifests a child's initial steps at differentiation by acquiring language, and also linguistic autonomy, which in Helen's case takes the form of individualized names for various anatomical parts: she calls her clitoris and labia alternately "Hahnenkämme" (cockscombs), "Vanillenkipferl" (vanilla croissants), and "Perlenrüssel" (pearl-snout). In using edible alternatives to clinical terms, she counters the cultural coding that would otherwise call for the purification of female genitals. In a more narrow sense than écriture féminine's or *The Vagina Monologues*' efforts to reclaim the realm of signification, as well as Mary Russo's female grotesques as the site of "semiotic delinquency," Helen simply attempts to create the terms with which she will experience her own body.[17] Sometimes her body parts even talk back, like when she imagines her anus protesting a doctor's rough treatment with a metal probe. Situating her voice at this site smacks less of irony or subversion than a child's willfully contrary response. That her experiences with doctors often resemble parent-child interactions becomes obvious when she proclaims "I will always clean up my own mess" and when she refuses to produce a postoperative bowl movement.[18]

A more mature and gendered marker of differentiation, however, becomes evident in Helen's control of the substances that exit and enter her body, which in turn provide a symbolic means of birthing herself. This process occludes the mother as biological presence and repository of cultural forms entirely. Throughout the novel, Helen cultivates and lavishly cares for avocado pits, which she inserts into and removes from her vagina in a sexually stimulating act that also mimics birth. (The fact that Helen even brings them with her to the hospital as she convalesces also underscores their metaphorical link to giving birth.) As she observes: "This is the closest I'll get to birth."[19] On the one hand, this act does indeed connect Helen to her mother's reproductive capacities and by extension the many women in the maternal family tree who suffered from psychological breakdowns. On the other, birthing avocado pits potentially ends this legacy with a symbolic stillbirth. Helen in fact later ensures its end by having herself sterilized soon after her eighteenth birthday. In this sense she "births" herself as a nonreproductive female and thus appears to remove all genetic taint from her body and its reproductive organs.

Given the text's elastic metaphors, however, ending the mother's influence is not as simple as passing a small inanimate object or the clinical removal of inflamed rectal flesh. Helen also imagines a more violent end to her genetic inheritance—a lightning bolt that cracks open the avocado pit and by extension the "Nichtstun" (doing nothing) of her female forebears. This fantasy conjures a forceful extraction, as well as the pain and messiness of an actual birth. It also translates into Helen's one violently self-destructive act in the entire novel: ripping open her postoperative wound and nearly bleeding to death, ostensibly to punish divorced parents who rarely come to visit her in the hospital. Implicit affinities, however, emerge in an act of overt antipathy, staged at the locus of the mother's overzealous hygiene. Most obviously, mother and daughter thus manifest similar self-destructive behavior. As much as Helen appears to express her sexuality in her own terms, she shows her anger in her mother's language so to speak.[20] More globally, wearing the body's material traces, here most dramatically in the form of blood, also evokes the early mother-child bond and a shared uterine space of overlapping selves. In this manner Helen's unhygienic ways could be less about flouting the mother's discomfort with bodily matter than recreating the earliest bond in life. Her open rejection of her mother thus goes together with implicit bonds that linger in unacknowledged ways.

Coming of age stories of course require an arduous process of differentiation, which Helen both dramatically and imaginatively enacts for us in her overdetermined birthing scenarios. Strikingly, her internal pep talks about the need to abandon her parents feel quite clichéd in comparison to the text's vivid imagery: as she lies in bed she has a realization: "You'll become an adult. You have to manage without them. Finally realize that you can't change them. I can only change myself. Exactly."[21] If we compare straightforward speech acts and coming-of-age generic conventions with Helen's ambiguous metaphors, we get the sense that how we understand identity, in both conventional and conceptual form, may be only part of the story.

When Helen rips open the surface of her body at the site of her removed hemorrhoid, she points to the complicated nature of the mother-daughter relationship as not only a dyad of antithetical parts but also as partially, if perpetually, fused. This act dramatically shifts attention from the surface to messy internal matter that challenges the boundaries so central to autonomous selfhood.[22] I would argue that even her earlier efforts to capture this wound as image betray the mother-daughter bond as well. Not long after her operation, Helen examines the wound in a hospital window reflection and then asks her male nurse to photograph it. In doing so, she creates the imago upon which her individuated selfhood will rest, specifically at the spot that presents a perennial challenge to the clean and proper boundaries that her mother so prized. Of course any kind of "mirror scene" as the foundation of identity offers at best the illusion of selfhood. The seemingly hard and fast contours on display remain a two-dimensional image, a kind of visual fiction that merely conjures rather than authenticates identity as fixed and knowable. And in Helen's highly original version of the mirror scene, she locates her identity at an orifice that brings inside and outside together, signaling as much a conjoined identity as differentiation via soiled boundaries that mock the mother's control. Thus what she perceives in the mirror is not necessarily the same as the manner in which the image resonates in the context of her story.

Along similar lines, many of Helen's actions in the novel suggest supreme control over all bodily orifices, particularly when they function as sites of pleasure that counter an otherwise painful past. Helen's enjoyment of anal sex, for instance, quite emphatically transfers early mother-child intimacy to her sexual partners, and all of her elaborate preparations for this act manifest exuberant adult pleasures and her ability to control how her sexuality will be expressed. As much as third-wave aims to achieve specifically female sexual satisfactions provide a useful frame here, both the semiotic and the psychological add important dimensions. As I have underscored, the signifying capacities of Helen's acts remain beyond her control, evident in critics who bring *Wetlands* down to the level of *Pippi Longstocking* and *Mad Magazine*. They also remain beyond her control insofar as they point to internal terrain only partially knowable, evident in enigmatic imagery meant to signal autonomy but that in fact also invokes the mother's perpetual presence. One is reminded here of Juliet Mitchell's proclamation in her seminal work, *Psychoanalysis and Feminism. Freud, Reich, Laing and Women* (1975): "At every moment of a person's life, he is living and telling in word, deed, or symptom the story of his life."[23] Identity thus emerges not only in relation to larger social/cultural definitions and the unique ways that we respond to them, but also in our responses to deeper psychic structures that predate cultural awareness. It has as much to do with what we need as with how we imagine ourselves being in the best possible sense, two goals that can be at odds with each other.

Given her vacillation between two extremes—pain, whether actual or imagined, and orgasmic pleasure—Helen embodies both a child's helplessness and an adult's defiant sexuality. This overlap helps us to understand *Wetlands* as a fringe variant on the classic coming-of-age novel, one with a less straightforward trajectory from innocence to experience than a scenario where omnipresent childhood experiences fold over into and provide the blueprint for adult selfhood.[24] At age eighteen, Helen is at best on the brink of adulthood and retains traces of childhood that get very tangled up with the adult sexuality she otherwise exhibits. Not only do the various bodily emissions featured in the text recall children's fascination with the same, they also factor into

Helen's imaginative sexual practices, like when she sometimes foregoes washing out the contents of her rectum before anal sex. To articulate her sexuality in her own terms is thus not only a measure of autonomy but also a sign of the infantile bedrock she steadfastly clings to, which brings adult sovereignty together with childlike obstinacy. The recurring phrase "I'm proud of that," for instance, mimics both a child's pleasure in mastering the demands of its surroundings and an obdurate need to rub our noses in bodily substances, making Helen simultaneously a dutiful and rambunctious daughter. As I will argue further below, sometimes her sexual practices are as egalitarian as they are idiosyncratic, making her a rebellious yet pliant adult.

Cross-Generational (Dis)Identification

Whereas melancholia in *The Pollen Room*, *Relax*, and *Lies* points towards eclipsed bonds of intimacy, Helen Memmel appears to embody what Madelyn Detloff has called a "dynamic of contempt as a condition of autonomous selfhood."[25] As I underscored in my introduction, Astrid Henry has critiqued the sharp-edged dyadic configuration called upon by some younger feminists, which lacks the implied overlap in the wave metaphor. Implicitly, a dyadic model also relies on a positivist notion of history in which succeeding generations presumably acquire the wisdom that their forebears lacked. As much as Henry provides a much-needed critique of the underlying assumptions informing the mother-daughter dyad, she also cites numerous theoretical paradigms that sustain this trope, as well as feed into a potently truculent form of affect.

In the introduction to *Not My Mother's Sister*, Henry cites Adrienne Rich's concept of "matrophobia" as the basic means for women to become individuated and free, as well as the "matricide" that Phyllis Chesler argues second-wave feminists committed in order to "step out onto the stage of history."[26] Rich also argues that matrophobic impulses actually belie a pull towards the mother and the danger of identifying with her completely. This notion aligns with what Diana Fuss, borrowing from Judith Butler, has argued is a refused or disavowed identification that has already been made in the unconscious. Henry also cites Julia Kristeva and her notion of the indissoluble and thus lethal bond between mothers and daughters, which renders matricide a form of suicide for the daughter.

Whether described as a "pull," a "refused identification," or an ultimately self-annihilating bond, the force invoked here feels more visceral than rational, an important consideration for generational constructs in feminism. Against the backdrop invoked above, the third wave is as much preprogrammed by atavistic impulses as it is conceptually superior to what preceded it. Yet on the surface, the larger modus operandi remains escaping the mother's perceived fate, whether her diminished patriarchal status or seemingly misconceived politics for rectifying this state. In its most egregious form, the "pull" towards the mother could take the form of a shared masochistic legacy, evident in *Wetlands*' succeeding generational madness and suicide.

Important to keep in mind, however, is a notion of identification as highly elastic, what Diana Fuss traces across her work *Identification Papers*, in order to supplement the various forms of disidentification above. This process cannot be limited to psychic processes that bracket and demonize the mother and/or cover over a disavowed identification with her. My extended attention to Fuss in the introduction to this volume laid the foundations for understanding identification as a process with the ability to reverse, multiply, and "contravene" itself in previous forms, which makes identity both unstable and open to change. It implies that even the deepest, most truculent forms of disidentification are subject to change. Thus what appears to be another dyad—identification versus (dis)identification—in fact blends a "play of difference" with "similitude in self-other relations."[27]

In my introduction, I invoked Roche's charge that Alice Schwarzer forgets about the "Mensch" in the "Frau," which set the terms for difference defined via exemplary versus flawed forms of behavior in relation to feminist politics. In most general terms, to be "human," with the liberal, humanist connotations this designation implies, hints at the mysteries of identity, whereas the word "subject" implies cultural programming. To be human is to be both exemplary, given our Enlightenment legacy, and to be prone to flaws. It involves deep psychological needs capable of trumping enlightened imperatives, or at the very least making for complicated, contradictory behaviors. To be human means to reside on both sides of the spectrum—that is, to identify with and strive for an ever more evolved selfhood, but one simultaneously mitigated by more primal imperatives capable of stoking less noble identifications. By combining the child and the adult, Helen also speaks to, as well as straddles, the divide between exemplary and flawed selfhood. What she shows us about being a "Mensch"—the simultaneous existence of the child and the adult—is thus far less invidious than masochistic tendencies or a genetic inheritance of mental illness.

Second- and third-wave feminisms tend towards one side of the equation, evident in German feminists from the 1970s pursuing an alternative feminist agenda presumably superior to the patriarchy versus a younger, more individualist generation fond of underscoring its less than politically correct pleasures. Rebecca Walker, whom some credit for naming the third wave, has articulated the latter position: "For many of us it seems that to be a feminist in the way that we have seen or understood feminism is to conform to an identity and a way of living that does not allow for individuality, complexity, or less than perfect histories."[28] Roche has added specificity to this charge by invoking, ironically, masochism, though hardly as a burdensome maternal legacy. In her exchanges with Schwarzer and in the lives of her protagonists, "less than perfect" plays out in the realm of sexuality, where it provides further ammunition for the cycle of contempt between (symbolic) mothers and daughters: "Ms. Schwarzer would like to outlaw sadomasochistic sex. But women are totally masochistic, even she can't change that. I don't feel like asking Ms. Schwarzer for permission when I really let loose in bed."[29]

With Roche in particular, it appears that the more politically incorrect her generation's imperatives are, the more they serve the purposes of differentiation rather than undiluted pleasure. I find it particularly striking that an older feminist—American journalist Katha Pollitt—offers a succinct and helpful response to the problem of unemancipated psychology and its relationship to feminism. When Deborah Solomon grilled her in a *New York Times* interview about stalking an ex-boyfriend on the Internet, Pollitt, who goes to nail salons with her daughter, responded, "Feminism doesn't mean you are some brick wall of impermeable stalwartness in every area ... [it] is not about presenting a perfect façade of strength to the world."[30] Her statement shows a great deal of understanding for contradictory behavior and the complicated terrain of inner lives.[31] Second-wave forms of feminism, however, have been less interested historically in examining women's choices in psychological terms that resist change, no matter how revolutionary and compelling the battle cry.

To its credit, *EMMA* devoted its second issue in 1977 to women's masochistic fantasies, featuring articles by American second-wave feminist Robin Morgan and Margarete Mitscherlich, a psychoanalyst best known for her and her husband's work on the difficulties of *Vergangenheitsbewältigung* (coping with the past) in Germany. Responding to

Nancy Friday's 1975 work *My Secret Garden*, *EMMA* journalists struggled with the finding that most women indulge in masochistic fantasies. Perhaps not surprisingly, though, the magazine encouraged women to reprogram them along more progressive lines. Scores of letters in the following issue, however, put a plethora of masochistic fantasies on display, providing an early indication to emergent feminists that not all psychic structures lend themselves to restructuring.[32]

EMMA also appeared to react to Helen's intimate shave with a 2008 essay by political scientist Regula Stämpfli called "Die Scham ist vorbei" (alternately translated as "The shame has passed" or "The female private parts are gone"). She put this practice, which extends across Eastern and Western cultures, into a larger global context, ultimately linking it, however, with an infantile, porn-inspired "look at me" brand of culture.[33] Of course Helen cultivates her own "look at me" practices, but her body ultimately shares little common ground with the waxed, buffed, and interchangeable bodies that Stämpfli critiques. Yet given the fact that she does participate to a degree in conventions of beauty, and does so in a forthright, unapologetic manner that recalls Pollitt's stance, she exhibits a hybridity that partly closes the gap between generational differences. If Helen reduces the second wave's collective sisterly solidarity to shared tampons, she also invokes its spirit by mocking the beauty industry and all the products that strip the surface of the female body clean. In this sense it becomes important to look beyond her overt rejection of the mother and examine enigmatic messages that belie otherwise emotion-laden theatrics. And what emerges complicates not only the mother-daughter bond in ways discussed above, but also the generational rubric as organizing principle for feminists.

Overt Anger versus Tacit Second- and Third-Wave Hybridity

In my introduction, I cited Katja Kauer's argument that the New German Girls channel older feminist autobiographical forms in their bestseller of 2008, though this intertextuality remains unacknowledged. Their example of overt rejection and tacit connection invites critique, of course, though Helen Memmel helps us to understand how this contrariness functions. Specifically, she reveals how anger takes on a rhetorical, performative quality when directed at a monolithic maternal form whose actual nature may be quite different than she imagines, given the narrative unreliability she acknowledges. This problem also speaks to many emergent German feminists' monolithic understanding of the various and contradictory feminist strategies and aims that preceded them. And very possibly the main protagonist's uses of Alice Schwarzer in *Wrecked* have less to do with the actual woman than her status as "feminist mother" and thus irresistible projection screen in Germany's larger mass-culture domain. To invoke her thus functions analogously to pop novels' uses of commodity culture in order to articulate their selfhood. At the same time, as I argued in chapter 1, playfulness in pop novels by women comes together with anger and unresolved issues of power, which thus shifts pop's subversive aims along more emotionally fraught but also potentially ameliorating lines. And of course Helen's relationship to pop culture extends beyond symbolic feminist mothers, given her highly idiosyncratic uses of beauty conventions. Thus she aligns well with popfeminist aims for "perforating" and "shaking up" popular culture with feminist strategies. If we look beyond Helen's anger and one self-destructive act, we find hybrid feminist forms that suggest unconflicted and perhaps even salutary intergenerational connections.

If we begin with Helen's alternatively childlike and adult qualities and associate them loosely with third- and second-wave tendencies respectively, we get a sense of the full spectrum of selfhood to which feminism of necessity needs to respond. As much as a childlike perspective manifests basic needs and desires that are less amenable to humanist correction, it also points to the playfulness with which third-wave feminism approaches cultural inscription. (More subtly, playfulness may suggest a general desire to move away from theory-based paradigms or progressive politics on a larger structural level.) Children both learn and conform, even as their playfulness injects an unpredictable quality into the manner in which they embrace cultural forms. In the spirit of a younger generation of feminists, Helen's random names for body parts, for instance, suggest an attempt to make linguistic forms signify in new ways. And the more arbitrary the connection between signifier and signified, the less linguistic acts presage the dynamics of neoliberal choice within a field of given forms underwritten by the patriarchy. At the same time, Helen's highly quirky names resemble a child creating her own form of idioglossia, which subtly underscores the insularity and self-involved quality of third-wave feminism's more individualist strains. By contrast, Roche's poignant words of reconciliation towards her mother in their *EMMA* interview bespeak the kind of detachment and emotional maturity lacking in the "look at me" tendencies otherwise evident among some younger feminists.

Put in a larger cultural-historical context, Helen's body combines a 1970s-style, second wave–mandated naturalness with a contemporary impulse towards stylizing, though of course without any help from commodity culture. She both embodies and blends the differences between then and now, indeed literally wears them on the surface of her body in a proud and pleasurable manner.[34] More specifically, Helen converts the self-reflexive interiority of autobiographical works by German women from the 1970s into an in-your-face exteriority. Verena Stefan's autobiographical novel *Häutungen* (English translation titled *Shedding*; 1975) provides an important counterpoint, since it employs corporal metaphors as the means to slough off a false consciousness. By comparison, one could dub Roche's novel "Dripping," given the way Helen publicly displays abject substances on the surface of her body. This approach mocks not only conventional, omnipresent standards of beauty, but also naïve beliefs in the possibility of achieving some zero-degree state beyond cultural inscription. Within a more contemporary literary frame, Helen's body also clearly contrasts those of male pop protagonists who drape themselves in the accoutrements of popular culture.[35] If she decorates her own surface on her own terms, giving pop's surface aesthetics bodily rather than consumer-based form, Helen nonetheless does so with the same forthright attitude as her male counterparts. To wit: she turns what should be a sign of her objectification—men ejaculating on her—into a crust she wears with pride, thus transforming male substances into something decorative rather than invasive.

Many passages in the novel appear unequivocally second-wave in spirit. When Helen turns off the television in her hospital room, she appears to foster the conditions for a more authentic form of femininity. This impulse becomes quite obvious when she critiques women who scrupulously tend to every aspect of their bodies: "Manicured women have done their hair, nails, lips, feet, face, skin and hands. Colored, extended, painted, peeled, tweezed, shaved, creamed."[36] She also invokes the tedium of "Rasurzwang," or the pressure to shave, and her ill-fated intimate shave would seem a dramatic indictment of the beauty industry's destructive effects.[37] Yet when performed by a partner, Helen experiences an otherwise tedious activity as sexually arousing, and overall she exhibits a talent for transforming typically dull and conventional acts of styling into something pleasurable. In fact, Helen takes Katha Pollitt's pleasure in visiting nail salons to a much more radical place. For instance, she uses facial makeup to amplify the natural coloring of her inner vulva and thereby create a pleasing contrast.[38] She also hints at the consumerist component of third-wave feminism with the observation "I haven't found pussy makeup at the drugstore yet. There's a gap in the market."[39] At the same time, as much as Helen shares a younger generation's pleasures in styling, her wildly contrarian means of doing so may again mock individualist, self-absorbed tendencies, perhaps most glaringly evident in the postfeminism that Tasker and Negra critique.

Equally important, given the playful nature with which Helen articulates her sexuality, she appears to eschew forms of sexuality that rely on dominance and submission, which feels in line with earlier feminists' dreams of parity between the sexes. Though she clearly engages in a "Machtspiel," or power play, with the absent mother, Helen rejects this frame in her sexual practices. For instance, when she imitates men who visit prostitutes with unwashed genitalia in order to play up the dominance/submission binary, Helen finds no difference in the amount of pleasure she experiences, concluding "I guess this power play just isn't my thing."[40] She thus rejects the patriarchal power hierarchies that animated the second wave, even as she continually enacts the mother-daughter power struggles of a third wave. Overall, one gets a sense of the divide between manifest discourse and actual lived experience, of overt discontent and implicit equanimity. In this regard, her example may go beyond the complex "mysteries" of identity I invoked before to explain contradictory behavior. Helen's example may in fact suggest an alternative selfhood, more dialogical than dyadic, which feminists have sought in the face of recent generational divides.

Valerie R. Renegar and Stacey K. Sowards have argued that "society is awash in false dichotomies," and patriarchy in particular "constructs false dichotomies that force women into either/or decisions where neither option is attractive."[41] Madelyn Detloff has also critiqued the dyadic models that structure female generational relations, particularly in academe where scholars are obliged to render the arguments of earlier scholars obsolete. She cites black women writers conjuring a "self-with-other" rather than "self vs. other" frame, or a dialogical mode of selfhood which emerges within a range of multiple, contradictory discourses not perceived as threatening to the integrity of one's identity. If contradiction is taken as a given, particularly for black women whose cultural heritage is characterized by plurality, it need not be a threat. The goal, in Chela Sandoval's formulation, is ultimately a "differentiated consciousness," which "recogni[zes] the importance of both alliances and differences within and among liberatory social movements."[42] Detloff views this model as an alternative to a dichotomy of individuation or annihilation, since it emphasizes affinities over boundary-dissolving sameness, as well as the continual renegotiation of simultaneous alliances and differences which are taken as a given.[43]

At best, *Wetlands* gestures towards dialogical selfhood by bringing differentiation together with affiliation in the form of unconscious mirroring, whether of the mother's destructive tendencies or of progressive, generationally specific feminist aims. What looks like a typical, heteronormative ending—that is, more mirroring of the mother's conventional life choices—could also be understood as the dialogical blending of seemingly antithetical elements. As I have argued, Helen engages in sexually pleasing practices—mostly with men, but sometimes with female prostitutes—that transform pain at the site of overdetermined orifices into pleasure. Ultimately, early childhood bonding and adult sexuality come together in her relationship with the male nurse Robin, whose gender-neutral name and profession bring masculinity and femininity together.[44] Initially, he maintains his professional equanimity in the face of Helen's sexual advances, even when they appear to arouse him. In this sense, his demeanor conjures an ideal parent-child relationship based on trust and respect. Yet Robin also submits to Helen's request to photograph her wound, as well as to return the flesh the doctors cut away. He thus sustains her identity in the terms she lays out, which make abject flesh foundational to her selfhood. When Helen's parents fail to arrive to take her home, she departs with Robin, thereby ensuring future care and—given the gestures with which she aroused him—future sexual satisfaction. In the largest sense, Helen uses him to attach her sexual pleasures to the deep, caring intimacy that her relationship with her mother lacked.

But even though he heals her in normative ways, Helen's relationship with Robin in fact challenges the basic dynamic of power underpinning visuality. This force either relies on a mastering patriarchal gaze or the kind of spectacle that undermines this gaze by tapping into hidden male anxieties. Helen's "look at me" exhibitionism, I would argue, goes beyond this model, so often embraced when young women imitate porn stars to either play to male fantasies or to embody the ever-elusive female desire that third-wave feminists so often seek. When Helen asks Robin to look at and photograph her wound, she is not participating in a culture where women gain power by letting themselves be objectified, no matter how much control they exert in the process. His initial refusal to do so makes it clear that a different dynamic is at work here. (In *Wrecked,* the wife also insists that her husband look at her anus and see the worms plaguing her there, which he blatantly refuses to do.) "Look at me" in this scenario means attention must be paid to deeply personal pain before she can transform her wound into the site of adult sexual pleasures. Control and choice here take on global proportions in comparison to the neoliberal satisfactions of women who pursue the same within the limitations of a meritocracy's definitions of success. Helen's actions thus reveal the full complexity of selfhood within and beyond the social/cultural forces that would shape it. In this sense, channeling the mother's self-destructive legacy by cutting open her wound while countering silence with theatricality and pain with pleasure could be less a form of dialogic simultaneity than a slow process of healing.

Dyadic Pairings as Borderline Distortions in *Wrecked*

If one senses a coming of age reaching its endpoint in Robin's correcting all the mother's shortcomings, it pays to be wary of happy, heterosexual pairings as the universal antidote to conflict. In fact, *Wrecked*'s wife and husband pairing provide incontrovertible evidence of family trauma continually determining the shape of adult intimacy. In *Wetlands,* the psychic need to separate from the mother, even if justified by traumatic life events, feels performative—as in artificial—when compared to the seemingly unconflicted, self-evident affinities that Helen shares with the preceding generation of feminists. In this manner, the actual mother may well be superfluous in relation to the daughter's symbolic uses of her. *Wrecked* ups the ante in both its realness and fantasy components. Once again, autobiographical trauma serves as the story's base—the death of Roche's three younger brothers in a 2001 car accident as their mother drove them to Roche's wedding. This horrific event plays out in the novel in a devastated daughter's/sister's attempts to resist suicide and create the semblance of a normal family life for her husband and young daughter. As the story of protagonist Elizabeth Kiehl progresses, the magnitude of the accident is mirrored in her grossly distorted perception of the mother, even though, as Elizabeth emphasizes, she was in no way at fault in the accident.

If we take Helen Memmel's stories about her mother at face value, despite her admission of being an unreliable narrator, we side with her plight as she strives for the first shoals of autonomy. Rather than admit to narrative deceptions in *Wrecked,* Elizabeth demonstrates borderline tendencies that divide the world into black and white extremes, an impulse she links to the accident and the effect it had of "completely changing [her] personality."[45] Previously, Elizabeth claims, she had been "looser, much looser."[46] Unlike the possibility of dialogic selfhood that Helen points to, Elizabeth underscores the egregiously destructive effects of dyadic relations and how they justify barring the mother entirely from her life. While she claims that the accident provided the "Todesstoß," or death knell, to an already sick and broken family, so much of the text suggests retroactive projections as the salve for trauma.

Wrecked brings together neurosis and antipathy towards the mother in its very first paragraph. Neurosis itself signals a kind of self-centeredness gone wonky, where perceptions are clearly out of sync with reality. "I'm scared to death," Elizabeth pronounces about the electric blanket that she and her husband heat up before having sex, "that this thing will start to smolder and I'll be burned alive or will choke to death on smoke."[47] Over the course of the novel, this fear clearly aligns with how she imagines her brothers' fate in the car accident. Strikingly, the novel also includes the same suicide scenario as in Helen's family, with its basis in Roche's maternal family tree. In *Wrecked*, Elizabeth's maternal grandmother attempts to gas herself and her young son, an incident which also may contribute to her fear of "choking to death." Beyond anxieties catalyzed by real life events, Elizabeth also describes a varied range of phobias, including a fear of elevators, heights, and falling skyscrapers, as well as more general problems with panic, compulsion, and shame. Strikingly, her young daughter appears to have her own manifold phobias, which Elizabeth does her best to quell in enlightened, therapeutic ways.

Whether fueled by genetics or life experience, Elizabeth's anxiety comes together on the first page with anger towards her mother. While fondling her husband's penis she thinks to herself, "From this point I betray my men-hating mother. She tried to teach me that sex is something bad. Didn't work with me, though."[48] When this statement appears in a paragraph where the protagonist otherwise betrays her distorted view of the world, it should hardly be taken at face value. And in case we do take her animus at face value, Elizabeth demonstrates throughout how preprogrammed the cycle of contempt actually is. She raises her daughter, for instance, in a dogmatically bourgeois and ecologically correct manner, the antidote to her free-spirited mother and peripatetic childhood, even though Elizabeth and her mother clearly share despotic behavior. She allows herself and her daughter, for instance, only two sheets of toilet paper after bowel movements and provides great detail about her stratagems for nonetheless achieving scrupulous cleanliness. Despite the careful boundary patrolling evident in both novels, Elizabeth's resemblance here to the mother in *Wetlands* suggests the interchangeability of women across generational divides. In fact, Elizabeth claims that many women in her family tree share her name, which also points to Roche's own mother, Liz, as well as the daughter in the novel, whose name is Liza.

A few pages into the novel, Alice Schwarzer brings more pressure to bear by taking up her position alongside the mother, both of whom Elizabeth imagines as "revenge goddesses" and super egos sitting on her shoulder when she has sex. She responds to their presence by critiquing the women's movement for making women too self-centered in bed and accuses feminists of denying the existence of vaginal orgasms. In contrast, Elizabeth proclaims, "In bed I noticed how little my feminist upbringing has to do with reality. In a completely clammy secret way and behind my mother's and Alice Schwarzer's back I thought: There is indeed a vaginal orgasm! Fuck yes!"[49] In a more subdued manner than Helen's zesty, off-the-wall sex practices, Elizabeth insists on her own "politically incorrect" pleasures, which include vaginal orgasms and anal sex. Yet these acts are as much reactive as straightforwardly pleasurable and suggest a daughter both wayward in relation to the mother and dutiful to a husband whose every desire she attempts to fulfill. (At one point she even reveals that her "Geilheit," or arousal, only exists in order to "mirror" [spiegeln] her husband's.) The novel's first twenty pages consist of a highly detailed description of how Elizabeth performs oral sex on him and are written in a manner akin to a sex manual. Her lengthy, detailed descriptions reveal pride over oral sex done well and underscore the role of "Dienerin," or servant, that she enjoys playing for her husband. One is reminded of Roche's insistence on masochistic sex practices not simply as a means to pleasure but rather as the way she articulates contempt towards Schwarzer's generation.

Unenlightened behavior takes various forms in the novel and provides yet another instance of ironic mirroring among differing generations. The mother's and Alice Schwarzer's imagined spying reprises itself when Elizabeth sets a trap to determine whether her husband has been watching porn films, with which she has a conflicted relationship. While she claims that their porn collection has no traces of violence towards women, they clearly fed her husband's desire to have sex with a variety of women. The three-way sex they perform in bordellos, however, always prompts Elizabeth's initial dread, and only at the end of the novel do we sense the possibility of what she truly desires, a three-way encounter with another man. Worse than Alice Schwarzer perched on her shoulder, Elizabeth compares herself to the Taliban or a character in an "Agentenfilm" when she puts strands of hair in DVD cases to determine whether her husband has opened them in her absence.

Elsewhere in the novel, further evidence of conjoined identities takes bodily form, for instance when Elizabeth recalls her early fascination with her mother's breasts. In the spirit of uninhibited progressiveness, the mother allows her to touch them. After the accident, however, such closeness takes on a smothering, lethal quality most obviously when Elizabeth imagines the convalescing mother pulling her down into a chasm and infecting her with madness. (One is reminded of Kristeva's enmeshed mother-daughter duo and the suicidal consequences of matricide.) Rather than masochism or suicidal behavior, "madness" in this case could take the form of borderline personality disorder tendencies evident in the mother's brand of affection. Elizabeth describes her mother's demeanor alternately as "Either I was allowed to be close to her or not at all" and "Either you're like me or I won't love you."[50] Strikingly, she appears to embrace this either/or intimacy when she declares "your pain is mine," then speaks of her desire to both dissolve into the mother and be alone. Elsewhere the novel reveals how she reprises her mother's "two faces" with both her daughter and her husband. Despite pronouncing her love for her daughter, Elizabeth also complains of being sucked dry and having a ruined life by this "selfish little baby bird."[51] Likewise the husband often serves as the target of Elizabeth's depression and aggression, but she also describes dissolving into him during the sex they have at the start of the novel. Her continual vacillating ("schwanken") between the mother and husband suggests a divided selfhood, alternately domineering and submissive.

Yet when Elizabeth uses a phrase such as "the ticking time bomb called mother," one begins to sense how much the car accident colors her perceptions.[52] In another instance of mirroring, Elizabeth's manner of punishing the mother—turning her back on her for good—subtly reprises another aspect of the accident, one detail that presumably justifies an extreme response. Not long after the mother awoke at the wheel, burned, bloodied, and broken, she was pulled out of the car, which soon after exploded. In that brief period of time, she neglected to look back to see if her sons were conscious or not, a detail which torments Elizabeth because she can never determine the degree to which they suffered in the ensuing explosion. Part of her imagined mother-daughter polarity—

of being either smothered or emphatically cut off—makes it possible for Elizabeth to identify with her brothers before and during their death, with the mother's seeming neglect leading to their annihilation.

The most revealing moment in the text, however, comes in the final pages when Elizabeth talks about all the life-saving techniques she has learned, including the uses of defibrillators and how to perform tracheotomies and mouth-to-mouth resuscitation. A simple sentence that stands on its own as a paragraph articulates why she needs to save a life: "All because she didn't turn around."[53] If life-saving measures constitute a constructive response to a horrific tragedy, Elizabeth's statement resonates for the novel in its entirety, which demonstrates the psychic need over and over again to punish the mother as the antidote to her own suffering. One small moment of postcollision bewilderment justifies again an extreme response. This scenario amplifies the developmentally normal need to separate from mothers, with all the animosity it underwrites, to the point where the mother's actual shortcomings no longer even register. *Wrecked* creates a scenario where anger is so out of whack with circumstances that it takes on a grotesquely performative quality, one that retroactively amplifies and distorts the mother's seeming faults so that the daughter can survive a tragedy. In this sense, the cycle of contempt is amplified to the point where its distortions become impossible to miss, which in turn forcefully exposes and implicitly critiques a daughter's egotism. This literary act of "showing" begins to resonate with Roche's act of telling her mother how sorry she was for her adolescent fury in the *EMMA* interview.

If *Wrecked* provides a form of critique by playing up the daughter's distortions, this approach was lost on Alice Schwarzer, who within days of the novel's publication penned an open letter to Roche. In it she clearly linked Roche's critique of 1970s-style feminism with a perennial mother-daughter struggle for power: "You're reacting to your strongly emancipated mother . . . but your mother was only reacting to her mother, your grandmother. And you in turn react to your mother by imitating your grandmother. Should this fatal interaction continue indefinitely? Don't we women want to end this vicious circle? Does your daughter have to turn into your mother?"[54]

Despite the largely autobiographical underpinnings of Roche's novels, conflating the author and her protagonists can be problematic. Male pop authors provide a useful point of reference, insofar as their public personas were so often quite different from their protagonists. Christian Kracht and Benjamin von Stuckrad-Barre as hip models in Peek and

Cloppenburg ads or as smug arbiters of culture in *Tristesse Royale* created personas very much at odds with the tormented lives of their protagonists. Know-it-all daughters who publically spar with iconic older feminists, I would argue, provide a variation on the same, especially when their protagonists underscore how artificial and destructive dichotomous thinking can be.

Artificiality in the form of role-playing in fact colors the entirety of the novel, mostly in relation to being a mother. Elizabeth uses the verb "darstellen" (to embody, but also to depict) when she compares her parenting style to her mother's, which inserts some distance between the role and the one enacting it. Before her bordello visits, she acts as if she is excited, but in reality feels "total anxiety." Frequent references to films and scenarios being like in films, as well as Elizabeth's simple statement "I'm a good actress," conjure both performativity and detachment, while reprising Helen's unreliability as narrator of *Wetlands*. When Elizabeth also pronounces "It's all my mother's fault!," one senses her simply play-acting the cycle of contempt, rather than embracing it for a justifiable reason.[55] And the borderline tendencies that she recognizes in the rhetorical question "Is this called Borderline?" make it possible to conjure the world in very straightforward, though contradictory categories that can be easily embraced and enacted with conviction.[56] If this particular form of "persistent twoness" points towards mental instability, *Wrecked* potentially distances its readers from the generational construct for aligning it with psychic structures, not ever more progressive paradigms of feminism. In this regard Roche's novel takes the logic informing texts by the New German and Alpha Girls to such an extreme that critique is clearly warranted. Ultimately, such an intense and one-sided investment in difference constitutes a form of willfulness, not a launchpad to conceptually new forms of feminism.

Conclusion

Both of Roche's novels connect performativity more to a psyche working through trauma than the project of resignification as modus operandi of gender studies in the wake of Judith Butler. Importantly, theatricality in tandem with egotism adds dimensions to a theoretical model that would move feminism forward by underscoring the artificiality of gendered roles. When these two forces interact they reveal the complexities that follow when individual selves respond to larger political imperatives. In the process, the individuality so prized by the third wave takes emphatic enough form to stall movement towards conceptually new and productive forms of feminism. Instead we become aware of the wide-ranging effects when a mother stands at the gateway to feminism. She serves as much as a projection screen tied to individual prehistories—in Roche's novels a legacy of female madness and/or a family tragedy—as the bearer of progressive politics. Yet as much as Roche's novels play up (dis)identification with the mother, thus echoing the arena of German feminism in the 2000s, the overall effect again encourages critical distance. And if we keep in mind the labile nature of identification, generational constructs could take other forms as well, resulting in affect that is more productive for feminism. The trajectory that Roche describes in her *EMMA* interview—from angry to appreciative daughter—makes this clear. An ever-unfolding story at the very least suggests the possibility of third-wave forms of feminism less grounded in individuality, as well as open to more collective forms of identification. As Astrid Henry has observed, "Where the third wave has appeared stuck ... is in moving beyond self-expression to developing larger analysis of the relationship between individual and collective experience, culminating in theory and political action."[57] Perhaps the trick is not roping them to their mother's brand of collective politics—what Roche's *EMMA* cover suggests—but letting a younger generation imagine its own ways of identifying with what preceded them, thereby forging new forms of solidarity.

Notes

1. Thanks are due to the Taylor & Francis Group for allowing me to reprint a revised version of an essay that appeared in *Oxford German Studies* 45.1 (2016), 83–99. This chapter originally appeared there as "Fractured Legacies and Dialogical Selfhood in Charlotte Roche's *Feuchtgebiete* (2008) and *Schoßgebete* (2011)."
2. Charlotte Roche, *Feuchtgebiete* (Cologne: Dumont, 2008); *Schoßgebete* (Munich: Piper, 2011).
3. Shoshana Felman, quoted in Judith Butler, *Excitable Speech: A Politics of the Performative* (New York: Routledge, 1997), 10.
4. See "Ohne dich wäre ich nicht ich," *EMMA* (May/June 2001), 56–61.
5. In another example of pop-culture literacy, Schwarzer channeled Marilyn Monroe and sang "Happy Birthday, Mr. Talk Show" to the talk and cooking show host Alfred Biolek on the occasion of his seventy-fifth birthday.
6. "Ohne dich wäre ich nicht ich," 60. The original German reads, "Ich war eben immer schon ein Fan von dir, Mama. Die anderen Mütter fand ich

doof, die waren Hausfrauen und so. Aber meine war immer politisch. Und trotzdem bin ich dann so ein Wirbelsturm geworden, der alles kaputtmachen wollte und das auch konnte. Es war schrecklich."

7. The film version of *Wetlands*—in German, *Feuchtgebiete* (David Wnendt, 2013)—takes a very different tack by making the mother a flesh-and-blood and often present figure, sometimes to melodramatic, sometimes comic, effect.
8. Roche, *Feuchtgebiete*, 120.
9. See Susanne Mayers, "Oh Muschilein. Charlotte Roche schreibt ein Sexbuch, und das Feuilleton vibriert. Warum die Feuchtträume einer TV-Moderatorin der Hit sind," *Zeit Online*, 6 March 2008, http://www.zeit.de/2008/11/Glosse-Literatur-Roche.
10. See Andrea Ritter, "Die Zotenköniginnin von Muschi-Land. Provokation oder neues Selbstbewusstsein—was steckt hinter dem Erfolg des Bestsellers von Charlotte Roche? Eine Expedition in die 'Feuchtgebiete' des Feminismus" (The smut queen of pussy land: Provocation or new consciousness—What is behind the success of Charlotte Roche's bestseller? An expedition into the wetlands of feminism). *Stern*, 12 May 2008, http://www.stern.de/kultur/buecher/3-charlotte-roche-die-zotenkoenigin-von-muschiland-619765.html. (The title is also a play on "Quoten," which rhymes with "Zoten," and alludes to the quotas the German government often sets to mandate women's increased participation in the working world.) Interestingly, Hannalore Schlaffer sees a strong link between *Wetland's* protagonist, as well as the protagonist of Helene Hegemann's controversial novel *Axotl Roadkill* (2010), with Pippi Longstocking and Zazie, the young heroine of Raymond Queneaus's 1959 novel. Both girls belong, she argues, to a longer history of the "Göre" (cheeky girl, hussy, brat). See Hannalore Schlaffer, "Die Göre—Karriere einer literarischen Figur." *Merkur: Deutsche Zeitschrift für europäisches Denken* 65.3 (March 2011), 274–79.
11. See "Feuchtgebiete am Theater—vom Terror der Körperlichkeit," *Süddeutsche Zeitung*, 30 September 2008, http://www.sueddeutsche.de/kultur/feuchtgebiete-am-theater-vom-terror-der-koerperlichkeit-1.698205; and Jenni Zylka, "Schleimporno gegen Hygienezwang," *taz.de*, 28 February 2008, http://www.taz.de/!5185966/.
12. See Sallie Tisdale, "Graphic Novel," *New York Times*, 16 April 2009, http://www.nytimes.com/2009/04/19/books/review/Tisdale-t.html.
13. In "Rescuing a Theory of Adolescent Sexual Excess: Young Women and Wanting," Sara I. McClelland and Michelle Fine observe, "Within medical, psychological, and cultural spheres, there has been significant debate around the subject of female sexual excess. Images of female eroticism, enjoyment, or pursuit have historically been linked with pathological categories, such as 'nymphomaniac' and 'slut'. . . . Although adult women have been somewhat successful in resuscitating a discourse of sexual excess for

them/ourselves, the sexuality of teen women has remained more securely locked within a judgmental box that treats female teenage sexuality as dangerous, risky, and excessive—or as victimization." See Sara I. McClelland and Michelle Fine, "Rescuing a Theory of Adolescent Excess: Young Women and Wanting," in *Next Wave Cultures: Feminism, Subcultures, Activism,* ed. Yvonne Tasker and Diane Negra (New York: Routledge, 2008), 33.

14. Claudia Liebrand argues that *Wetlands* resembles a psychological case study, but with roots in eighteenth century works such as Georg Büchner's *Lenz.* Elsewhere, she also links the text, if understood as a critique of male-centered pornography and destructive societal structures, to the "Betroffenheitsliteratur" (literature of concern) of the 1970s, as well as Ingeborg Bachmann's "Todesartenzyklus" (death cycle) which includes the novel *Malina* (1971). See "Pornographische Pathografie. Charlotte Roches *Feuchtgebiete,*" *Literatur für Leser* 34.1 (2011), 13–22.
15. Roche, *Feuchtgebiete,* 19.
16. Ibid., 18.
17. Carrie Smith-Prei makes a similar argument in "'Knaller Sex für alle': Popfeminist Politics in Lady Bitch Ray, Charlotte Roche, and Sarah Kuttner," *Studies in 20th and 21st Century Literature* 35.1 (Winter 2011), 25: "The mass-market and male-driven women's beauty industry subversively inspires Roche, herself a recognizable pop icon, to configure a 'female grotesque' in her novel *Feuchtgebiete.*"
18. Roche, *Feuchtgebiete,* 16; Heike Bartel argues that Helen's childlike names for her body parts render Roche's project to create alternatives to otherwise tired patriarchal language unsuccessful. As will become clear over the course of this chapter, the larger point may be the coexistence of the child and adult in Roche's protagonist. See "Porn or PorNO: Approaches to Pornography in Elfriede Jelinek's *Lust* and Charlotte Roche's *Feuchtgebiete,*" in *German Text Crimes: Writers Accused, from the 1950s to the 2000s,* ed. Tom Cheesman (Amsterdam: Rodopi, 2013), 99–123.
19. Roche, *Feuchtgebiete,* 40.
20. This one self-destructive act leads Claudia Liebrand to question whether Helen suffers from borderline tendencies. I would argue that one instance alone in a text otherwise characterized by adult sexual pleasures renders this interpretation less convincing. But, as I will demonstrate, Roche's protagonist in *Wrecked* not only consistently demonstrates borderline tendencies but even recognizes them as such. See Liebrand, "Pornographische Pathografie," Charlotte Roches *Feuchtgebiete.*" *Literatur für Leser* 34.1 (2011), 13–22.
21. Roche, *Feuchtgebiete,* 185.
22. Roche's *Wrecked* also includes the anus in its narrative, specifically in a case of worms that prompts the protagonist to recollect a family tragedy of horrific proportions.

23. Juliet Mitchell, *Psychoanalysis and Feminism: Freud, Reich, Laing, and Women* (New York: Vintage Books, 1975), 14.
24. The fact that Roche initially intended to write a sex manual and later labeled *Wetlands* a feminist manifesto invokes the hybridity of feminist texts, from the textbook-style approach of *Our Bodies, Ourselves* to Benoîte Groult's autobiography *Salz auf unserer Haut* (Salt on our skin), which describes a gradual sexual awakening that begins at age eighteen and takes a literary form that some critics likened to porn.
25. Madelyn Detloff, "Mean Spirits: The Politics of Contempt between Feminist Generations," *Hypatia* 12.3 (Summer 1997), 79.
26. Astrid Henry, *Not My Mother's Sister: Generational Conflict and Third-Wave Feminism* (Bloomington: Indiana University Press, 2004), 9–10.
27. Diana Fuss, *Identification Papers* (New York: Routledge, 1995), 2.
28. Quoted in Valerie Renegar and Stacey K. Sowards, "Contradiction as Agency: Self-Determination, Transcendence, and Counter-Imagination in Third Wave Feminism," *Hypatia* 24.2 (Spring 2009), 6.
29. The original German reads, "Frau Schwarzer möchte Sadomaso-Sex verbieten. Frauen sind aber total masochistisch, das wird auch sie nicht mehr ändern können. Ich habe keine Lust, Frau Schwarzer um Erlaubnis zu fragen, bevor ich im Bett richtig loslege." Quoted in "Monogamie—ein riesiger Fehler," *Süddeutsche Zeitung*, 21 May 2008, http://www.sueddeutsche.de/kultur/bildergalerie-nimm-mich-jetzt-auch-wenn-ich-stinke-1.218176-2.
30. See "Questions for Katha Pollitt: Women's Studies," Interview with Deborah Solomon, *New York Times Magazine* (23 September 2007), 17.
31. Roche herself faced similar grilling. When an interviewer noted her shaven legs and a more conventional approach to femininity than her literary protagonist, she described how her earlier colleagues at *Viva* had continually berated her for not shaving her underarms. One senses her giving in rather than taking Pollitt's unapologetic stance towards the inconsistencies of selfhood.
32. See "Unsere masochistischen Sex-Phantasien," *EMMA* (September 1977), 6–13.
33. See Regula Stämpfli, "Die Scham ist vorbei." *EMMA* (January/February 2008), 60–61. She writes: "During the eternal search for a man, American women, otherwise so emancipated in the realms of politics, economics, or science, transform themselves into girls who never grow up, who beg for attention in pathetic ways. They go very far in their almost pathological search for new experiences and recognition. They strip, do lap dances, and accompany their friends, colleagues, and husbands into shabby clubs, shout even more raucously than all the boys present and like dragging their girlfriends along best. In the American 'look at me' culture, every means for offering up their sexuality, and with it themselves, is justified."
34. Maria Stehle identifies a variety of feminist aims in regard to Helen's selfhood: Helen aligns herself with a 1970's feminism that encouraged women

to explore, enjoy, and love their own bodies, even as she explores sexual practices that an earlier generation would have understood as submissive and humiliating. Likewise Helen embraces a third-wave predilection for porn, but also brings body hair, fluids, and smells into the picture, in an over-the-top rendition of a second-wave natural body. See Maria Stehle, "Pop, Porn, and Rebellious Speech: Feminist Politics and the Multi-Media Performances of Elfriede Jelinek, Charlotte Roche, and Lady Bitch Ray," *Feminist Media Studies* 12.2 (2012), 237–38. I would also add that Helen initiates her own kind of girl-power movement by sharing bodily fluids with girlfriends.

35. Katja Kauer assesses the extent to which *Wetlands* itself could be understood as a pop novel. Roche's work as a *Viva* video jockey aside, the novel construes adolescence, she argues, from an adult's perspective, but minus a moralizing critique or any semblance of narrative authority; see *Popfeminismus! Fragezeichen! Eine Einführung* (Berlin: Frank & Timme Verlag, 2009), 123.
36. Roche, *Feuchtgebiete*, 106.
37. Helen is quite detailed in this regard: "Because my ass presumably also belongs to sex, it has to submit to this modern pressure to shave like my pussy, my legs, my underarms, the area above my lips, both big toes, and the tops of my feet. The area above my lips doesn't get shaven of course but rather plucked because as we've all learned you otherwise get an even thicker mustache. As a girl you're obliged to avoid that. Earlier I was very happy unshaven but then I began with this nonsense and can't stop anymore" (Roche, *Feuchtgebiete*, 9–10).
38. Critics have pointed out the implicit racism of passages where she describes black women's genitalia in very graphic terms.
39. Roche, *Feuchtgebiete*, 124.
40. Ibid., 122.
41. See Renegar and Sowards, "Contradiction as Agency," 11.
42. Quoted in Detloff, "Mean Spirits," 80.
43. Ibid., 92.
44. Claudia Liebrand also points out the gender reversal of the man playing the role of nurse, with all the care and tending this role requires. See "Pornografische Pathografie," 18.
45. Roche, *Schoßgebete*, 228.
46. Ibid., 24.
47. Ibid., 7.
48. Ibid.
49. Ibid., 17. The original German reads, "Im Bett habe ich gespürt, dass meine feministische Erziehung meilenweit an der Realität vorbeigeht. Ganz klamm-heimlich und hinter dem Rücken meiner Mutter und dem von Alice Schwarzer habe ich gedacht: die haben unrecht! Ich spüre doch fast jedes Mal: Es gibt ja wohl einen vaginalen Orgasmus! Verfickt noch mal!"

50. Ibid., 112, 28.
51. Ibid., 167.
52. Ibid., 162.
53. Ibid., 275.
54. "Du reagierst auf deine so forciert emanzipierte Mutter ... Aber deine Mutter hat nur auf ihre Mutter, deine Großmutter reagiert. Und du wiederum, du reagierst nun auf deine Mutter—und machst es wie deine Großmutter. Soll diese fatale Wechselwirkung immer so weitergehen? Wollen wir Frauen diesen Teufelkreis denn nie durchbrechen? Muss deine Tochter nun etwas werden wie deine Mutter?" "Hallo Charlotte," no longer appears on Alice Schwarzer's website but is alluded to in numerous articles, including "Alice Schwarzer zu Charlotte Roche. Du hast nicht die Lösung. Du hast das Problem," *Der Tagesspiegel,* 16 August 2011, http://www.tagesspiegel.de/kultur/alice-schwarzer-zu-charlotte-roche-du-hast-nicht-die-loesung-du-hast-das-problem/4504560.html.
55. Roche, *Schoßgebete,* 18.
56. Ibid., 204.
57. See Astrid Henry, "Solitary Sisterhood: Individualism Meets Collectivity in Feminism's Third Wave," in *Different Wavelengths: Studies of the Contemporary Women's Movement,* ed. Jo Reger (New York: Routledge, 2005), 83.

CHAPTER FOUR

Girls Gone Wild
Ulrike Meinhof, Uschi Obermaier, and Feminist Fantasies of '68

In *Time Binds: Queer Temporalities, Queer Histories,* Elizabeth Freeman theorizes a present that is always split, though not by the signifying processes that give it shape, but rather "by prior violence and future possibility."[1] Drawing on Jacques Derrida's work *Specters of Marx*, she emphasizes the "hauntological properties" that resonate around this rift. According to Derrida, what emerges in Marxist thought is an "ethics of responsibility toward the other across time—toward the dead or toward that which was impossible in a given historical moment, each understood as calls for a different future to which we cannot but answer with imperfect and incomplete reparations."[2] As much as we remain bound to history, the other who resides there asserts itself in ways that perpetuate further fragmentation—that is, that splits the "forward-moving agency" of selfhood. As a consequence, Freeman argues, "time does not heal but further fissures history."[3] This framework provides a useful starting point for generational constructs, both the fundamental divides that define them and their teleological trajectories towards less imperfect solutions for oppression and thus a brighter future. By pointing us backwards in time, this framework obliges us to meditate on what was and to acknowledge unfinished business. It becomes less about "affective displays of frustration and even intense dislike" of an earlier generation for undermining progress than empathy for the "impossibilities" of a given historical moment and recognizing our perpetually insufficient remedies for them.[4] Ideally, this process would oblige a younger generation of feminists to think about the forces that determine their relationship to older feminists, as well as to cultivate their own analeptic approach to the once and future forms of oppression that of course remain.

Cultivating empathy extends beyond the realm of ethics alone insofar as this aim often aligns with artistic processes intended to recreate history. Significantly, this aim also stands in relation to the fantasies and projections that filter the past, which results in rich, but not necessarily cohesive, layering. Freeman's work actually begins with analysis of a scene from Nguyen Tan Hoang's video *K.I.P.* (2000) that blends grainy, dated gay porn with the reflection of the director's face watching it on a TV monitor. While she expertly dissects the video's various forms of temporal dissonance and their implications for spectatorship across different time periods, she also reflects on the meaning of the images for someone in the post-AIDs era. Rather than buttressing a progressive logic whereby increased visibility correlates with increased freedom, these images "jam" historical sequences by evoking what Hoang never experienced but "clearly mourns for"—a time in the 1970s and early 1980s when urban gay men could "enjoy casual sex without latex."[5] Equally important, the video's title not only invokes a famous porn star from that era but it also, as Freeman points out, recalls the phrase "rest in peace." One senses a past that is irretrievably gone, as well as a horribly altered landscape where illness shut down non-normative forms of eroticism and where ghosts should command our respect.

In understanding a contemporary audience's relationship to both the student movement and the birth of feminism in Germany, acknowledging the role of fantasy—whether nostalgic or hostile—is of course fundamental. Equally important for this chapter, which switches to the realm of film, is the extent to which fantasy-bound representations of a long-eclipsed moment in time stoke identification across difference and compel continued investment in never fully realized political projects. Wolfgang Kraushaar's numerous volumes on the student movement have provided a comprehensive historical overview and analysis of the difficulties in understanding a "myth" and a "code," two words that appear in one of his early book titles.[6] He thus situates history within a larger cultural imaginary, with the word "code" conjuring subsequent generations' truck with the era for their purposes. This vantage point signals a blend of preexisting artistic codes with the concrete historical traces that come to define an era, while raising the question of which artistic filters have represented another era's feminism and to what ends. To what extent do they cultivate empathetic, restorative relations across generational divides? How do they conjure feminist aims and fantasies, whether from an earlier moment or retroactively from a contemporary feminist perspective? In what ways do these filters align with larger cinematic approaches that range from the conventional to the experimental?

Whereas Hoang's video draws on the repertoire of experimental approaches, the two films that this chapter addresses—*Der Baader Meinhof Komplex* (The Baader Meinhof Complex; 2008) and *Das wilde Leben* (released in English as *Eight Miles High*; 2007)—are decidedly mainstream in their approach, despite art house elements.[7] They depict iconic female figures for the era of '68, Ulrike Meinhof and Uschi Obermaier respectively, two women who continue to inhabit the larger public imaginary nearly a half a century later. In simplest terms, Meinhof embodies the intellectual theorist/left-wing terrorist and Obermaier the fashion model and "Kommune 1" resident whose image became synonymous with sexual liberation and youth culture. (At the risk of overstating the contrast, Obermaier was also deemed to have the political consciousness of an "amoeba.") Whereas left-wing terrorism resonated in relation to 1970's feminism in troubling ways, Obermaier's legacy provides fertile ground for contemporary feminists who make eroticism central to their politics. As I will demonstrate in this chapter, Edel's film offers a hedge to inflated rhetoric that viewed female terrorists as an outgrowth of feminism, whereas Bornhak's depiction of Obermaier revels in the sex-positive energies of girl culture, as well as the third wave more generally. In the process, contemporary spectators implicitly witness both the political impossibilities of a given historical moment that stoke empathy and erotic affinities that bridge generational divides. Even though neither Meinhof nor Obermaier embraced emergent feminism, they nonetheless function in these two films as ciphers for feminism's ever-evolving energies and its influence on a larger realm of representation.

As much as connections can be made to Freeman's understanding of unconventional temporalities in Hoang's film, it should also be pointed out up front that both of the films under discussion here remain, as I emphasize above, in a largely mainstream register, one in which identification has long rested on a spectator's capacity to empathize as well as lose herself in cinematic fantasies. Significantly, the first aim, with all its liberal, humanist energies, shares ground with early feminists' attempts to uncover women's experiences, and in this regard *The Baader Meinhof Complex* activates a dated but still important feminist strategy for representing gender. Along similar lines, in *Eight Miles High*, Uschi

Obermaier's agency in the visual realms of fashion and tabloid journalism enacts a more contemporary feminist notion of performativity that calls attention to the artificial bases of selfhood. This chapter thus moves away from the kinds of fractured subjectivities that literary interiority is so adept at depicting and instead focuses on past and future feminist approaches to representation as they play out in mainstream film. It concerns itself with the mother-daughter trope in the implicit but nonetheless familiar terms—that is, as overtly political and/or transgressively sexual—that represent a key historical era for older feminists.

If this process, particularly where it overlaps with dominant cinema conventions, lacks some of the complexities I have traced in previous chapters, it nonetheless aligns with the possibilities that Diana Fuss highlights in *Identification Papers*—meaning identification's ability to "continually ... evolve and change, to slip and change under the weight of fantasy and ideology."[8] This observation tallies with Freeman's analysis of Hoang's video if one assumes that ever-changing identifications across time factor into the temporal fissures that she describes. And if this splitting takes the form of a contemporary perspective layered over history, the filmic medium could potentially bolster the affiliations that fuel social movements across generations. At the same time, this chapter will also trace the pitfalls of dominant cinema as a window onto feminism, including the shrinking of feminist fantasies, such as uncovering authentic voices and celebrating performative agency, into cliché. In fact, *Eight Miles High* demonstrates an investment in both possibilities, as if performativity were synonymous with autonomy, a notion that Judith Butler has explicitly challenged.[9] When representation shifts along politically progressive lines, it does not necessarily yield larger insights for feminism about how to continually reimagine itself in the face of ever-shifting identifications and their challenge to a larger collective identity.

Fantasies of '68, Cliché, and Corrective Impulses

Before examining *The Baader Meinhof Complex*, a brief detour is warranted by the manner in which it activates older strategies for representing '68 and how this affected its reception in ways that occluded feminist politics. Wolfgang Kraushaar's scholarship on '68 highlights our thoroughly mediated relationship to this era. Strikingly, he often relies on highly visual metaphors—for instance, when he compares our perceptions to a kaleidoscope whose elements continually shift to create new impressions.[10] He also quotes at length a passage from Hans Magnus Enzenberger's "Erinnerungen an einen Tumult—Zu einem Tagebuch aus dem Jahr 1968" (Memories of tumult—regarding a diary of the year 1968). Here Enzenberger emphasizes how his experiences lie "buried under the dung heap of the media, 'archive materials,' panel discussions, the veteran styling of a reality that has become unimaginable in an underhanded way." Most strikingly, Enzenberger compares his memories to what sounds like a classic art house film:

> My memory, this chaotic, delirious director, delivers an absurd film whose sequences don't fit together. The sound is asynchronous. Whole shots are underlit. Sometimes the screen is just black. A lot has been recorded with a shaky camera. I don't recognize most of the actors ... the whole process is a mystery to me. ... It wasn't possible to "understand" everything all at once, to "make heads or tails of it," to "find the point of it." The contradictions scream to the heavens. Every attempt to make the tumult intelligible necessarily ends in ideological gibberish. Memories of the year 1968 can only take one form: that of collage.[11]

If one combines the collage principle invoked above with Enzenberger's film analogy, what he describes may be akin to something more like montage, a technique often used to denote the passage of time but whose origins in Soviet cinema were decidedly political. Most important, the passage above anticipates the disjunctive, media-laden layers that have become, paradoxically, a familiar means for rendering '68 in seemingly authentic fashion.

R. G. Renner had identified blurry boundaries between the real, the imaginary, and the simulated in films such as Volker Schlöndorff's *Die Stille nach dem Schuss* (released in English as *The Legend of Rita*; 2000), which specifically undermine the possibility of fixed ideological meaning.[12] Unlike the more obvious left-wing vantage point of his earlier *Die verlorene Ehre der Katherina Blum* (*The Lost Honor of Katherine Blum*; 1975), this later film offers a more circumspect vantage point. Its altered tone likely responds to the realities of GDR life revealed in the post-wall era, which tempered left-wing idealism. Renner cites the film's mix of slow motion and sped-up imagery, East and West rock music, everyday aesthetics and expressive color meant to invoke interiority as the filmic means by which Schlörndorff creates an ideologically indeterminate message.[13] The trajectory that his example suggests implicitly posits a less unified approach as more politically mature or more capable of rendering a complex reality.

Yet critiques of what one could more broadly define as a postmodern approach are now so familiar that they can preordain a negative reception, one that extends beyond academia to the larger public sphere. This was the case with *The Baader Meinhof Complex*, which above all came to embody the manner in which once avant-garde approaches get neutralized when they enter the mainstream and suffer the fate of being written off as cliché.[14] As Ulrich Kriest observed in the opening paragraph of a 2008 *film-dienst* essay, "Every new film about the RAF [Red Army Faction] automatically becomes part of a difficult-to-contain river of images and cinematic images and television shots and photographs. The terrain appears to be minutely pruned to a minute degree, memories mix with anecdotes, images become slogans.[15] The additional strands of an all-too-familiar critique deserve further mention here, if only because they shut down in such a global way the need to parse the film's codes and search out occluded messages related to feminism. Significantly, various critics accused *The Baader Meinhof Complex* of lacking a specific point of view towards its protagonists, whose actions presumably warranted the filmmaker's disdain. *Der Spiegel*, for instance, argued that the film aimed to "show but not to interpret."[16] Filmic elements that fueled this critique included a ceaseless flow of images within quickly edited, action-packed sequences that allow "barely any time to breathe."[17]

A postmodern approach, of course, can yield not only an apolitical vantage point but also abet the cooptation of once subversive aims, a process evident in the dichotomous pairing of "radical" with "chic." As Sarah Waters has argued, this designation reduces '68 to "pure image, a hollowed-out symbol emptied of its political and historical significance."[18] To be sure, '68 has long lived on in its consumer culture manifestations. Both Mattias Frey and Mary-Elizabeth O'Brien have documented a critical mass of RAF pop forms dating back to the millennium. These include the 2001 magazine *Tussi Deluxe*'s fashion shoots of models posing in 1970's clothing in ways resemble the RAF's familiar media images. Around the same time, the RAF red-star logo superimposed over a machine gun, as well as a hand grenade and the designation "Prada-Meinhof," began appearing on T-Shirts, as did black turtlenecks and crushed velvet pants. And singer Jan Delay released an album the same year with the song "The Sons of Stammheim."[19] Yet this pop-culture hall of mirrors also lends itself quite readily to artistic forms of metacritique, perhaps most flagrantly on display in Canadian underground filmmaker Bruce LeBruce's porn depiction of RAF members, *The Raspberry Reich* (2004). Politically motivated terrorist acts give themselves over to radical chic, but also more broadly feed into a spectator's forbidden pleasure principle, a process that would ideally spawn self-awareness about the untoward nature of our investment in the RAF.

Yet Edel's film contains enough self-conscious elements to offset critiques of the film's presumed apoliticism insofar as they implicitly comment on our relationship to '68, particularly in the mythic guises that Kraushaar describes. *The Baader Meinhof Complex* often stages its characters in ways that suggest the power of the visual. One witnesses, for instance, shots of bystanders photographing RAF exploits, an act that yields some of the iconic images that the film frequently cites.[20] But by putting the camera into bystanders' rather than photojournalists' hands, Edel implicates the extra-filmic audience within the RAF's seductive pull. Another striking example is the uncanny manner in which he reproduces RAF wanted posters, though with celebrities posed as their historical counterparts.[21] As much as citation seems the motivating factor here, the overall effect speaks to the slippage between criminal activity and celebrity status, or in LeBruce's less subtle mise-en-scène between arousal prompted by violence or by sexy cinematic doubles.[22] As Andreas Baader proclaims at one point in Edel's film, "shooting and fucking are the same."[23]

Media-based montages appear frequently as well, and in the barrage of visual and acoustic reportage about the RAF, *The Baader Meinhof Complex* abets confusion between its narrative events and their portrayal within a screen-filled mise-en-scène. This particular hall of mirrors in turn points to obsessive desires that would endlessly replay an unfolding real-life drama, a dynamic that extends to the RAF members and their relationship to the frenetic myth-making machinery surrounding them. Often they appear to feed off and obsess over their own story as it unfolds, since we frequently see them glued to television sets and later to radios in their Stammheim jail cells. In a related vein, in the media circus surrounding their trial, Baader and Gudrun Ensslin play to their audience, often garnering applause in the process. Self-conscious performance alongside the film's mixed-up media layers create an insular dynamic whereby the actual text of political dissent becomes one more element in an acoustic echo chamber. Audiences within the filmic space who chant en masse at demonstrations add to the effect, while perhaps echoing a more contemporary audience's piecemeal understanding of history. The large crowd at a Rudy Dutschke speech at the Freie Universität Berlin, for instance, chants "Ho Chi Minh," then chants his name in a similar manner in front of the Axel Springer building after Dutschke has been shot. This scene ends with a lone bare-chested figure that shouts "Dresden, Hiroshima, Vietnam." Articulated within the film's echo chamber, however, historical parallels shrink to rhythmic mantras rather than pointing to the wider context that motivated left-wing activism and subsequent terrorism.[24]

If *The Baader Meinhof Complex* makes spectators acutely aware of the media's part in shaping our obsessive fascination the RAF, it leaves out one particularly salacious element: the charge that left-wing terrorist acts committed by women were directly linked to the feminist movement. A preprogrammed response based on familiar critiques of postmodernism—as apolitical, as too imbricated within commodity culture—is problematic if it shuts down analysis of individual filmic codes that speak to or even correct this omission. What interests me again of course are the feminist-inflected elements that get lost in the shuffle. As I discussed in the introduction to this volume, feminism's own forms of performative citation always meet up with the vagaries of reception, or an audience's ability to perceive something potentially subversive within the arena of popular culture. Strikingly, Edel's depiction of Ulrike Meinhof often uses dominant cinema techniques that make fewer demands on spectators, yet at the same time implicitly respond to that larger extra-filmic discourse regarding feminism and left-wing terrorism. I would also add that Edel's approach to Meinhof not only counters the film's postmodern techniques and aims, it also needs to be seen in relation to his attempt to conjure history "how it was."[25]

Efforts to render '68 authentically draw from a larger arsenal of techniques than pastiche alone and can aim for effects beyond depicting mediated selfhood. Taking its title and material from Stefan Aust's best-selling, 667-page work of 1985, long the standard history of the RAF, *The Baader Meinhof Complex* draws as much on a concrete source as a cacophonous cultural imaginary. Not surprisingly, the demands of adaptation figured into the film's reception as well.[26] One gets the sense that the need to recapitulate the same time frame that Aust documents—from Meinhof's early days as a journalist to the RAF suicides in Stammheim—resulted in an exhausting viewing experience. When fidelity served as the measuring stick in the traditional book-to-film comparison, critics were sometimes frustrated by the film's attempt to pack the entirety of Aust's text into the film's extended 150-minute running time. (At the same time, the layers of adaptation on display in the film—of history as filtered through Aust's work, through the citation of iconic images and the media filters on display within the filmic space—

reveal how a postmodern approach can be equally taxing.) *The Baader Meinhof Complex*'s gargantuan production values—a budget of twenty million euros, 123 speaking roles, and 6,300 extras—suggest to what extent fidelity remains the favored arbiter of a successfully rendered filmic reality. Edel's and producer/screenplay cowriter Bernd Eichinger's biographies bear mention here, since they attended the Munich Film School in the early 1970s and consider themselves '68ers. Stating that he wanted to tell the story as authentically as possible, Edel cited his then nineteen- and twenty-year-old sons as a motivating factor: "Normally you make a film for a particular audience but this time it was different. I wanted to tell and show them everything that I know and found out so that they could form their own opinion about what happened then and what I witnessed."[27]

With this stated aim in mind, one should not be surprised that both Edel and Eichinger explicitly distanced themselves from Hollywood techniques in their approach. Edel did not want to create a "work of enlightenment," and Eichinger himself observed that "there are no heroes in this film, no one with whom one can identify. There's also no plot in the strictest sense, no linear narrative. Instead, it's solely the monstrosity of events, which grabs the attention of the audience and which keeps the story moving forward."[28] Ambiguously rendered characters and events aside, Eichinger's desire to "grab the audience" and "keep the story moving" sounds very much in the spirit of Hollywood. Though he described the film's structure as a "shredded dramaturgy," in an interview with *Sight and Sound* he also referenced what could best be described as a narrative hook: the answer to the question of why a "respected journalist [left] her two children and start[ed] shooting people."[29] This frame, or course, poises us to expect some access to Meinhof's interiority, despite Eichinger's observation that "you can't check inside people, but you can check what comes out."[30] In general terms, creating a sense of Meinhof's motivations also belongs within the realm of adaption strategies insofar as her written and public statements need to be articulated in relation to her life circumstances and actions. Taken together, these elements no doubt reveal incongruities—for example, the decentered consciousness that lends itself to postmodern approaches. More importantly for my purposes, the particularities of one woman's experiences stand in relation to the blanket assumptions about women and terror that characterized the era. Against this backdrop, *The Baader Meinhof Complex* could aim as much for the kind of correctness and care that we associate with adaptation as for ambiguity and metacritique.

One last aspect bears mention before I trace the film's depiction of Meinhof vis-à-vis Eichinger's narrative hook, and this point is both basic and crucial. The word adaptation refers to the changes—meaning the artistic choices—made in order to render the object or story at hand in a manner best suited to a particular medium. The imperatives of fidelity should become less acute, less likely to adversely affect a work's reception if one works with this definition. Beyond the evolving artistic approaches are also evolving political sensitivities that factor into adaptation and their inevitable shift from progressive to clichéd with the passage of time. Renner's argument about Schlöndorff's less ideologically discernible standpoint in *The Legend of Rita* compared to *Katharina Blum* provides a case in point. Evolving political sensitivities among audiences impact reception as well; even two-dimensional images and an acoustic echo chamber can be perceived in multifaceted, politically colored ways. In what follows I will demonstrate that Edel has created a retroactive correction of facile links between emancipation and unbridled anarchy.[31]

The Baader Meinhof Complex, Feminism, and Dominant Cinema

In 1977, at the height of RAF crimes, *Der Spiegel* published a cover story that can only be described as hysterical in tone. The magazine's labeling of female terrorists as "shooting girls" (schießende Mädchen) provides this volume's most salient example of "mad Mädchen," though minus any trace of the ironic playfulness that was to come roughly twenty years later. *Der Spiegel's* view of RAF women as fiercely aggressive, as "girls with Saturday night specials in cosmetics cases," played up not only gendered but also class-based perversions. "Good bourgeois daughters from well-heeled families," the cover story proclaimed, gave in to "self-destructive impulses that [brought] them down to the level of murder or manslaughter."[32] Vojin Sasa Vukadinovic has also situated *The Baader Meinhof Complex* in relation to such heated discourse, which extended well beyond the media: "As the military clashes between the RAF and the FRG [Federal Republic of Germany] increased, self-declared experts on feminism from the government, academia, clergy, and media began to propogate the thesis that feminism was the actual thrust behind militant Marxism-Leninism in West Germany. They based this assertion not on a substantive engagement with the politics of anti-imperialism, but on the presumed high percentage of women in groups like the RAF."[33] Vukadinovic also cites Günter Nollau, then part of the Federal Ministry of the Interior, who observed as early as 1971, "So many girls are part of this.... Perhaps what is now becoming clear is that this is an excess of women's emancipation."[34]

The first issue of *EMMA* appeared in the fall of 1977, and Alice Schwarzer's early editorials struggled with assertions in *Der Spiegel's* cover story and elsewhere in the "Männerpresse" that violent women were an outgrowth of feminism. Without condoning the actions of female terrorists, she pointed out the patriarchal nature of the society they attempted to undermine, a vantage point that casts women's anger as a logical response, rather than irrational force. Psychoanalytic paradigms, however, bolstered the latter category; Schwarzer cites, for instance, the notion that female violence stems from an unfulfilled incestuous love of the father that turns into rage. Of course medical discourse has a way of overlapping with long-standing and dubious cultural fantasies, for instance in images of "Amazonen," or "female warriors carrying off the booty of flesh ... who take over characteristics of the male role" that Schwarzer references.[35] She also helpfully points out the obvious double standard at work in our understanding of gendered violence: "A male bank robber can still be a Robin Hood, a female bank robber is a tragic figure whose child one takes away."[36] If one looks beyond societally or medically sanctioned misogynist fantasies, history itself offers other examples of female violence—Schwarzer cites women who participated in the French and Russian revolutions—which makes it difficult to reduce female terrorists to an aberration unique to their own historical moment.

EMMA also featured an editorial by famed psychoanalyst Margarete Mitscherlich, better known for her and her husband Alexander's seminal work on *Vergangenheitsbewältigung, The Inability to Mourn* (1967). Given the nuttier psychoanalytic explanations about women and violence, her voice in the pages of *EMMA* constituted a means to fight fire with fire. Perhaps not surprisingly, she shifted the emphasis away from female to collective psychology, or the need to identify an enemy in response to internal problems and divisions: "Some critics let the tendency come to full flowering that inner problems and divisions can be helped via a new orientation towards the enemy."[37] What surprises, however, is how Mitscherlich locates this German brand of McCarthyism, as she calls it, on both sides of the political spectrum—among those who would revive fascist response to dissent with the death penalty and terrorists who confuse the political situation in the 1970s with Nazi rule.

In the largest sense, both Schwarzer and Mitscherlich critique undifferentiated rhetoric and the mass forms of behavior that can result. Their highly analytic approach casts two public female figures as the voice of reason, as well as the arbiters of a moral high ground. Both aspects of their contribution to a larger debate relate to *The Baader Meinhof Complex*'s depiction of Ulrike Meinhof, though, overall, Edel's approach can feel more straightforward—and sometimes flatfooted—than analytic. One example that relates not to Meinhof but another female RAF member deserves mention in this regard. It could be understood, like Schwarzer's and Mitscherlich's editorials, as a direct response to heated rhetoric. *Der Spiegel*'s cover story singled out RAF member Susanne Albrecht for exhibiting "the outermost boundary of human perversion" because she used her friendship with Jürgen Ponto's daughter to gain entry into their home.[38] After she announced "Hallo, es ist Susanne," her RAF cohorts brutally gunned down Ponto, prompting *Der Spiegel* journalists to indignantly ponder "Who could imagine someone showing up for an assassination with flowers?"[39] *The Baader Meinhof Complex*, however, reenacts this assassination with Albrecht bitterly weeping during their escape, then plays up her outrage over a murder with which she had not reckoned. Simply put, Edel stages a woman's part in a terrorist act in a much less sensationalistic manner that counters *Der Spiegel*'s account of girls gone wild.

Staging is one of film's basic and less medium-bound elements, given its roots in theater. It provides a baseline in *The Baader Meinhof Complex*'s overly mediated mise-en-scène, however one-dimensional it feels in relation to the film's otherwise art-house-style elements. Yet if Edel aimed to correct an era's excesses, one wonders if this task necessitates more direct, less ambiguous strategies for representing RAF women in particular. Historically, Meinhof may have indeed provided a voice of reason compared to other RAF members if one considers her early role as a journalist and theorist. Ensslin and Baader, by contrast, have been linked to the literary and filmic touchstones that colored their political acts. Ensslin, often viewed as the good bourgeois daughter, used high-art references to mythologizing ends, creating RAF code names culled from *Moby Dick* for her cohorts. Baader purportedly identified with James Dean, Marlon Brando, and Jean Paul Belmondo's sexy anarchist in the French New Wave film *Breathless* (1960) and was a fan of Hollywood action films such as *Bonnie and Clyde* (1967) and *The Wild One* (1953).[40] This aspect of their historical personas of course lends itself to pastiche as the means for conjuring politics imbued by art and commodity culture. Edel takes a different tack with Meinhof, her trajectory in the film starting from a place of privilege and fleeting contact with popular culture, the latter signaled by the women's magazine just below her face in one of the film's first shots. One gets less a sense of a decentered than a false consciousness, the latter implying an either/or choice between opposing vantage points. To initially reside in the wrong camp provides a handy launchpad for a traditional narrative arc based on increasing wisdom.

As Mary-Ellen O'Brian has argued, Meinhof's transition from left-wing journalist and wife of a philandering husband to committed terrorist structures *The Baader Meinhof Complex,* providing "connective tissue" between the film's montage-based sequences.[41] Against the historically heated rhetoric, Edel couches her story in terms of a woman finding her voice, evident in the way the film's echo chamber sometimes grants it near voice-over status when she appears to witness and explain, as well as judge, otherwise chaotic sequences. Early on when Meinhof reads aloud a letter to the Shah's wife, Farrah Diba, protesting injustices in Iran, her voice carries over to the next sequence when the Shah arrives in Berlin and his goons brutally beat German protesters. O'Brien underscores how these initial scenes culminate in Meinhof's commentary on a television talk show: "The truth is that the protests of these students have exposed our state as a police state, that the police and press terror on 2 June in Berlin reached a climax, and that we understand that freedom in this state means freedom for the police nightstick." O'Brien notes her privileged positioning within the sequence, with Meinhof providing a "plausible" interpretation of the scenes we have just witnessed. Meinhof's use of the word "truth," however, combined with her role as talking head on a news analysis program—perhaps the closest one can get in a self-reflexive filmic space to detached, voice-over style observation—casts her as principled adjudicator. Strikingly, she looks directly into the camera as she finishes her observations.

Even if these early scenes are too brief for Meinhof to have evolved beyond her initial privileged position entirely, the film repeatedly underscores her efforts to weigh moral options and make the right choice. Often we see her silent reaction to interlocutors like Baader and Ensslin, and she lurks in the background at a courthouse and listens as Ensslin's parents give an interview in which they express support of their daughter. Immediately afterward we see her at the typewriter, as if to transcribe their spirit into a potent political tract. The protest scene at the Axel Springer building ends with her gaze surveying the damage in a shot that lasts roughly five seconds.

Figure 4.1. Still: *The Baader Meinhof Complex* (2008)

It is through her eyes that we witness that lone figure who shouts "Dresden, Hiroshima, Vietnam." Her evolving selfhood resonates even more alongside the film's two-dimensional Andreas Baader, with his love of leather jackets, fast cars, and tendency to call RAF women "Fotzen" (cunts). Despite her ultimate breakdown, subtle visual coding transfers the "voice of reason" role to Brigitte Mohnhaupt, thereby extending Meinhof's shaping presence to the next generation.[42] Mohnhaupt first appears in the film, for instance, in the same kind of intense, silent reaction shot that had previously characterized Meinhof. She is also shown typing political tracts, her words articulated in voice-over fashion as well. Most important, Mohnhaupt takes the "voice of reason" role to the next, metacritical level. When she states that the RAF members in Stammheim determined their lives right up to their death, she admonishes the next generation to "stop seeing them as they weren't." Given the film's confusing display of the RAF's myriad media incarnations, spectators should heed her words as well.

Edel's use of mainstream elements blend seamlessly, I would argue, with a second-wave-style narrative of "Selbstverwirklichung" (self-actualization), a word Gudrun Ensslin's father uses to describe his daughter's trajectory during that courthouse interview. This notion also appears to rub off on Ensslin's mother, who observes that her daughter's example made her less afraid in her own life. If Hollywood films often provide an enlightening message, Edel tailors his to educate spectators along gendered lines. The process of sloughing off a false, specifically patriarchally defined consciousness of course aligns well with second-wave objectives and provides the blueprint for feminist classics such as Verena Stefan's autobiographical work *Shedding* (*Häutungen*; 1975).[43] As clichéd as the idea of "self-actualization" may sound within a contemporary feminist arena, it counters the rhetoric of irrational, unnatural behavior among RAF women. It should be emphasized again that his approach is not analytic, but rather, in the spirit of mainstream cinema, more visceral, which also constitutes another means for fighting fire with fire. History dovetails with melodrama in this manner as well: the film begins with Meinhof lovingly admonishing her two daughters to come out of the water, and Edel is careful to capture Meinhof's torment when she ultimately abandons them to pursue revolutionary aims. He thus gives the cliché of "self-actualization" very specific and historically verifiable contours. Patricia Melzer's work on maternal ethics and political violence is relevant here because she has documented Meinhof's efforts to protect her children even after she went underground. She observes: "Meinhof's actions point to the fact that the safety of her daughters was very much on her mind and that she attempted to ensure their wellbeing while also committing to armed struggle."[44]

The film's gendered contrasts and dichotomous doublings not only provide the kinds of foils familiar to audiences of Hollywood films, but also highlight Meinhof's singularity. While other films have also played up Baader's sexual swagger and pop-culture-inspired two-dimensionality, *The Baader Meinhof Complex* situates him as well in relation to feminism.[45] At one point, for instance, he proclaims that women's emancipation has simply led to their right to scream at men. Elsewhere, Baader's simplistic rhetoric plays directly into the film's medial cacophony: his establishing shot shows him adding more fluid to bombs because, as he claims, "bigger bombs make for bigger headlines." His words thus collapse the distance between politically motivated violence and a frenzied media response, as if both sides feed on one another. Edel elevates Meinhof above the fray with her repeated articulations of the theoretical underpinnings of RAF violence. However morally problematic her words, they command attention in a way that Baader's catchphrases do not.

Male-female polarities bookend *The Baader Meinhof Complex* as well, with the voices of Janis Joplin and Bob Dylan providing our acoustic entry and exit from the film. Joplin's song "Mercedes Benz" accompanies initial shots of naked women on an FKK (Freikörperkultur, or free body culture) beach in Sylt. "Blowin in the Wind" plays as Hanns Martin Schleyer (president of the German Employers Association) is shot in the head as the film ends. If Joplin's voice invokes free-spiritedness in specifically female form, her lyric about expensive cars also anticipates the privileged, upper-middle-class world that Meinhof is shown to inhabit in subsequent scenes. Edel uses the standard trope of visual doubling to ironic effect as well: the film's first shot captures Meinhof in a cocoon-like beach cabana, her face above a women's magazine featuring Farah Diba on the cover. Soon after, we hear Meinhof's letter to Farah Diba, which admonishes her for a privileged life and urges her to return from her beach vacation and confront the dire circumstances of Iranians. Coupled with Joplin's song, visual doubling with Farah Diba makes Meinhof's limited self-awareness about her own socioeconomic privilege hard to miss.[46] The film's other acoustic bookend, "Blowin' in the Wind," feels less layered in comparison. Dylan's lyrics emphasize repeated queries:

> How many roads must a man walk down
> Before you call him a man?
> . . .
> How many times can a man turn his head
> And pretend that he just doesn't see?
> . . .
> How many times must a man look up
> Before he can see the sky?
> . . .
> How many deaths will it take 'till he knows
> That too many people have died?

As much as Dylan no doubt speaks here about humankind more generally, the gender polarities evident in *The Baader Meinhof Complex* encourage spectators to associate one of the RAF's most notorious crimes with measures of masculinity. In this regard, Edel appears to simply reverse the polarizing rhetoric that spotlighted female over male violence.

Not all of the film's binaries are male-female, however. Repeated shots of Meinhof's two daughters in the first half of the film provide a visual doubling that echoes not only the Meinhof/Farah Diba pairing, but also that between her and Ensslin. Such shots encourage spectators to compare and contrast, an exercise that structures our relationship to characters in elemental ways, rather than obliging us to ponder the film's metacritiques and their implications for us as well. In the process, the sexual coding that structures our understanding of Meinhof and

Ensslin becomes apparent. An early shot of Ensslin shows her naked in a bathtub as she converses with a new member whom she invites to join her. Soon after, Baader enters the room and briefly strokes her breasts. By contrast, in the film's first scene of Meinhof and her daughters on the FKK beach, her nakedness is carefully shielded. (Later, when Brigitte Mohnhaupt becomes the RAF's core figure, we see a shot of her in the shower, but obscured by a shower curtain, and her one sex scene is also less graphic than female nudity elsewhere in the film.) The beach scene also includes a medium close-up of the woman Meinhof's husband will soon have sex with, her naked body exposed from the waist up. Contrasting visuals encourage spectators to associate an exposed female body not with a sexually progressive era but as the counterpoint to Meinhof as intellectual, as keenly aware of patriarchal double standards that sanction male rather than female libertine behavior. Strikingly, when Meinhof's husband tries to film her at the beach she shields herself from the camera. And despite his support of Meinhof's early journalistic success—we see him toast her in an early party scene—Edel reduces his part in the film to the same sexual dimension that underpins Baader's persona.

Whereas Ensslin appears not only overtly sexual throughout but also very much in thrall to Baader, Meinhof cuts her ties to her husband early on and never uses sexual wiles to advance her cause.[47] The fact that Ensslin gets captured in a store trying on clothes, which may be historically accurate, also works to underscore her superficial character, as does the fact that she ultimately chooses Baader over Meinhof.[48] Together Ensslin and Baader bring a party atmosphere and sexual swagger to the guerilla training camp they visit in Jordan, the same locale in which the gravity of Meinhof's circumstances becomes clear when she must decide the fate of her daughters. In terms of both early feminist values and mainstream film conventions, Meinhof clearly occupies the moral high ground. The film's depiction of Ensslin also borders, in places, on lending support to the reactionary arguments about violent women as unnatural. An early scene shows her holding her infant son and smoking a cigarette, though she quickly hands him off and begins to spout RAF dogma in response to a television news report. Unlike Meinhof's daughters, Ensslin's son then disappears from the narrative, and we see nothing of her real-life efforts to remain a presence in his life, even after her incarceration.[49]

Vukadinovic has argued that *Der Baader Meinhof Complex* not only taps into but in fact underwrites antifeminist media vitriol towards female terrorists, citing several elements in the film: a female member raises her hand first when RAF members vote on whether to execute Hanns Martin Schleyer's driver and body guards during his abduction; the way the film cites reified images of gun-toting women; catty competitiveness between Ensslin and Meinhof for the position of leader; and Baader as loyal follower in thrall to his girlfriend Ensslin, his screaming fits evidence of a subservient position. Such individual fragments, whether clichéd images or general examples of assertive female behavior, might add up to an antifeminist film if one considers *The Baader Meinhof Complex* primarily as pastiche, with no mitigating narrative structure to add other levels of meaning. Ironically, by emphasizing the film's traditional elements—the familiar and here female-coded narrative arc of "Selbstverwirklichung"—I, too, am highlighting clichés, which Edel clearly employs. Yet given their overlap with the kinds of narratives that fired up German feminists in the 1970s, they provide an artistic means for countering the hysterical antifeminist rhetoric of the times. The larger question that remains is whether less flat-footed approaches might achieve the same aim. Is it possible, for instance, to articulate a feminist perspective that also acknowledges how much collective politics tap into individual as well as egotistic or even psychologically unstable impulses? This is, of course, another way of saying that it must work with the interior realm where identifications perpetually shift in unpredictable ways. Schlöndorff's progression from an overtly left-wing position in *Katharina Blum* to the kind of representational tactics in *The Legend of Rita* that suggest something more divided and circumspect, as Renner describes it, provides a useful point of comparison. Could his latter positioning be carried over into the realm of feminism, where mass cultural sympathy for the underdog may still be too precarious to coexist with critiques of the underdog's blind spots?

Mary Harron's film *I Shot Andy Warhol* (1996), I would argue, successfully combines a feminist sensibility with exposure of its female protagonist's predilection for theatricality, at times narcissistic and self-serving. Valery Solanis was an early militant feminist, the author of the manifesto "The Society for Cutting up Men," and the woman who shot Andy Warhol at point-blank range and nearly killed him. Over and over again, Harron's film documents the virulent sexism aimed at women, particularly Solanis, by Warhol's male coterie. They refer to her hair, for instance, as a "monstrosity" and admonish Solanis to fix it and put on lipstick. Candy Darling serves as the ultimate embodiment of successful femininity for them; s/he not only epitomizes Hollywood glamor but also serves as the best kind of woman because, as one acolyte proclaims, she lacks a "cunt." While the film helps us to understand the motivations behind her criminal act, it also contains its own meta-levels of meaning, which significantly work for and against our sympathies for Solanis.

James M. Harding has situated her criminal act in relation to Warhol's cut-and-paste aesthetic, with Warhol's bullet-ridden body a more literal rendition of this approach as well as his larger belief that anything could be art.[50] (Famous photos after the shooting show Warhol exposing his stitched-up, patchwork torso.) In larger terms Solanis took an otherwise apolitical postmodern aesthetic and made it highly political by linking it to female rage. At the same time, Harron subtly underscores Solanis's moments of un-self-reflexive posturing and how they implicate her within the artificial world she critiques. One scene shows her watching the Miss America Pageant on TV, during which many women threw their bras into garbage cans. Her reaction—"that should be me"—overtly exposes the narcissistic aspects of her personality, which *I Shot Andy Warhol* is careful to repeatedly capture. In other words, Solanis appears to be just as interested in being the center of attention as critiquing patriarchal standards of beauty. A later scene shows Solanis and a male revolutionary spending an afternoon together having sex, shooting off guns, and mouthing militant slogans. Ironically, the bullet belt that Solanis wears draped across her chest looks like the kind of sash that women wear at Miss America pageants.[51] Again, one gets the sense that her politics sprang not only from concretely misogynist treatment, but also her own attraction to theatrical display. Harron thus appears both sympathetic to her plight but also aware of how politics and theater can come together in ways as self-serving as they are sympathetic to the oppressed.

Truly Wild? Uschi Obermaier, Pop Art, and Popfeminism

If Edel's dated feminist and artistic means for portraying Meinhof retroactively correct the era's reactionary rhetoric, Achim Bornhak's depiction of Uschi Obermaier in *Eight Miles High* taps into the subsequent pairing of "radical" with "chic," as well as "feminist" with "sexy." To align Obermaier with feminist aims, however, requires justification to avoid seeming like a complete fantasy projection that ignores the actual circumstances of her life. After all, the quote I referenced earlier about her having "the political consciousness of an amoeba" is actually taken from the afterword to her autobiography, *High Times. Mein wildes Leben*, on which Bornhak's film is based. Taken from a series of interviews with Olaf Kraemer, which he transcribed and then turned into a book and then a screenplay, *High Times* documents her rise to iconic fashion model and student movement "it girl," as well as relationships with fellow "Kommune 1" resident Rainer Langhans, Hamburg club owner Dieter Bockhorn, and rock stars such as Keith Richards and Mick Jagger.

In his afterward, Kraemer details a negative response to Obermaier's story, which was initially rejected by thirty publishers, based on both filmic conventions and the sense that Obermaier was responsible for reactionary arguments about '68 and the women's movement:

> Was she too brutal, too Lilith-like and too hedonistic for a traditional heroine's journey, the kind that film loves? Can you defy the dramaturgic and biographic mandate of transformation and still invite sympathy? ... There would be many intense, partly irrational arguments in our team about Uschi's character in the screenplay and her significance for '68, about the role she played for our country and still plays now. Judgments ranged from "she was just a groupie, she has the political consciousness of an amoeba! You should make a film about Ulrike Meinhof instead!" to "she personifies modern woman" and "she's at the root of the Methuselah plot"—which is all accurate, but nonetheless the truth lay elsewhere for me.[52]

On the one hand, Kraemer wisely underscores the difficulties of getting at the truth of Obermaier's experiences without considering, as well as contributing to, her status as projection screen. (His stance obviously counters Edel's and Eichinger's investment in telling their story as authentically as possible.) In fact, Kraemer even describes taking the final version of the screenplay to Obermaier for her approval. Using Rainer Langhans as a lesser foil, Kraemer's portrayal suggested, as he put it, "the wildest man still appeared to be a woman."[53] The extent to which this depiction could be understood in feminist terms is debatable, especially if being "Lilith-like" is not so different from the female Amazons that Schwarzer cites as evidence of cultural fantasies about rapacious women. Along similar lines, one wonders if Kraemer's depiction of Obermaier's sexual experiences simply constitute a nonviolent but equally suspect example of girls gone wild. To understand Obermaier's life as having any connection to feminism, then and now, requires a close look at her words and *Eight Miles High* as adaptation of them, as something more than Kraemer's fantasy of a feral female. As I will demonstrate, one finds not only traces of old and new feminist strategies in both book and film, but also echoes of 1960's female pop artists' metacritical strategies for self-representation.

Dubbed a "wild and sexy film," *Eight Miles High* depicts the often scantily clad, if sometimes naked, Obermaier as, according to the *New York Times,* "a one-woman counterculture."[54] This statement combines, as classical autobiographical selves often do, singularity with representative status—contrary elements that speak to the manner in which the tabloid press singled her out at demonstrations and created an icon. Coupled with periodic voice-overs taken from *High Times,* Obermaier's media incarnations in the film, evident in shots of newspaper headlines and magazine articles, anchor her story in concrete historical traces, however overdone this approach has become. In a similar vein, montage sequences also capture Obermaier's fashion shoots, which extend the film's self-conscious display of media forms to a realm where fantasies are quite explicitly concocted. Whether *Eight Miles High*'s media layers resonate beyond cliché-ridden elements like flashing cameras and glam poses is the question. At the very least, when overcooked Springer Press–style headlines leap out at the spectator, they invoke the kinds of communal fantasies that exceed the particulars of Obermaier's story.

One of these headlines describes her as "living the dream of a generation." As vague as this phrasing sounds, in a contemporary context the word "generation" alone resonates, reminding us that collective aims, particularly in Germany, can vary greatly depending on age or identification with a particular time or place. While this statement firmly links Obermaier to her own historical moment and its utopian tendencies, the "dream" she lives, if aligned with the performative agency she exhibits throughout, has a more indeterminate temporal frame. Often we see her active participation in fashion shoots that conjure '68 via pleasurable dressing up and femininity itself as a form of masquerade that can be donned or removed. In this manner, *Eight Miles High* pursues a different strategy than *The Baader Meinhof Complex,* which mixes up media forms with the historical moment they document, thus exposing our obsessive fantasies, as well as our inability to recognize their artificial bases. By emphasizing basic visual coding—that is, Obermaier as either naked or fetchingly attired—*Eight Miles High* creates a more clear-cut divide between fantasy and reality, or a conventionally homogenous filmic space with psychologically transparent characters. Third-wave strategies that draw on theories of gendered masquerades, as well as an empowering sexuality, of course vary in the degree of complexity they ascribe to selfhood. Judith Butler, as I underscored in my introduction, was careful to emphasize "possibility of agency" within performative strategies, itself always undermined by the fragmented nature of selfhood. Girl culture in some of its most basic manifestations, as Katja Kauer has argued, consists of little more than a traditionally stylized, fetishized femininity, however cheekily performed. Given the conventional aspects of *Eight Miles High*, the question becomes whether its third-wave resonances end up lacking in complexity as well.

Dominant cinema elements are not hard to spot in the film, once again often taking the form of predictable foils that play up inequities or bald-faced ironies, particularly when Kommune 1 men such as Langhans are depicted as the ultimate "Spießer" (squares). After much lip service to revolution and free love, for instance, he proclaims to his comrades, "I would betray the revolution for this woman." While his proclamation celebrates Obermaier's singular sex appeal, it also pits Marxist theory against conventionality. Alienation from Marxist theory and its indifference to women's oppression, of course, fueled the birth of feminism in Germany. Equally important, women were also in a position to see beyond progressive theory to the traditional social structures that motivated male student activists as well. *EMMA*'s 2008 special issue on '68 included the slogan "Free the eminent socialists from their bourgeois dicks" (Befreit die sozialistischen Eminenzen von ihren bürgerlichen Schwänzen) in a large-type, bolded paragraph on its first page.[55]

Yet Bornhak's sympathy for women in the student movement and once radical aims packs less punch when it comes forty years later and again speaks to the power of convention. Certainly enough time has elapsed for provocateurs to assume the mantle of the underdog who ultimately triumphs. Yet Obermaier's life story, particularly its implications for female power in visual terms, cannot be so tidily subsumed by familiar narratives. *EMMA*'s 2008 special issue on '68, for instance, pointedly separated her out of its celebration of women in the student movement. It provided the following bold-text lead-in about early feminists: "They were not only the objects of '68 but also the subjects of their own history, beyond Uschi Obermaier."[56] Yet some of the images included—of topless female students at a demonstration and more topless protestors on the cover of a magazine—implicitly draw Obermaier back into the history of '68 as she, too, displayed her body for political ends. Significantly, the meanings of this act potentially point both forward and backward in time, towards both contemporary rhetoric about female sexuality among younger German feminists and art historians' reassessment of 1960's female pop artists.

While I have referenced above girl culture's investment in sexuality, chapter 1 of *We Alpha Girls* offers more specific contours. It includes a section with the heading "Feminists are shrewd and sexy," in which its authors make the basic claim that the "new feminism deals with the topic of sex in a much more relaxed way. Feminists today are more about lots of sex and good sex."[57] The book also includes a chapter titled "Explosive Sex for Everyone" (Knaller-Sex für alle), which critiques second-wave notions of porn as catalyst to violence against women. Such paeans to female sexuality may lack the complexities and subversive potential of speech acts traced by Judith Butler in *Gender Trouble*, but they do recall 1990's Riot Grrrl culture as exemplary of raucous erotics.

Yet recent feminist reevaluations of 1960's female pop artists provide a longer history and contemporaneous frame for Obermaier's participation in the pop-culture domain of her own times. Though previously rejected for drawing on the same sexist and sometimes pornographic forms as male pop artists, female pop art now radiates pop-inflected sexual empowerment to many art historians. As Kalliopi Minioudaki observes, "Consummating their pleasurable consumption of popular culture, while either critically exposing its trappings for women or radically transvaluating them for their own empowerment, several women Pop artists engaged themselves in an inassimilably diverse—critical, affective, humorous, autobiographic, and often all of the above—critical dialogue with it.[58] Pop artist Pauline Boty provides a particularly resonant example because she bolsters her own sexuality via an unlikely pop source. As Minioudaki argues, in her art she looked to Marilyn Monroe as a liberating model of "sexual empowerment rather than [as] a casualty of Hollywood spectacle—a harbinger of the liberating change that the sexy fashions and girls of swinging London promised sexually-unsure females."[59]

In *Eight Miles High* celebrity photos of Brigitte Bardot and James Dean hang on the walls of Obermaier's girlhood room, a detail taken directly from her autobiography. On the one hand, they anticipate the jet set she will eventually join at the height of her celebrity. Yet against a female pop-art frame, Bardot's image could signal at least two shaping forces on Obermaier's ultimate trajectory: women as agents, not objects, of consumption; and female sexuality as empowering, not demeaning. Both book and film make her sexuality central, its force prompting Rainer Langhans to dub her a "Lustautomat" (sex machine). Highlighted not only against his "Spießigkeit" (conventionality) but also another male Kommune 1 residence's impotence, it takes central stage in explosive scenes with her various lovers. Yet what makes her sexuality more than Lilith-like hedonism and/or a pop embrace of pleasure writ large are its effects on her surround as much as its carnal force. A close reading of various scenes that rely on conventional elements—desiring gazes, visual mirroring, and complementary elements—hint at its shaping influence.

An early scene shows a photographer capturing Obermaier dancing in a Munich club, creating images that will land her on the cover of the magazine *Twen* and launch her rise as an international fashion model. Soon after, she hitchhikes to Berlin in a van full of hippies, their colorful clothes and drug paraphernalia compelling her own fascinated gaze. Shot/reverse shots when she enters Kommune 1 then emphasize Obermaier's and Langhans's desire for each other as the other residents strike their famous up-against-the-wall pose and Langhans subsequently conducts an interview with the press naked. A few scenes later, a shot shows him and Obermaier sitting side by side on a bed, back-lit in a way that makes them less distinct, while also creating a halo around their hair. Each of them sports a wild, tousled mane, which join when they kiss to obscure their faces and create a complete merging.

Desire in these scenes extends beyond sexual attraction per se insofar as one senses as well the seductive pull of the counterculture life and the "long hairs," as one hears them labeled more than once from those on the outside looking in. The staging and visual effect of Obermaier's and Langhans's sexual merging, however, suggests less the attraction of the exotic than a magnetic, narcissistic pull, as if each of them saw themselves reflected in the other. In line with a straightforward narrative arc, Obermaier no doubt simply sees in Langhans the wild life she craves; his projections, I would argue, operate more on a metacritical plane very much aligned with retroactive, third-wave fantasies of performative power. It is the media-savvy Obermaier, after all, who successfully transforms countercultural aims into images that will be widely disseminated. On a more subtle level, however, her influence even manifests itself within the presumably anarchical, if alpha-male space of the Kommune 1. Ironically, as much as she initially parrots Langhans's rhetoric and ways, Obermaier also seems to inspire both his and, later, Dieter Bockhorn's attempts to become more fashionable. Over the course of the film, each of them dresses in increasingly style-conscious ways, with scarves and other fashion accessories that could be taken from one of Obermaier's fashion shoots. Langhans first appears naked before gradually transitioning to a look that fits in well at Keith Richard's decadent country manor. In fact, his wild mane of hair seems to mutate into the furs that Obermaier sometimes sports in fashion shoots, which later provide a key visual element in Bockhorn's fur-lined club and apartment, and in the bus they travel in through third-world countries.

If one senses a commentary on the way counterculture gets co-opted, with radical elements turning chic, it is important to consider the larger implications when a woman drives this process. When a Kommune 1 female resident admonishes Obermaier for wearing makeup and the latter responds by calling her an "old hag" (alte Gurke) who is jealous of her looks, one senses postfeminist cattiness towards a presumably lesbian, man-hating older generation. Yet comparisons between male and female forms of nakedness in the film suggest more complex underpinnings to the issue of female empowerment in visual terms. The staging of her arrival at Kommune 1, at the very moment the residents strike that famous naked pose for the press, underscores their fundamental inability to manipulate the realm of signification. Strikingly, Obermaier applies makeup as she approaches the commune, hearing at the same time a whiney voice issuing from its windows: "this is simply FKK," to which a second voice replies "if you want something subversive, you'll have to think of something else." Consequently, the spectator is positioned to view Kommune 1 posturing as rather unimaginative and unseductive compared to the fashion shoots the film later depicts. More generally, the fashion shoots position the Kommune 1 naked tableaux as one more form of posing among many, not the ultimate image of authenticity.

Equally striking in this regard is that the Kommune 1 residents, by positioning themselves "up against the wall," assume the body language of capitulation to the larger powers that be, as if to signal from the outset that their gesture has already been neutralized. The fact that a subversive act is automatically linked to FKK reveals the difficulty in signifying a wild and free life if naked bodies simply point backwards in time to something that already was and that has less to do with counterculture than promoting a particular form of healthfulness. Significant as well is that FKK bodies are not idealized bodies, the kind that inspire the media attention that Obermaier continually receives. Another scene in the film shows the Kommune 1 residents seeking this attention as well as they pour over morning newspapers together, only to find that the media gravitated to Obermaier at demonstrations, not the rest of them. To change the status quo, they need to strike the pose of authenticity in a manner that resonates with a wide audience, what Obermaier achieves in her career as a fashion model with carefree, if unreflective, ease. She makes the wild life look sexy; the men, by contrast, end up looking vaguely foppish in their overly stylized outfits.

At the same time, *Eight Miles High* grants Obermaier straightforward moments of seeming authenticity that complement her finesse in artifice and posturing. In other words, she escapes the critique the film otherwise directs towards Kommune 1 naivety about creating powerfully anarchical images. The film begins and ends with her standing naked in the ocean, Bockhorn's funeral pyre burning on the waves in the distance. One senses authenticity underwritten by a ritual process of purification, especially after one sees how much men demand from her, which include Bockhorn's conventional expectation that she marry him and have children. She exemplifies here the classic '68er's dream of throwing everything overboard, with distinctly feminist undertones. When Obermaier reflects in voice-over whether she would have done anything differently in her life, she answers with a simple "no," after which the film ends. Both visually and in narrative terms then, Obermaier affirms her own trajectory and ultimate unfettered selfhood. Again, if *Eight Miles High* lets her—not her Kommune 1 cohorts—embrace a cliché here, Obermaier's autobiography offers a more resonant and potentially subversive image that invites comparisons with female pop artists of the same era.

In reflecting on an image of herself that captures her topless and in unzipped jeans, Obermaier invokes an aggressively articulated sexuality that trumps the conventions of 1960's *Playboy* photography: "The photos in jeans and naked with a sunburn were the very first sex photos that didn't come across as airbrushed in a pussyish way—and they made me famous. I stared right into the camera and my titties stuck out at the lens like two weapons. Compared to the half-shameful and hidden porn photos of the time these shots were totally powerful and an intense expression of their time. I looked strong. Like an attacker."[60] Minioudaki argues that some female pop artists, particularly Evelyne Axell and Pauline Boty, specifically articulated a protofeminist use of the pin-up, undermining female passivity with a "bad-girl" pose and a strategic exhibitionism of radical narcissism.[61] While Obermaier's image recalls the "wild-woman," Lilith-ish persona that predates her, the time lag between the late 1960s and now, as well as the vagaries of reception, open up other possibilities. If her words channel a third-wave ethos—one that enabled women to imagine themselves exercising control over the signifying capacities of their bodies and actions—they potentially nudge audience reception to a more progressive place. The fact that Kraemer's transcribed interviews took so long to find a publisher and filmmaker might have to do with the fact that by the mid-2000s, feminist discourse had provided a more positive read on what a previous generation might have written off as hedonistic.

At the same time, the idea of "seductive subversion," to quote the title of a recent catalogue of female pop artists from the 1960s, in no way negates the adage that "sex sells," with or without a feminist filter to temper objectification. And it sells even better if, like Obermaier, one is conventionally attractive. Comparisons to the more radical manifestations of girl culture are useful here, especially if one considers the "irritating" semiotic games that Riot Grrrls and Gangsta Bitches and Hardcore Dykes played with their otherwise sexist designations. No doubt they stoked more discomfort than libidinal pleasure in their enactment of femininity. Other examples from a variety of cultural contexts offer powerful examples of jarring encounters with the female body. These include Austrian performer Valie Export, who created "Tap and Touch Cinema" and "Action Pants: Genital Panic" in the late 1960s. The first involved constructing a "movie theater" to enclose her torso, which also provided access for anyone to reach through its curtain and touch her breasts. The latter described the crotchless pants that Export walked around in at an art cinema in Munich, her genitals exposed at eye level to the seated audience. More recently, the video "Rub" (2015) by Canadian musician and performance artist Peaches featured many exposed genitals belonging to women of varying shapes and skin color, as well as sexual acts motivated by clitoral pleasure. Nothing within the montage-like stream of images corresponds at all with conventional male-directed porn.

Conclusion

I began this chapter by emphasizing temporal fissures, or how reactions to earlier historical moments can stoke our sense of unfulfilled political goals, thereby providing a powerful bind. Insofar as dominant cinema taps into and shapes our endlessly elastic capacity to identify, it provides a straightforward means for stoking empathy among otherwise disgruntled young feminists vis-à-vis their mothers' generation. This process becomes even more straightforward where feminist strategies of representation overlap with those of the dominant cinema. But I would like to conclude by emphasizing what gets lost in the process. Despite Ulrike Meinhof's feminist-inflected "Selbstverwirklichung" in *The Baader Meinhof Complex,* her political tracts (read in voice-over) and ultimate choice to join the RAF cast her as an agent of history, a role traditionally reserved for men. This role's formulaic parameters become apparent in the film's action-packed sequences, which sometimes position her front and center. By contrast, fashion metaphors lend themselves to Uschi Obermaier's ascendant trajectory in *Eight Miles High* given how power aligns with performativity alternately donned and cast off. With some pleasurable sex and chic fashion thrown into the mix, one senses a predetermined, "having it all" (post)feminist fantasy, meaning power in professional and personal terms. Since this fantasy aligns with a larger neoliberal meritocracy, it offers no radical alternatives to deep-seated societal structures. Basic assumptions about individual agency remain in place, but overlain with cinematic fantasies that turn things to women's advantage. Nowhere do we get a detached, critical view of fragmented selves whose very nature is less amenable to mainstream film's need for cohesion and resolution.

Instead both films implicitly show us the movement's shaping influence on our understanding of two historically fraught female figures. More generally, however, the way these films use a feminist frame feels again more straightforward than artistically enigmatic since they stop short of telling us something new about a social movement and its impact on female selfhood. Casting Meinhof's trajectory, however misguided, as a fraught but failed form of "Selbstverwirklichung" again borrows structuring and mutually sustaining elements from both dominant cinema and second-wave-inspired fantasies. Yet if Edel's cacophonous echo chamber had included feminist and/or antifeminist voices, it might have generated new perspectives less conducive to a neat narrative arc that traces its protagonist's evolution. Again, Mary Harron's depiction of Valerie Solanis provides a striking example of a fragmented, incongruous selfhood, one that exposes how theatricality can feed narcissism and activism simultaneously. Meinhof's psychological breakdown in prison may have resulted from her own internal divisions, but *The Baader Meinhof Complex* casts it more as the effect of Baader's and Ensslin's ostracizing her, which stokes our sympathy rather than detachment.

Obermaier as the more overtly theatrical character compared to Meinhof would seem a likely figure to display contrary elements, yet the strongest distancing device the film offers is her comically thick Bavarian accent. The fact that *Eight Miles High* combines third-wave performativity and sexual empowerment with a traditional coming-of-age narrative and another instance of "Selbstverwirklichung," also has the effect of excising otherwise resonant layers. Like the Alpha Girls and New German Girls who imagine themselves creating a new brand of feminism but unwittingly channel the voices of the previous generation, *Eight Miles High* displays a similar blind spot. In order to create its own kind of cohesive narrative, the film melds together a performative and experiential version of selfhood, giving us a protagonist highly skilled in artifice but also deeply invested in the search for an outside authentic space. A more unconventional approach might have yielded less synthesis or again some form of metacritical commentary on contrary aims. Charlotte Roche's protagonist in *Wetlands* provides a useful point of comparison because her uses of bodily fluids bring together the authenticity mandated by the second wave with the highly stylized bodies of a subsequent generation. The overall effect is not so much cohesiveness but a new way of thinking about the very categories of artifice and authenticity.

Ultimately, both films give us historically fraught female figures rendered less unsympathetic by a feminist framework, but one general enough to tally with mainstream filmic dictates. Within this arena we expect to see the transformation and empowerment of a traditionally disadvantaged group, but in a manner that stops short of fundamentally reimagining traditional power structures. Chapter 5 will look at two films that gesture towards both dystopian and utopian horizons, while closely examining the effects of progressive aims on female protagonists in particular. Mothers and daughters factor into their narratives as well, once again providing deeply personal, identity-shaping power struggles. First, I look at the teenage daughter of RAF members in Christian Petzold's *Die innere Sicherheit* (released in English as *The State I Am In*; 2000) and then two sets of mothers and daughters in Fatih Akin's *Auf der anderen Seite* (released in English as *The Edge of Heaven*; 2007). Strikingly, the outcome as much as the content of these two films creates the kind of overt contrast that initiated my analysis of Meinhof and Obermaier as filmic entities. Petzold depicts a young girl who gives herself over to consumer culture, and Akin a German-Turkish mother-daughter pairing that unites in the face of oppressive Western and Eastern forces. *The State I Am In* suggests the bleakest possible consequences for a commodity-based selfhood as alternative to leftist tenets, whereas *The Edge of Heaven* taps into the presumably sapped revolutionary energies of an earlier moment. For the purposes of this study, these two films shift emphasis away from a medial, performative selfhood back to the utopian possibility of collective solidarity.

Notes

1. Elizabeth Freeman, *Time Binds: Queer Temporalities, Queer Histories* (Durham: Duke University Press, 2010), 9–10.
2. Ibid., 9.
3. Ibid., 10.
4. Birgit Mikus and Emily Spiers, "Fractured Legacies: An Introduction," *Oxford German Studies* 45.1 (2016), 16.
5. Freeman, *Time Binds,* 13.
6. See Wolfgang Kraushaar, *1968 als Mythos, Chiffre und Zäsur* (Hamburg: Hamburger Edition, 2000).
7. *The Baader Meinhof Complex,* directed by Uli Edel (Constantin Films, 2008). DVD (mpimedia group, 2010). *Eight Miles High,* directed by Achim Bornhak (Babelsberg Film, 2007).
8. Fuss, *Identification Papers* (New York: Routledge, 1995), 9.
9. Judith Butler, *Excitable Speech: A Politics of the Performative* (New York: Routledge, 1997), 15.
10. See Wolfgang Kraushaar, *Achtundsechzig. Eine Bilanz* (Berlin: Propyläen, 2008). He writes, "1968 is not only polarizing, it's also a puzzle whose fragments hardly let themselves retroactively create a coherent image, it's a kind of kaleidoscope whose pictorial elements always shift to create new impressions" (49).
11. Quoted in Kraushaar, *1968 als Mythos, Chiffre und Zäsur,* 51. The original German reads, "Die Erfahrungen liegen begraben unter dem Misthaufen der Medien, des 'Archivmaterials', der Podiumsdiskussionen, der veteranenhaften Stilisierung einer Wirklichkeit, die unter der Hand unvorstellbar geworden ist. Mein Gedächtnis, dieser chaotische delirierende Regisseur, liefert einen absurden Film ab, dessen Sequenzen nicht zueinander passen. Der Ton is asynchron. Ganze Einstellungen sind unterbelichtet. Manchmal ziegt die Leinwand nur Schwarzfilm. Vieles ist mit wackelnder Kamera aufgenommen. Die meisten Akteure erkenne ich nicht wieder . . . Mir ist dieses Vorfahren schlierhaft . . . Es war nicht möglich, das alles gleichzeitig zu 'verstehen,' sich 'einen Vers darauf zu machen', es 'auf den Begriff zu bringen'. Die Widersprüche schreien zum Himmel. Jeder Versuch, den Tumult intelligible zu machen, endete notwendig im ideologischen Kauderwelsch. Die Erinnerungen an das Jahr 1968 kann deshalb nur eine Form annehmen: die der Collage."

12. R. G. Renner, "1989 und die Folgen. Deutsche Gegenwartsgeschichte im Nachwendefilm," *Pandaemonium germanicum: Revista de Estudos Germanísticos* 16 (2010), 42.
13. Ibid., 38.
14. I am indebted to Christina Gerhardt, who presented a paper at the 2009 German Studies Association Conference titled "*The Baader Meinhof Complex*: Cinema on the RAF, 1970s to the Present." It alerted me to the various voices I cite here in the reception of the film.
15. Ulrich Kriest, "'Action Speaks Louder than Words.' Oder: Warum niemand den Film *Der Baader Meinhof Komplex* braucht," *film-dienst* 20 (25 September 2008), 7.
16. See Andreas Borcholte, "Eichingers 'Baader-Meinhof-Komplex': Die Terror-Illustrierte," *Spiegel Online*, 18 September 2008, http://www.spiegel.de/kultur/kino/eichingers-baader-meinhof-komplex-die-terror-illustrierte-a-578786-2.html.
17. See Michael Althen, "Polit-Porno: 'Der Baader-Meinhof-Komplex,'" *Frankfurter Allgemeine Zeitung*, 24 September 2008, http://www.faz.net/aktuell/feuilleton/kino/video-filmkritiken/video-filmkritik-polit-porno-der-baader-meinhof-komplex-1105334.html. He writes: "Vor lauter Aktionen, Anschlägen, Attentaten bleibt kaum noch Zeit, Atem zu holen."
18. Sarah Waters, "Introduction: 1968 in Memory and Place," in *Cultury History and Literary Imagination*, vol. 16, *Memories of 1968: International Perspectives*, ed. Ingo Cornils and Sarah Waters (Brussels: Peter Lang, 2010), 17.
19. See Mattias Frey, *Postwall German Cinema. History, Film History, and Cinephilia* (New York: Berghahn, 2014), 174–75; and Mary-Elizabeth O'Brien, *Post-Wall German Cinema and National History: Utopianism and Dissent* (Rochester, NY: Camden House, 2012), 47. Both of them quote the "Sons of Stammheim" lyric: "The terrorists are finally gone / and there's peace and quiet / And you can drive your Mercedes safely / without it exploding."
20. I am indebted here to a 2009 German Studies Association paper by Svea Bräunert, which underscored the film's self-conscious framing shots. She has subsequently published *Gespenster Geschichten. Der linke Terrorismus der RAF und die Künste* (Berlin: Kulturverlag Kadmos, 2015).
21. The fact that so many A-list German actors signed on for this project also speaks to the RAF's continued allure.
22. Ironically, if you Google "RAF" and then click on "images," Edel's simulated wanted posters appear alongside the originals.
23. Bruno Ganz's and Heino Ferch's appearance in the film as Horst Herold, the director of the Bundeskriminalamt or German FBI equivalent, and his assistant, exemplifies another form of layered mediation. Casting both men as representatives of the police state makes sense if one thinks of their previous pairing as Adolph Hitler and Albert Speer in Oliver Hirschbiegel's 2004

film *Downfall*. As much as the first shot of Ganz links him to Willy Brandt wanting more democracy and to include the APO (extra parliamentary opposition linked to the student movement) in parliamentary processes, and as much as he articulates the need to understand the RAF rather than "cut off heads," he still retains the lingering aura of a cult film and popular object of YouTube mash-ups. The Nazi associations he brings to the role implicitly point to recent and historical anxieties about "Datenschutz" (data protection) and the extent to which the government had gained too much power during the 1970s.

24. As Ulrich Kriest has argued, the overall political discourse gets lost in films about the student movement: "If one looks at the body of films on this topic, then only one area remains completely under-illuminated: the political discourse of the RAF that can be found in its writings, briefly put: the question regarding transcending the system, the serious intellectual engagement with strategies of overcoming capitalism and imperialism" ("'Actions Speak Louder than Words,'" 9).

25. Both academic and print media reception of the film often cite the extremes that Edel and Eichinger went to in the name of fidelity, specifically using the same number of bullets as the RAF members had in the recreation of a shoot-out scene.

26. Aust had been an editor at *Konkret*, the leftist journal that Meinhof wrote for, and later became editor-in-chief of *Der Spiegel*. In a more personal vein, he was the one who rescued Meinhof's twin daughters from a refugee camp in Lebanon.

27. See Borcholte, "Eichingers 'Baader-Meinhof-Komplex.'"

28. He continues: "Rather than a linear narrative the film consists of puzzle pieces, which the audience has to piece together themselves in order to get the overall picture. In practical terms, this means that characters appear, a lot of the time they remain nameless, and when they play no further part in the story they disappear again" (ibid.).

29. James Bell, "After the Revolution," Interview with Bernd Eichinger, *Sight and Sound* 12.26 (December 2008); Andrea Dittgen poses the same question in "Radical Chic," *Sight and Sound* 18.12 (December 2008), 26.

30. Quoted in Bell, "After the Revolution," 26.

31. Hans Weingartner's 2004 film *The Edukators*, which tells the story of three contemporary activists, also appears to enact corrective measures in relation to '68 by subtly reprising the era's gendered blind spots. Only the female lead has a steady—and exploitative—job; her two male cohorts, by contrast, understand oppression in more abstract terms and initially pursue their activism without her. In this manner Weingartner recreates but ultimately corrects the boys' club feel of the student movement.

32. "Die Terroristen. Frauen und Gewalt," *Der Spiegel* 31.33 (8 August 1977), 25, 22.

33. Vojin Sasa Vukadinovic, "The Baader Oedipus Complex," in *A Companion to German Cinema*, ed. Terri Ginsberg and Andrea Mensch (Chichester, England: Wiley-Blackwell, 2012), 470.
34. Quoted in Vukadinovic, "The Baader Oedipus Complex," 470.
35. Alice Schwarzer, "Terroristinnen," *EMMA* (October 1977), 1.
36. Ibid.
37. Margarete Mitschlerlich, "Sündenböcke," *EMMA* (November 1977), 5.
38. "Die Terroristen. Frauen und Gewalt," 22.
39. Ibid. To *Der Spiegel*'s credit, its cover story featured an interview with the criminologist Helga Einsele, who provided a larger historical frame and less hysterical tone. Above all she pointed out that violent women were nothing new, citing terrorist women in Russia and Ireland in the early part of the twentieth century. She also described the cold-blooded murder committed by Wera Sassulitsch in 1878 in which she shot a Russian civil servant at point blank range. If anything was different among 1970's female terrorists, she asserted, it had to do with quantity, not quality. She then explained extreme violence among RAF woman as a product of the insular conditions under which they lived and the resulting loss of contact to reality. See "Die Täter leben in absoluter Inzucht. Spiegel-Interview mit der Frankfurter Kriminologin Professor Helga Einsele," *Der Spiegel* 31.33 (8 August 1977), 28–29.
40. Eichinger mentions in an interview a famous incident when Sartre visited Baader in jail and pronounced him afterwards to be "incredibly stupid." Cited in Bell, "After the Revolution," 26.
41. She describes the character of Horst Herold as a "semi-identification figure" as well, since he narrates and interprets both the State's and the terrorists' agenda, his insights anticipating the circumstances of post-9/11 audiences. See O'Brien, *Post-Wall German Cinema and National History*, 230–31.
42. Even her loss of voice, as O'Brien argues, underscores Meinhof's privileged narrative status: "Meinhof's hysterical crying fit when arrested and her transformation into a hallucinating neurotic in solitary confinement are glimpses into her psyche that other characters are not afforded" (*Post-Wall German Cinema and National History*, 229). Reinhard Zachau has pointed out how the film offers a far less disturbing image of Ulrike Meinhof's arrest than the iconic newspaper shot of her being manhandled by the police officers who captured her. In it a hand props her chin up as if to present her to the media, while Meinhof looks down and grimaces. In the film an awed silence ensues when the police realize whom they have captured, and as Meinhof slumps and weeps, one of them merely grasps her elbow in support. See Reinhard Zachau, "Death Images in *The Baader Meinhof Komplex*," *Glossen* 33 (November 2011), http://blogs.dickinson.edu/glossen/archive/most-recent-issue-glossen-332011/reinhard-zachau-glossen-33/.
43. One very blatant irony deserves mention here. Sarah Colvin's volume on Ulrike Meinhof emphasizes the many contrary projections she inspired in

the press, from a "fearless and self-sacrificing" Joan of Arc to victim of her fellow revolutionaries. Yet no one has yet engaged with the underside of Meinhof as feminist icon, evident in her rejection of "the liberal women's movement in German as 'Votzenchauvismus' (cunt chauvinism)." See Sarah Colvin, *Ulrike Meinhof and West German Terrorism. Language, Violence, and Identity* (Rochester, NY: Camden House, 2009), 5.

44. Patricia Melzer, "Maternal Ethics and Political Violence: The 'Betrayal' of Motherhood among the Women of the RAF and June 2 Movement," *Seminar* 47.1 (February 2011), 98. She continues: "The contact with the twins cemented her continuous identity as their mother, and it demonstrates that they were at the center of her thoughts. Her desire to let them know that seemed as strong as her need to feel their presence in her life in prison: she writes that she thinks of them constantly and begs them to visit, write, and send new photos to augment the ones she knows by heart" (ibid.).
45. Christopher Roth's 2002 film *Baader* is often cited, and critiqued, for its overtly pop-inflected depiction of Andreas Baader and mix of historical events with fictional fantasies.
46. Mary-Elizabeth O'Brien has also noted the irony of Joplin's and Farah Diba's presence in this scene, arguing that both underscore the double standard from which Meinhof operates (*Post-Wall German Cinema and National History*, 225).
47. Mattias Frey also comments on the polarized view of Meinhof and Ensslin in the film, and he refers to their characters as "the hot heart and the cool brains of the organization" (*Postwall German Cinema*, 71).
48. Strikingly, one scene shows Meinhof visiting Ensslin in prison, and during their conversation the latter deems theory a form of "masturbation."
49. Melzer provides a wealth of evidence, often in the form of letters, of Ensslin's commitment to her son Felix. She writes, "During her first year in prison, Ensslin creates a variety of drawings for Felix and knits and crochets for him a continuous flow of gifts that attest to her constant thoughts of him.... At times she seems overwhelmed by emotions for the boy and refutes... doubts about her maternal commitment, emphatically claiming that she never desired to be separated from [him]" (*Maternal Ethics and Political Violence*, 92).
50. Her S.C.U.M. manifesto, he argues, links the cutting up of men with "the most innovative aesthetic strategy of the avant-garde, namely the subversive cutting up, recontextualization, and radical juxtapositions that are the basic techniques of collage itself. Inasmuch as this allusion identifies the cutting up of men with a tradition of experimental art, the manifesto, in its implicit embrace of collage aesthetics, rhetorically positions itself as a hostile usurper and unassimilable agent, commandeering an avant-garde aesthetic strategy that it employs to disrupt the avantgarde itself." See James M. Harding, "The Simplest Surrealist Act: Valerie Solanas and the (Re)Asser-

tion of Avantgarde Priorities," *TDR: The Drama Review. A Journal of Performance Studies* 45.4 (Winter 2001), 148.
51. I am indebted to a former Davidson student for suggesting this wonderful reading. Thank you, Eric Reeves.
52. Olaf Kraemer, *High Times. Mein wildes Leben* (Munich: Wilhelm Heyne Verlag, 2007), 292–93. The original German reads, "War sie zu brutal, zu Lilith-haft und zu hedonistisch für eine traditionelle Heldinnenreise, wie sie der Film so liebt? Kann man sich dem dramaturgisch und biographisch wichtigen Prozess einer Transformation entziehen und trotzdem eine Sympathieträgerin sein? ... Immer wieder gab es heftige, zum Teil irrationale Auseinandersetzungen unter den Beteiligten über Uschis Charakter im Drehbuch und seine Bedeutung für '68, über die Rolle, die sie für unser Land gespielt hat und immer noch spielt. Die Einschätzungen ihrer Person gingen von 'Das war doch bloß eine Groupie, sie hatte das politische Bewusstsein einer Amöbe! Macht lieber einen Film über Ulrike Meinhof!' Bis zu 'Sie verkörpert den modernen Typus Frau' und 'Sie ist die Wurzel des Methusalem-Komplotts'—was alles zutreffend ist, doch die Wahrheit über sie lag für mich noch einmal woanders."
53. Kraemer, *High Times*, 293.
54. See Nathan Lee, "The Life of a World-Class Sex Kitten," *New York Times*, 11 July 2008, http://www.nytimes.com/2008/07/11/movies/11eigh.html?_r=0.
55. "Die 68erinnen," *EMMA* (May/June 2008), 74-75. Strikingly, Hans Weingartner's *Die Edukators* also subtly highlights the bourgeois bases of otherwise egalitarian theory. Its most pronounced Marxist theorist nearly derails the protagonists' political aims in the oedipally charged encounters he stages with the wealthy industrialist they have kidnapped. And only by the end of the film are the two men in the group able to give up the idea of monogamous male-female relationships to accept "free love" between them and the female protagonist, evident in the film's final shot of the three of them lying in bed together.
56. Ibid., 74.
57. Meredith Haaf, Susanne Klingner, and Barbara Streidl, *Wir Alpha-Mädchen. Warum Feminismus das Leben schöner macht* (Hamburg: Hoffmann und Campe Verlag, 2008), 23.
58. Kalliopi Minioudaki, "Proto-Feminisms: Beyond the Paradox of the Woman Pop Artist," in *Seductive Subversion: Women Pop Artists 1958–1968*, ed. Sid Sachs and Kalliopi Minioudaki (New York: Abbeville Press, 2010), 108.
59. Kalliopi Minioudaki, "Other(s') Pop: The Return of the Repressed of Two Discourses," in *Power Up: Female Pop Art*, ed. Angela Stief and Martin Walkner (Vienna: Kunsthalle Wien, 2010), 140.
60. Kraemer, *High Times*, 111. The original German reads, "Die Fotos in Jeans und nackt mit Sonnenbrand waren die ersten wilden Sexfotos überhaupt,

die nicht pussymäßig geschleckt wie im *Playboy* rüberkamen—und sie haben mich berühmt gemacht. Ich schaute genau in die Kamera, und meine Titties stachen wie zwei Waffen in die Linse. Im Vergleich zu den halb verschämten und verdeckten Pornographiefotos aus der Zeit waren diese Aufnahmen total kraftvoll und ein intensiver Ausdruck ihrer Zeit. Ich sah stark aus. Wie eine Angreiferin."
61. Minioudaki, "Other(s') Pop," 142.

CHAPTER FIVE

Counter-Cinema, Crossing Bridges, and Future Feminisms

Christian Petzold's **The State I Am In** *(2000) and Fatih Akin's* **The Edge of Heaven** *(2007)*

In her seminal essay "Women's Cinema as Counter-Cinema" (1975), Claire Johnston has argued that conventional cinema's structuring categories create gender-coded myths in order to transmit sexist ideology. Drawing on Erwin Panofsky's work on stereotypes in early cinema, she cites a longer tradition that positions "man inside of history," whereas woman appears "ahistoric and eternal."[1] If women change at all, she continues, their "modifications [are only] in terms of fashion."[2] The previous chapter demonstrated how conventions that blend dominant cinema approaches with familiar feminist strategies of representation can easily ossify into cliché. Johnston's observation above helps us to understand how two historically fraught female icons take over the role of agent of history, thereby reversing male/female polarities. This seemingly radical shift, however, should also be understood as a cosmetic change at best insofar as it belies social realities that continue to disadvantage women and/or obliges them to don a new but predetermined set of defining characteristics. Significantly, Johnston's essay approaches representation via metaphors that often pit reconfigured surfaces against truly ruptured ones.

In seeking alternatives for capturing women's experiences, she rejects the idealistic possibility that the "'truth' of [women's] oppression can be 'captured' on celluloid with the 'innocence' of the camera."[3] Such a realist, sociological approach, she argues, denies the "myths" underpinning representation, a designation that resonates beyond cliché to evoke a timeless and pervasive, if fictive, truth. Instead of searching out occluded voices, hidden experience, and oppressed circumstances that invite identification, film should, she argued, interrogate its own language and manufacture new meanings in relation to sexist ideology. This approach is more radical than attaching new signifieds to familiar signifiers, since it aims for dissonance and rupture. Johnston deems filmic icons to be the "weakest point" in the mythmaking machinery; how they stand in relation to the myths they represent can potentially "disrupt the fabric of the male bourgeois cinema."[4] For women in particular this means creating "a dislocation between sexist ideology and the text of the film."[5]

Johnston's efforts to imagine a truly alternative cinema for representing women's experiences provide a useful starting point for the two films this chapter will address: Christian Petzold's *The State I Am In* (in German, *Die innere Sicherheit*; 2000) and Fatih Akin's *The Edge of Heaven* (in German, *Auf der anderen Seite*; 2007).[6] Female protagonists feature prominently in both directors' best-known works, in each case comprised of trilogies that situate German history, culture, and contemporary global forces in relation to women's lives. *The State I Am In* was followed by Petzold's *Ghosts* (*Gespenster*; 2005) and *Yella* (2007), which together comprised his Ghost Trilogy. Though the word "ghost" suggests historical invisibility vis-à-vis the films' female protagonists, Petzold instead shows them wandering through liminal spaces that counter established iconography and narratives. In the process, uncanny elements unsettle our sense of a German "Heimat" (homeland), and ultimately two of his trilogy protagonists are expulsed from it entirely in car accidents. Akin's *The Edge of Heaven* was preceded by *Head On* (*Gegen die Wand*; 2004), and together these two films are part of a trilogy, which includes the 2014 film *The Cut*, called "Love, Death, and the Devil" (Liebe, Tod, und Teufel). If translated word for word—*Gegen die Wand* meaning "against the wall" and *Auf der anderen Seite* meaning "on the other side"—each title highlights stymied or utopian mobility, embodied in *The Edge of Heaven* by women who cross over via death or transgenerational, transcultural solidarity. Spatial metaphors in both *The State I Am In* and *The Edge of Heaven* suggest less women's fixed positioning vis-à-vis larger ideological forces than dramatic examples of detachment and/or mutability.

If an alternative cinema for women necessitates ruptures in filmic language, an important starting point for Petzold's and Akin's films is also genre and the extent to which its various characteristics resist or invite breaches in meaning. The two poles in *The Edge of Heaven* I cite above—death and utopian forms of unity—point in the direction of melodrama, a genre whose associations with convention are particularly strong. Such pronounced antithetical outcomes also speak to individual desires often obstructed by familial and social pressures. Only death or artificially constructed Hollywood endings out of sync with an inimical surround provide a form of escape. Douglas Sirk's melodramas serve as an important reference point, and not only given the outcome of a film such as *Imitation of Life* discussed in chapter 1—that is, female bonds forged in and through generational/racial discord and on the occasion of a mother's death. Sirk's lineage manifests itself in Rainer Werner Fassbinder films, including his own Bundesrepublik Deutschland Trilogy, a touchstone for both Petzold and Akin. His trilogy titles—*Die Ehe der Maria Braun* (*The Marriage of Maria Braun*; 1979), *Lola* (1981), and *Veronika Voss* (1982)— are virtually synonymous with his female protagonists, whose lives are intertwined with Germany's economic miracle. If, as Johnston argues, "icons" constitute a weak link for transmitting ideology, Fassbinder's three female protagonists stand in precarious relation to mythical maternal figures as repositories of national identity. Bertolt Brecht's "pale mother" provides a familiar example of Germany as matriarch, though he inserts distance between icon and domain when she sits "besmirched" among her bellicose progeny. Fassbinder's theatrically iconic women (two of the three trilogy protagonists are actresses) distance us from the ambition and industriousness of the economic miracle if one considers how overtly male characteristics come together at times with fetishistically displayed femininity. Economic success sometimes becomes a matter of getting in bed, as Maria Braun does, with the right partners.

Though melodrama may have influenced the shape of these films, Fassbinder's interest in Sirk's melodramas emphasized an unexpected characteristic, specifically a female interiority that potentially undermines otherwise predetermined action. In 1971 Fassbinder stated: "I have seen six films by Douglas Sirk. Among them were the most beautiful in the world."[7] Aesthetics in his films actually work to highlight rather than repress the ideological workings of the filmic spaces they conjure. A film such as *All That Heaven Allows* (1955), for instance, achieves this aim with color-coding that reflects interior desires otherwise proscribed. Fassbinder's *Lola* similarly uses color as a form of emotional expressionism, and his earlier overt homage to *All That Heaven Allows*—his 1974 international success *Ali, Fear Eats the Soul*—explicitly evokes its predecessor's stark red zones of contained sexuality.[8] Beyond alluring aesthetics, Fassbinder was also taken by "action" defined in psychological terms: "In Douglas Sirk's movies the women think. I haven't noticed that with any other director. With any. Usually the women just react, do the things that women do, and here they actually think. That's something you've got to see. It's wonderful to see a woman thinking. That gives you hope. Honest."[9] Though awkwardly patronizing, Fassbinder's observation opens up the possibility of less predictable outcomes than convention would allow when women meditate on their circumstances. Perhaps not surprisingly, both Fassbinder and early feminists revived interest in Sirk's films during the 1970s, recognizing more subtle levels of meaning beneath what Thomas Doherty identifies as melodrama's obligatory elements: swelling strings, sobs and sacrifices, all contained within in a "buttoned-down, girdled milieu."[10] If female interiority provides a conventional counterpart to male action, it is also the realm where contradictions are perceived and processed; reaction, in turn, has the potential to communicate some form of disjuncture to filmic audiences.

The extent to which color provides both a natural and intrusive detail within a Sirkian mise en scène invites comparisons with Petzold's starkly realistic but also vaguely alienating filmic spaces. Much has been written about his unique cinematic techniques and more generally of the Berlin School of filmmakers with which he is aligned. Petzold, Thomas Arslan, and Angela Schanelec attended the Deutsche Film- und Fernsehakademie in Berlin in the early 1990s, working with avant-garde and documentary filmmakers Hartmut Bitomsky and Harun Farocki. Later Berlin School filmmakers include Ulrich Köhler, Christoph Hochhäusler, Benjamin Heisenberg, Maren Ade, and Valeska Grisebach, all of whom studied film elsewhere in Germany but share stylistic affinities with the "first generation." As Marco Abel has defined them, typical characteristics include "long takes, long shots, clinically precise framing, a certain deliberateness of pacing, sparse usage of extradiegetic music, poetic use of diegetic sounds, and, frequently, the reliance on unknown or even nonprofessional actors who appear to be chosen for who they are rather than who they could become."[11] If at all present in Petzold's films, dominant cinema techniques are considerably muted. More important, as Abel argues, political content articulates itself in aesthetics meant to evoke affective sensations instead of filmic elements that require semiotic decoding, a "rupture" that goes beyond Johnston's iconography-based framework. The extent to which something akin to critique emerges within this register relies on his films' ability to evoke pleasure that belies ultimately egregious bodily effects.

This contradiction is particularly relevant to *The State I Am In*, the story of a girl named Jeanne whose parents appear to be former Red Army Faction (RAF) members on the run in a contemporary landscape. Over the course of the film, we witness her and her parents' return to Germany after their money is stolen from a Portuguese hotel. Here they hide out in a Hamburg villa, from which Jeanne makes excursions to a nearby town, including brief trysts with Heinrich, a young man she met in Portugal who also returned to Germany. If pleasure that belies pain sounds vaguely like a left-wing critique of capitalism's destructive effects on selfhood, *The State I Am In* aligns this double bind with presumably liberating movements as well. Abel underscores Michel Foucault's and particularly Gilles Deleuze's shaping influence on Petzold, specifically how they link gratification to power structures. Along these lines, Petzold views the new institutions that appeared in the 1960s, "those hedonistic communities, the patchwork families ... and the shared apartment-living situations, which were established in direct opposition to the traditional father-mother-child neurosis," as "actually embod[ying] the modern control society ... that suddenly exert[s] [its] force upon people."[12] Likewise, when contemporary global forms of capitalism stoke pleasure in ever more broadly and swiftly dispersed forms, they simultaneously prevent subjects from perceiving the "ever tightening noose around their neck."[13]

Jeanne's introspective, observant demeanor throughout *The State I Am In* potentially adds another layer to the film's experientially-oriented mise en scène. Bodily effects notwithstanding, it opens up the possibility of critical detachment, particularly towards RAF crimes and lingering left-wing tenets that preordain her outlaw existence. This stance would make sense given Jaimey Fisher's observation that Petzold's films distinguish themselves in the way his characters "psychologically process, even fantasize, the uneven spaces produced by global and globalizing capitalism."[14] Yet the film's title points away from any kind of analytic purview. If "thinking women" react to oppressive circumstances in unexpected ways, "innere Sicherheit" (internal security), by contrast, suggests a more primal need, particularly if one considers Jeanne's age. Some of the film's critical reception refers to her as a twelve-year-old girl, making her perhaps the only actual Mädchen in this volume. In developmental terms, she is thus a far more nascent being than a teenager or young adult. At the same time, if Jeanne's age prompts us to think of *The State I Am In* as a coming-of-age tale, she may in fact be emblematic for Petzold's protagonists in general, whose "agency, though not denied, is severely compromised."[15] Sensation and affect also invoke more a child's manner of engaging with the world and thus would seem a less likely path towards political or historical consciousness. Most important, I would argue that Petzold's affective register also carries metaphorical meanings that resonate beyond the pleasure/control double bind.

Strikingly, when ambient or natural sounds replace contrived or musical acoustics, spectators are made aware of perception itself. Obliquely rendered ideological presences in the film—in the parents' RAF imperatives, the legacy of German fascism that crops up in places, and more subtly in commodity culture as alternative for a young teenager—thus subtly align with a larger canvas of perceived phenomena. Like natural noises, ideological forces tend to blend in unless one consciously pays attention to them. Equally important, *The State I Am In* also creates the conditions for disjuncture, graphically enacted in a crash at the end of the film when Jeanne is thrown from a car and left bloodied and broken in a desolate field. When perception enters the realm of pain, spectators become aware that her world's ideological underpinnings not only offer nothing to an evolving self, they also do the most literal kind of damage possible. In this manner Petzold "tears at the language of film" by aligning ideology with sometimes barely perceptible natural elements that gather force and achieve catastrophic proportions by the film's radically dystopian ending. This outcome also undercuts feminist fantasies then and now: not only does it literally silence the teenage protagonist, but also the spare landscape on view counters the consumer world with which she had begun to construe her voice. In this sense Petzold creates a form of disjuncture not only in relation to sexist ideology, but also to feminist uses of commodity culture for its own political ends.

Though Akin's film is characterized by geographical movement between East and West, it ends with a Petzold-like shot of a young man standing motionless before the Black Sea, the sounds of lapping waves captured in an extended take. This meditative, still endpoint is less about perception per se, or how ideological forces align with ambient noise we may or may not register, than a process of reflection. In a story where East and West constantly reverberate against each other, often evident in sexist oppression that shifts form but remains a constant, neither side becomes a self-evident site of ideological supremacy. Spectators are poised not only to perceive but also to compare and contrast and think through preformed assumptions. Strikingly, Wolfgang Kraushaar conjures the image of a "partially still open horizon" when reflecting on the elusive nature of '68, its historical shape, and its long-term consequences.[16] *The Edge of Heaven* obliquely alludes to this era via contemporary activism in Turkey, significantly far away from Hamburg, where a professor cites Goethe's cautionary stance on revolution in a lecture. In Akin's film it is the women, particularly a German mother and Turkish daughter, who give the utopian horizons associated with the student movement concrete form. This achievement becomes evident partly in reconfigured signifiers aligned with both Eastern and Western oppression. Specifically, these two women transform religious and economic forces that oblige women to repent or reduce them to objects of exchange into the foundation of transcultural, transgenerational solidarity. Rather than ending their story in stasis and passivity, Akin shows them stepping onto an Istanbul street together, the Turkish daughter deeply penitential for her part in the death of the German mother's biological daughter. In effect, they perform a kinder form of exchange in the ersatz mother-daughter bond they form as salve to this loss, as well as to the death of the Turkish mother. Ultimately, Akin's story of familial bonds is less about tearing the fabric of film than attaching melodrama's contrived resolutions to abandoned political utopias, thereby creating a salve for contemporary social and cultural divisions. Most importantly for this volume, *The Edge of Heaven* depicts shifting forms of identification among mothers and daughters as an antagonistic, acutely painful, but ultimately always evolving, process. To the extent that both parties consciously recognize its mutability, as well as choose to embrace affinities alongside differences, the possibility of building bridges emerges. Ultimately, Akin's film suggests ways of fostering solidarity among rebellious daughters and aggrieved mothers.

One final point of commonality deserves mention: both *The State I Am In* and *The Edge of Heaven* center their narratives on familial discord and fundamental differences between parents and children. In observations about the film, Akin lines up the political alongside the familial: "There were so many political aspects I wanted to touch on. But I also wanted to tell a story about mothers and sons, fathers and daughters—about hope as the last refuge we have as human beings."[17] Both of the films' narratives resonate not only alongside generational struggles among feminists but also the legacy of '68 in a contemporary landscape of gendered and cultural divides. While families ideally provide the ur-locus of "Sicherheit," individuation of course requires a degree of rebellion, whether directed towards misguided feminist mothers or Nazi-tainted fathers. On a less overtly historical plane, traditional families came to embody to '68ers the foundation of a hierarchical social field—that is, the locus of authoritarian structures to be overthrown. In a sense, Petzold fulfills this anarchical aim with the parents' likely demise in the car crash, though again that barren field as endpoint strips away ideological forces tout court. And throughout the film he plays up affinities as much as disjuncture, in the former case between authoritarian parents and teachers and the Nazi past they rail against.

Akin takes a different tack by drawing on a longer humanist legacy as corrective to the antiauthoritarian excesses of '68. If change does indeed begin at the family level, the young Turkish man who stands before the sea anticipates a returning father, as well as solidarity across differences wrought by their mutually fraught German and Turkish identities. The Turkish daughter and German mother, by contrast, seem poised to extend their own form of familial-based solidarity across a concrete national divide. The less open-ended feel when they step onto an Istanbul street together resonates even more strongly in the context of German feminism, where local as opposed to global concerns have more often set the agenda for 2008's Alpha and New German Girls. As I suggested above, *The Edge of Heaven* suggests a path forward for feminists mired in difference, which the film amplifies by situating difference in relation to power-laden family hierarchies. Yet it also strips away biology, which infused mother-daughter dyads with survivalist undertones. Biology not only becomes superfluous in the deep bonds formed by the German mother and Turkish daughter, it also takes more metaphorical shape in a process whereby they learn to reinfuse and sustain each other across difference. In the utopian spirit of the film, this process aligns with the solidarity I imagined in the introduction of this volume, not as a quiescent endpoint but as the energies infusing continually shifting interstices between affinity and difference. Ideally their "survivalist" aim is to preserve a larger whole.

Interiority and Cruel Affect in *The State I Am In*

One of the first shots of Jeanne in *The State I Am In* shows her wearing ear buds as she roams a beach in Portugal, not far from the hotel where her fugitive parents have taken up residence. Given her young age, this image evokes a petulant adolescent attempt to shut out the world, as well as to internalize elements that cultivate identity in carefully chosen, individual terms. Certainly this gesture makes sense in a film where the RAF and National Socialism hover as examples of a collective or national identity. The latter force sometimes takes uncanny form: an orphanage in the woods in Germany, for instance, is called the "Anne Frank Heim." This name estranges in that a woodland refuge unexpectedly points not to fictive archetypes but to history and a real, not folkloric, girl lost to it. If Jeanne in ear buds again signals rebellion along psychic lines with their own idiosyncratic contours, youthful influences on her coming of age reveal their own historically consonant nature as well. In fact, Petzold's spare, generic-looking topographies ironically make it even more possible for history to resonate within the present than overt visual signifiers of the past presumably would. The latter's invisibility shifts things again to an affective register, like ghosts whose presence is more keenly felt precisely because they slip in and out of view. Ghosts thus do the work of familiar, clichéd iconography of a particular historical moment that no longer prompts a strong response. And they reside in random, fleeting elements that feel in tune with generic landscapes but that nonetheless resonate beyond them.

Early on, Jeanne meets a boy named Heinrich on the Portugal beach, who later becomes her boyfriend, and he tells her to shut her eyes and begin imagining.[18] He then describes the Hamburg villa where Jeanne will subsequently take her parents to hide. Incongruous filmic details make it difficult to determine whether the scenes unfolding in Jeanne's mind anticipate a coming reality or remain pure fantasy, but his gesture nonetheless initiates her escape into a subjective space. This choice makes sense when historical, ideological, and ultimately consumerist forces fail to provide stable scaffolding for an emerging identity; at the very least, fleeing into an interior, psychic realm should make it possible to reimagine otherwise paltry bases of selfhood along more empowering lines. Yet the notion of "escape" resonates ambiguously if one considers the history of their newfound home. Some critics have recognized it as the "Villa Stahl," which once belonged to a famous Nazi architect. This setting thus allows Petzold to suggest unwitting affinities between left-wing terrorists and the generation they deplore. And as much as this second woodland shelter invokes history, it too, like Anne Frank's secret annex, is both hiding place and prison. Since it initially appears in Jeanne's imagination, *The State I Am In* subtly connects interiority with prisons of one's own making.

Within a longer historical and literary frame, excessive interiority has hindered radical change in Germany, particularly if one thinks of Goethe's shaping influence as cited in *The Edge of Heaven*. To find some kind of interior security, to translate the film's title literally, runs the risk of cultivating a problematic insularity, amplified all the more when juvenile personas escape an oppressive reality in this manner. Youth culture in the form of *Sturm und Drang* literature, of course, provided the backdrop to the twenty-four-year-old Goethe's bestselling *Die Leiden des jungen Werther* (1774), in which romantic obsession leads to self-destruction. In *The State I Am In*, the filmic space is less defined by literary allusions than a fairytale-like mise en scène, which becomes all the more evident when Jeanne begins regularly crossing a bridge from the woods to explore the pedestrian zone of an adjacent town. Compared to Goethe's protagonists, who inhabit an ambiguous zone between adolescence and young adulthood, Jeanne vacillates between a primal search for "Sicherheit" (safety)—what her distracted, hard-bitten parents clearly have not provided—and an adolescent impulse to rebel. Fairytales, of course, enable young children to make sense of the world with basic rubrics of good and evil. Their oblique presence in the film, as well as a young teenager's subjective perspective as filter, remind us that ideology can perform a similar function, especially when it tries to pass off its own versions of good and evil as timeless givens. As I ar-

Figure 5.1. Still: *The State I Am In* (2000)

Figure 5.2. Still: *The State I Am In* (2000)

gued above, Jeanne's coming of age hardly points in the direction of an evolved historical consciousness as likely endpoint. Instead, "rebellion" articulates itself within the limited topography between the parents' woodland hideout and the town's generic pedestrian zone.

While fairytales provide a compass for navigating between antithetical poles, the uncanny qualities of seemingly straightforward narratives undermine any sure footing. Indeed, what feels safe and secure to children lost in the woods, here the sudden appearance of a house that entices with the possibility of pleasurable warmth and sustenance, also creates the conditions for their possible demise. And danger exists at both ends of the spectrum if one considers the kind of archetypical cruel parenting that drives children from home and hearth to begin with. In *The State I Am In*, we find not only criminal parents who endanger rather than protect their child, but also an enticing commodity culture that provides the means for escape and rebellion. Petzold's double bind is thus not only about pleasure that belies a "tightening noose," but also, in the more literal, fairytale version, a flight from parents who abuse their children to an alluring, candy-covered house as a deceptive form of salvation. As much as Jeanne is drawn into a world of t-shirts and shiny plastic bags, Petzold conjures the town as a kind of bland, dead zone of commodity culture. Tellingly, Jeanne sometimes appears either in lavatory stalls or next to a dumpster, which aligns her with the waste that commodity culture must depose of in order to perpetuate itself.

In the woodland villa, Petzold perverts the "Heim" as a zone of "Sicherheit" by showing both parents' repeated attempts to keep Jeanne confined within a childlike state. One shot, for instance, captures them in bed with their teenage daughter lying beside them. The father also buys Jeanne a sweatshirt to keep her warm, which she rejects for having the cartoon figure Biene Maja on it. Ironically, their control sometimes vaguely resembles a post-"deutscher Herbst" (German autumn) world of surveillance cameras, given how the parents police Jeanne's activities. After she has sex for the first time, for instance, the mother appears very suddenly, almost as if she had been watching her.[19] What exactly constitutes security also becomes difficult to determine in a film where police and terrorists look vaguely alike, particularly when both groups are captured together in long shots. Also significant in this regard is a teacher whom Jeanne later encounters, who rails at his students in an ironically authoritarian manner during a screening of *Night and Fog* (1995) for not being moved by the film's horrific images. In fact, he ultimately chastises Jeanne forcefully enough for her to flee the room in humiliation.[20] Overall, one witnesses how hiding out in the "Heim" means confronting a cloying, dictatorial, almost perverted parentalism.[21] Petzold's fairytale frame thus signals more than a child's limited means for understanding the world. It clearly demonstrates how the "heim" (home) turns "unheimlich" (uncanny) when family structures "secure" identity in misguided ways.[22] Indeed, Heinrich later assumes, based on Jeanne's outfit, that she belongs to the Jehovah's Witnesses.

Petzold represents Jeanne's need to escape with recurring elements: three times in the film, other characters—a terrorist, her mother, and her boyfriend—strike her, and at three different moments she utters the phrase "I have to go." Tim Hardin's 1960's song "How Can we Hang onto a Dream" accompanies the opening scene and includes the line "she's leaving home." Entering the town's pedestrian zone feels like a logical geographical and symbolic move insofar as Jeanne can thus put literal distance between herself and her parents and embrace the capitalistic structures they abhor. In the best possible scenario, everyday consumer culture, given its ubiquity and nonelitist attributes, should enable Jeanne to articulate basic needs and desires in a manner that her parents' elitist dogma cannot. (More than once, characters in the film also reference *Moby Dick,* an arcane canonical text rendered even more abstruse by the RAF's coded uses of it.)

After returning to Germany, Jeanne begins encountering other young people almost immediately, including a female wearing a Diego Maradona t-shirt, which Jeanne ends up borrowing later on in the film in what feels like a basic form of imitation. One is reminded that the same actress, Julia Hummer, played a troubled young female in Petzold's 2005 film *Ghosts*. T-shirts feel emblematic in that film as well, especially when the lead character and the woman who seduces and betrays her briefly wear ones with the word "Girlfriends" on them. Not only does the naïve protagonist appear to learn the complexities of adult relationships by literally trying them on, the duplicitous girlfriend also reveals the specious nature of commodity culture's alluring mirrors. Their attire also invokes 1990's girl culture, though the protagonists of *The State I Am In* and *Ghosts* appear far too unevolved to cultivate its characteristic ironic detachment. Instead, when Heinrich observes to Jeanne at one point that her "uniform consists of disguises," consumer culture begins to overlap with the film's other historical and allegorical hiding places.

Rebellion that ends up embracing convention is, of course, not a new narrative. Petzold, however, adds estranging elements by making the very idea of rebellion "other" to itself, and not only by revealing ironic affinities between left-wing terrorists and Nazis.[23] Another example of popular culture in the film—a Beach Boys poster for the *Endless Summer* album that hangs on a villa wall—resonates beyond adolescent dreams to subtly comment on the parents' vagabond existence. Retroactively then, the first song we hear—Tim Hardin's "How Can We Hang onto a Dream"—resonates along similar lines.[24] To either challenge or escape traditional societal structures constitutes a kind of adolescent fantasy that ultimately proves untenable. At one point, Heinrich chastises Jeanne for not knowing who Brian Wilson is, and his life story adds another dimension, one that closes down the possibility of Jeanne's escape into commodity culture. In a sense, his is a narrative with a foregone conclusion, much like the parents' perhaps equally predictable demise in the final car accident. Given their drug abuse, celebrities such as Wilson and Maradona embody the downside of a hedonistic "endless summer," providing the classic example of consumerism in its most negative form. Thus rather than offering Jeanne the means to cultivate her identity in her own terms, consumer culture may simply lead her to self-destruct.

More important is again Petzold's uncanny rendering of terrorism vis-à-vis consumer culture. What should be antithetical extremes end up overlapping to create dissonance. In reflecting on the kinds of effects he aims for, Petzold has emphasized the need to register the mysteriousness and complexity of ordinary spaces. Our task as spectators is not to take in "things we are asked to decode," like "one object means richness, another old age, yet another youth, etc." Instead we should "find youth *in* old age, or death *in* mourning."[25] *The State I Am In* gives such basic components more concrete historical but equally incongruent form in the overlapping realms of fascist history, liberating movements, and the dead zone of contemporary capitalism.

When Jeanne is thrown from the car in the film's final scene, the mise en scène circles back to the kind of wide-open space with which it began on that Portugal beach. Without the allusive layering evident elsewhere in the film, this landscape renders Jeanne's fate very difficult to determine. At the very least, her battered body in this scene, and the blood that trickles from her mouth after she has been struck, constitutes a concrete, physical presence as counterpoint to Petzold's fairytale mise en scène, historical ghosts, and lifeless commodities. One is reminded of Michael Rutschsky's proclamation in *Erfahrunghunger* (1980), his seminal New Subjectivity work: "The socialized individual dissolves in a swarm of threatening discourse, and that drives one to seek self-realization, self-determination beneath language, in perception in the body, if necessary in fear and pain."[26] If the first part of this sentence points to the damage done by ideological forces, one wonders if Petzold's perception-oriented filmic practice, its endpoint here in extreme bodily distress, could at all be related to the project of "self-realization," with or without feminist underpinnings. Read metaphorically, Jeanne's forceful ejection from the car could be understood as a rebirth in a landscape shorn of historical, ideological, and consumerist trappings. It counters her parents' more regressive trajectory: towards the end of the film they have begun to resemble her, their bank robbery disguises reprising her earlier Jehovah's Witness look. Petzold, however, refuses to provide any glimpses of Jeanne's emerging self from this point forward.

If we circle back to Johnston's essay, the possibility of self-realization may be beside the point if the larger aim is rupturing traditional filmic language in order to expose the disjuncture between ideology, sexist or otherwise, and the text of the film. Yet one wonders if Petzold's filmic practice ends up rupturing things to the point where nothing remains for a feminist film practice. I would argue that we should indeed keep the project of "self-realization" in mind, especially given how much *The State I Am In* resonates alongside New Subjectivity's search for selfhood in an alienating discursive surround. The challenge becomes understanding how bodily pain, as well as the pleasure that buttresses the classic false self of commodity culture, signifies not authenticity but instead calls attention to an affective register. This realm, in turn, potentially tells us something about a contemporary, neoliberal surround, which in Petzold's trilogy is navigated by women, all of whom put pain and injury on display. (*Ghosts* opens with a group of men chasing and beating one of its female protagonists; *Yella* begins and ends with its protagonist lying lifeless on a beach, her empty staring eyes looking eerily like Janet Leigh in the tub in *Psycho*).[27] Feminist and film theory, as well as the ramifications of bodily affect and/or semiotically transmitted messages, make it possible to situate *The State I Am In*'s ending in relation to feminist aims across a longer spectrum.

Lauren Berlant has argued that pain, hurt, and oppression constitute a form of identity politics through which oppressed groups become visible and make claims for recognition. Feminism, with its own narratives of suffering, has contributed to a dynamic whereby pain serves as the "true core of personhood and citizenship."[28] Berlant dissects and critiques this emotional realm, however, particularly how it construes identity in relation to nation. Pain, she argues, is not a self-evident entity that provides a reliable measure of justice and fairness. It can also provoke a variety of responses, not all of which pave the way for structural change. And even when pain does inspire what Berlant calls a "violent" sentimentality, this response may simply constitute a defense mechanism against one's culpability in the suffering of others. The larger problem becomes a nation "built across fields of social difference through channels of affective identification and empathy," a dynamic which belies the workings of power.[29]

What not only remains in place but also place gets buttressed by emotion is a larger, erroneous narrative that promises happiness and a good life in which there will be no pain. Equally problematic when increasingly dramatic scenarios of suffering compete against one another is how the everyday, ordinary, ongoing suffering of others is eclipsed. How things play out in this latter realm relates to the double bind that Abel underscores—specifically pleasure that belies an ever-tightening noose. Berlant argues that in order to have the good life, "contemporary capitalism makes a bargain with 'the personal,' ... which is that people can have dignity in its domains only insofar as they comply with the inevitability of insecurity in the capitalist world and take on as their own image of agency snatching what they can of assurance, insurance,

[and] amelioration."[30] In other words, the "good life" relies on unstable capitalist structures that no longer guarantee one's ability to flourish. Yet subjects are expected "to take whatever value is accorded to them and find a way of being within it; and to spin negative value into the gold of an always deferred future, meanwhile coping, if they can, in the everyday."[31]

The State I Am In exposes this dynamic in various ways, working within both concretely visual and less gaugeable affective realms. Jeanne's suffering is not dramatic in either a melodramatic or political sense; what we witness instead are everyday, perpetual frustrations that nonetheless prefigure not only the deferral but also the complete eradication of the "good life" in an empty field. By this I mean we witness a variety of dead ends that crop up on a regular basis in Jeanne's life, not only in lavatory stalls but also the changing rooms of clothing stores and in a mother who blocks her way through the woods after she returns from a tryst with Heinrich. Significantly, Petzold closes down on the problematic "sentimental" response which Berlant critiques—one that presumably leads to concrete change but in fact corresponds with specious promises of a future good life—by minimizing our ability to identify with Jeanne. Her often mute presence, her slumped shoulders and baggy jeans, her endless meandering within dully generic landscapes offer nothing in the way of pleasurable spectacle or a cohesive narrative trajectory. What could be simply a Brechtian means for promoting critical detachment, however, may in fact divert affective response to a more subtle realm of bodily sensation. In the process, we perceive as much as we witness the perversely thwarted nature of seemingly everyday lives.

In a less overtly spatial/metaphorical sense, the various dead ends that Jeanne encounters impede the affective feel of capitalism that Abel identifies in Petzold's films—that of fleetingness and weightlessness, of always being in motion but never arriving someplace that feels secure and homelike.[32] Prototypical scenes of cars in transit in all three of Petzold's Ghost Trilogy films serve to conjure a pleasurable trajectory that *The State I Am In* in particular, I would argue, emphatically blocks. (Elsewhere in the film, the entire family drives to a field where money has been buried, only to find old, worthless currency. When they visit a former RAF member now living in bourgeois comfort, he casts them out rather than offering financial support.) Abel's argument aligns with Deleuze's analysis of the sensations that spectators receive and act on, which exceed the parameters of a mimetically or semiotically coded filmic space and the accompanying process of ideological inscription. Instead, affective intensity provides what Deleuze refers to as a "line of flight," enabling spectators to transform and do things in excess of their cultural positioning. Elena del Rio has also argued that such affect makes it possible to "think of the unthought."[33]

A film such as *The State I Am In*, however, keeps ideological inscription perceptible enough to create a contrapuntal intensity. The kinds of ideological contradictions that normally play out within the narrative space shift in this manner to the realm of disparate bodily sensations. Del Rio has described an "unpredictable, disorganized, rhythmic alternation" between images "belonging to explainable narrative structures, and those that disorganize these structures with the force of affective performative events."[34] While *The State I Am In* stokes the sensation of swift transport to a better place, a secure "Heim," it also incorporates the perpetual thud of thwarted movement. What qualifies as the "unthought thought" is how fluctuating affective intensities in the realm of the everyday give the lie to the false promises of capitalism, its ever-deferred and chimerical good life. As much as we witness the evidence of false ideological imperatives, of perpetual dead ends in lavatory stalls, affect pulls us along towards buried money and bourgeois comfort.[35] Petzold shows us again and again anticipatory versions of the film's barren endpoint, but powerful sensations have the ability to overrule the film's overt messages. And as much as he avoids melodramatic excess, this dynamic is, to borrow a key word from the title of Berlant's most recent work, very cruel. It is perhaps all the more so when it leaves a child, someone not in a position to think through things and cultivate detachment, with literally nothing.[36]

Carrie Smith-Prei and Maria Stehle have situated Berlant's *Cruel Optimism* in relation to contemporary forms of feminism, specifically their "attachment" to "liberation from oppressions, freedom (of expression), choice of sexuality, or economic equality . . . which cruelly promise . . . clarity of meaning (goals, intent) and productivity (success, failure)."[37] In kicking the stool out from beneath a girl before any of these aims can crystalize, Petzold exposes how fallacious the entire project of self-realization remains within a larger, neoliberal framework. Equally important to keep in mind is Angela McRobbie's trenchant critique of neoliberalism's effects on feminist politics, which I referenced in the introduction to this volume. Taken together, Petzold's film and McRobbie's insights leave us in a very barren place indeed. In comparison, Fatih Akin's filmic practice offers utopian alternatives.

Bridges and Utopian Endings in *The Edge of Heaven*

Fatih Akin figures centrally in Sabine Hake and Barbara Mennel's *German Cinema in the New Millennium*, with the final section of their anthology devoted to his "representative role as auteur in a new global art cinema."[38] He quite emphatically embodies the fluid dynamic they delineate in their introduction, or a nonhyphenated German *and* Turkish selfhood that challenges "fixed categories of identity" and "the binary logic of native and foreign, home and abroad, and tradition and modernity."[39] In situating the history of Turkish German films in relation to the labor of the "Gastarbeiter" (guestworkers), they argue that German cinema has a long history of creative exchanges, as well as international and transnational relations. This circumstance makes film professionals "the quintessential guestworkers and the cinema ... the very model of cultural hybridity and cosmopolitanism."[40] Unlike the limited agency we would associate with temporary labor historically denied full participation in German society, the Turkish German filmmakers that Hake and Mennel's volume addresses should be viewed as "actors on a national and transnational state [who] intervene in, and respond to, local and global frames of reference."[41]

Given the complicated plot of *The Edge of Heaven*, a brief synopsis is warranted. The film depicts three parent-child relationships: the Turkish father Ali, who lives alone in Bremen and whose life centers around visits to prostitutes and the race track, and his son Nejat, a professor of German literature at the university; the Turkish mother Yeter, who works as a prostitute in Bremen and sometimes services Ali, and her daughter Ayten, who is a member of an antigovernment resistance group in Istanbul; and the German mother Susanne, whose earlier life suggests some student-movement idealism and whose faith in the European Union smacks of German superiority, and her daughter Lotte, a university student in Bremen. In a crisscrossing narrative where these characters nonetheless often just miss each other, Ali initiates the action by paying Yeter to be his live-in companion. After he strikes her in anger one day, she dies and he is sent to prison. Nejat, who had learned of Yeter's desire for her daughter to have an education, travels to Istanbul to find her. Yet Ayten has fled to Germany to escape arrest and to search for her mother. Here she meets and falls in love with Lotte, who in turn is moved by her idealism. When Ayten's petition for asylum is rejected and she is forced to return to Turkey, Lotte follows her. Here Lotte dies unexpectedly, shot by a gun she attempted to procure for Ayten's fellow antigovernment activists. Susanne, who had bitterly rejected Lotte's attempts to seek Ayten's release from a Turkish jail, then comes to Turkey to achieve this end. Here she meets Nejat, who has relocated to Istanbul to run a German bookstore. The film ends with his search for Ali, who was deported back to Turkey after his release from a German jail.

At first glance, *The Edge of Heaven* reanimates an early trope in German Turkish cinema, what Hake and Mennel describe as the "overdetermined figure of suffering and entrapped Turkish woman, a key witness in both feminist critiques of patriarchy and liberal arguments for secular democracy."[42] In a film where five protagonists traverse the borders between Germany and Turkey, the sixth one, the Turkish mother and sex worker Yeter, at most enjoys brief transit in the form of a Bremen streetcar ride. But even here fundamentalist Turkish men harass her to repent for her work as a prostitute, a circumstance that presumably does indeed warrant feminist critique and casts secular democracies as a more evolved alternative to religious strictures. *The Edge of Heaven* depicts Yeter primarily in confined spaces—not only streetcars, but also in her basement bordello room, and in the small apartment where she becomes a live-in sex worker—all obvious spatial markers of a circumscribed life.

When mobility falls away in a contemporary global context, however, female oppression and enlightened democracy as salve provide at best obligatory starting points. Additionally, Yeter's livelihood points to market forces only partially amenable to the individual choice and agency that both feminism and democratic structures prize. Though many interpretations of *The Edge of Heaven* emphasize how mobility in the film corresponds with global flows of culture, Yeter reminds us that capital remains part of this process as well.[43] It perhaps goes without saying that Yeter's body—as commodity and later corpse—provides a particularly invidious and gendered form of capital that exposes market forces' unchecked power. Deniz Göktürk's citation of Anna Tsing's work in her reading of *The Edge of Heaven* provides a useful reference point in this regard. Tsing emphasizes that people, wares, and data do not flow in an unencumbered and similar fashion; "friction" can result in the interactions between local and global interests, which in turn point to imbalances in economic resources and politically powerful interests.[44] Suffice it to say, a migrant sex worker as opposed to guestworker has the potential to muddle local perceptions of global labor flows, as well as to amplify the power differential in otherwise democratic exchanges of money for labor.

Strikingly, Akin emerged as a filmmaker with *Kurz und schmerzlos* (released in English as *Short Sharp Shock*; 1998) during the 1990s, a period during which the archetype of the suffering Turkish woman disappeared, ultimately giving way to a postmillennial shift towards genre cinema as the dominant mode for Turkish German films. In the process, "old dogmas of privileging politics over aesthetics, realism over fantasy, suffering over pleasure, and an aesthetics of estrangement over emotional engagement" disappeared as well.[45] Fassbinder's filmic homages to Sirkian melodrama, of course, contained their share of "old dogmas" that did indeed atomize suffering, often via estranging elements.[46] Akin clearly calls upon Fassbinder's self-conscious framing shots throughout *The Edge of Heaven*, which extend beyond evidence of Yeter's literal containment. (Wooden beams in two of the main characters' homes and a fenced-in garden provide the means elsewhere to contain and delineate the protagonists. As I will argue below, one of the male characters leads an existentially circumscribed life despite establishing shots of him traveling to Turkey and later the Black Sea.) Two sets of ethnically marked mothers and daughters also recall Sirk's *Imitation of Life*, with its example of tragically severed ties via both death and cruel estrangement.[47]

If melodrama mandates the suffering of women, and in this case reanimates a dated Turkish female trope, it also opens up the possibility of utopian and/or Hollywood endings. In the context of Turkish German film in a global context, such resolution might come in the form of cultural hybridity implicit in the German film industry's Turkish German "guestworker" variant, whose example redefines otherwise hampered lives. At the same time, Akin tempers the ebullient underpinnings of cosmopolitan cultural flows not only via the dramatic "friction" of a female corpse; in the spirit of Fassbinder, he also plays up the use value at the heart of all relationships, even the most deeply intimate and loving. Importantly, such complexity renders the film's utopian ending perhaps less melodramatic than attainable insofar as it acknowledges and works through the *Realpolitik* at the heart of human interactions.

Akin bookends *The Edge of Heaven* with two traveling sequences, which feature the Turkish son Nejat in search of his father, the German émigré Ali who is eventually expatriated back to Turkey for his act of manslaughter. Unlike the confinement that characterizes Yeter's and, to a lesser extent, the German mother Susanna's lives, Nejat and Ali put volitional and juridically mandated mobility on display. Varying types of mobility, in turn, point back to the presence or absence of hyphens in binational identities. Ali's fate suggests discrete and incompatible identities that predetermine perpetual shifts between two poles; Nejat's profession as university professor of German literature would seem to display mobility in the form of assimilation and professional achievement. Oddly, though, very few cross-cultural artifacts appear in his private sphere, which looks like a quintessential book-filled academic's abode. (A shot through a doorway emphasizes his double containment within walls of books in both rooms.) This omission stands out given the cultural hybridity that films such as Akin's earlier *In July* (2000) celebrate, which Anthony Kwame Appiah has called "nothing less than a love letter to the notion of a new unified Europe."[48] Similarly, Roger Hillman and Vivien Silvey have analyzed the "romance of cosmopolitanism" in Akin's *Soul Kitchen* (2009), with its transnational mix of citizens, food, and music.[49] In abandoning his profession and moving to Turkey, where he opens up a German bookstore in Istanbul, Nejat embodies less the ease of a transnational, cosmopolitan identity than the tug of origins mostly eclipsed in his German existence. Significantly, when he lectures on Goethe's cautionary stance towards revolution, Nejat cites his metaphor of a rose blooming prematurely, with potentially detrimental effects. He thus presents a fundamental voice within the German "Leitkultur" as an immobilizing force. (Nejat's stasis before the Black Sea could, in fact, partly reflect this legacy.) And despite his relocation to Istanbul, his German bookstore there feels like a protective enclosure as much as an attempt to stoke cross-cultural cosmopolitanism beyond his shop. In this sense and despite his literal return to Turkey, Nejat's transnational mobility is not entirely salutary.

In his own way, Ali has also assimilated, but to everyday forms of capitalist exchange and speculation. Ironically, I would argue that his duel identity implies a less hyphenated existence than Nejat's, even if his bare bones existence betrays nothing of the cosmopolitanism one would associate with a binational university professor. Rather, Ali embodies the "fluidity" of patriarchal oppression that inheres in evolving East/West identities. Early scenes show him visiting Yeter in her brothel, then taking her to the racetrack and offering her a wage to become his live-in companion. His offer no doubt provides an appealing alternative to continued harassment from Turkish fundamentalists. Yet when Ali strikes her for challenging his objectifying behavior, inadvertently causing her death, his violence amplifies their verbal assault on the streetcar. The film depicts Turkish SWAT teams in Istanbul tracking down female activists, including Yeter's daughter Ayten, as they pursue their revolutionary aims to ensure free education for all Turks. In demonstrating against the AK Party, its devout Muslims, and its anti-Kurdish nationalism, these women invoke, on the one hand, the secular, revolutionary legacy of Ataturk. Ironically, as much as their efforts align with Western values, in the context of the film they implicitly cast Goethe as one more oppressive male force who would preserve a status quo detrimental to women. And when Ayten later wanders by the words "Rebel Studies" spray-painted on the cafeteria wall of Nejat's Hamburg university, one gets the sense of revolution reduced to the conceptual paradigms of a disciplinary field and the spatial parameters of a lecture hall.[50]

Mobility among the female characters takes its own literal and, in relation to a larger literary and global context, sometimes overdetermined, sometimes startling, forms. Yeter does in fact cross the border back to Turkey, but only in death as her coffin rolls along a conveyor belt transporting cargo from a plane. Though perhaps preordained in multiple ways—by melodramatic conventions articulated in the "suffering Turkish woman" of Turkish German cinematic history, by sex work that already marks her as an exchange commodity, and by the shrinking confines of her life—this image nonetheless startles. Mobility here underscores the logic and mechanistic underpinnings of "just-in-time capitalism," and its brute effects on a female body feels completely out of whack with the buoyant transcultural fluidity cited above in other Akin films. Later, when the German daughter Lotte's corpse arrives in Germany in the same fashion, in a shot that merely reverses the movement of Yeter's coffin across the screen, transcultural frameworks start to feel superfluous. Death here extends beyond its conventional, ethnically marked archetype to claim a second woman of German origins, one who enjoys the mobility of an educated, English-speaking middle class. Clearly, some form of feminist framework is warranted, and not one that emphasizes performative agency as the salve for intolerable circumstances.

Akin's intertextual literary frame does, however, enable Lotte to rewrite the role her name clearly alludes to—young Werther's impossible love object. Played by an actress with blond curls and stark blue eyes, Lotte in Akin's film becomes intensely and romantically involved with Ayten, and rather than self-destruct she pursues her to Turkey, where Ayten has been incarcerated after an unsuccessful attempt to obtain asylum in Germany. Unlike the narcotic effects of Goethe elsewhere—in Nejat's "Leitkultur"-sanctioned immobility, in the fact that a newly arrived Ayten sleeps through his Goethe lecture—Lotte transforms her own Goethe legacy in an emphatically proactive manner. At the same time, her death at the hands of two young boys with a stolen gun feels as accidental as Yeter's from Ali's physical abuse, which mitigates our sense of misogyny as a fully volitional force, particularly in a world of mechanized, digitized flows. Equally important, as much as cosmopolitan hybridity constitutes a positive transcultural force, Akin also shows us its underside, what I referred to earlier as the waste that capitalism must continually remove in order to perpetuate itself, in distinctly gendered form. The question becomes what kind of feminist framework still insists on transnational forms of misogyny, despite the inevitable charges that this approach reprises dated, naïve beliefs in global sisterhood and ignores first-world women's complicity in larger forms of oppression. Is it still possible nonetheless to fire women up to fight the good fight when this particular project feels so hopelessly out of touch with contemporary forms of feminism?

At the very least, Akin offers the narrative means for working through female complacency in the face of another woman's suffering by highlighting the evolution of the German mother, Susanne. If Nejat as voice of Germany's historically reticent relationship to revolution and Ayten as would-be radical offer a seemingly clear-cut gender divide, Susanne muddies things by combining complacency with authoritarian behavior, buttressed by a sense of cultural superiority. Twice she observes to Ayten that Turkey's antidemocratic excesses will be corrected as soon as it joins the European Union. When Ayten proclaims "Fuck the European Union," Susanne responds with the authoritarianism at the heart of hierarchically-defined familial structures, forbidding Ayten to use bad language in her house. Elsewhere, Susanne's manipulations of her daughter Lotte echo the way Ali wields economic power over Yeter. As Lotte's political consciousness begins to form, inspired by Ayten's fight first to obtain asylum in Germany and subsequently to be released from prison in Turkey, Susanne maintains control by either procuring or withholding money for lawyer's fees. Despite her own dully domestic life of pitting cherries in her cool blue kitchen, Susanne hardly suffers the same circumscribed existence as either Yeter or Ayten.[51]

Gender is, of course, only one aspect of a privileged German identity that makes it difficult for Susanne to identify with oppression, patriarchal or otherwise. Even if references to her free-spirited youth, when she hitchhiked through Turkey on her way to India, align her with the generation of '68, she instead embodies this legacy's ossification. (Her last name "Staub" [dust] seems relevant here.) In reflecting on the positive changes that followed in the wake of '68, Kraushaar includes "a relative democratizing in most areas of society."[52] Given the extent to which the student movement achieved this measure of success, Susanne's complacency about the European Union fixing Turkey's antidemocratic problems may reflect more than cultural superiority. One senses as well the expectation that non-Western countries pursue the same post-Enlightenment trajectory as Europe. To uphold one model of success, of course, bodes badly in a film that so emphatically and sympathetically depicts difference. More pointed, though, in a narrative that ultimately highlights intense familial bonds, is simply Susanne's diminished empathy, both for Ayten's plight and her daughter Lotte's passionate attempt to help her.

Yet Susanne evolves over the course of the film, and in this regard Goethe's influence takes on added nuance. Mennel cites Helge Martens's observation that he "preferred an evolutionary world view following exact and consistent laws.... The evolutionary creation through water, in phases and rules."[53] She also invokes Andrew Piper's understanding of Goethe's late writing as being shaped by a "geo-logic" that articulated an evolving sense of space and time circa 1800, ushering in "a new relativity of the idea of 'location.'"[54] This development is analogous to the changes wrought by the digital era—specifically how "transnational mobility, digital media, and the increased speed of transportation and information technology have changed narrative conventions, perception of time and space, and the structure of intimacy and familial relations."[55] In *The Edge of Heaven,* this contemporary force reveals itself in a narrative structure in which doublings, pairings, and crossings, Mennel argues, echo digital media's simultaneity of movement, nonlinear, and multidirectional aspects. Yet the old-fashioned "bibliophilia" that she also identifies in the film—Nejat's museum-like German bookstore, the novel he gives to Ali, and Lotte's diary—conjures temporality determined by words unfolding linearly across a page and the process of reflection they initiate. Historically, Mennel writes, this realm aligns with "national high culture based on a canon, traditional left-wing politics defined by a distinct philosophical-political system, regional attachments, an understanding of space and time rooted in prescientific knowledge and lack of surveillance technologies, and foundational religious and mythical beliefs that underwrite humanist values and enable human encounters."[56] If we think back to Goethe's preference for evolution over revolution, the former could also be understood metaphorically as a form of enlightened transformation—what the speed, spontaneity, and unmediated nature of digital culture presumably hinders. While bibliophile elements point backwards to a larger humanist tradition, they also, I would argue, suggest a corrective to revolutionary fervor in general, as well as to one key aspect of the German student movement that targeted family structures.

Unreflective zeal constitutes one general aspect of what Kraushaar describes as the "maximalist" elements among student activists—that is, those who rejected reform that required working within a parliamentary system.[57] Susanne's observation to Ayten—"Maybe you're just somebody who likes to fight"—casts her in a similar light, while diminishing the particularities of her political beliefs. If not defined in biological terms, evolution could be understood as adaptive skills that close the gap between complacent parents and recalcitrant children. Difference and division, of course, comprise an important piece of family structures insofar as children need to separate themselves from and rebel against parents in order to ensure an individuated, autonomous selfhood. Strikingly, every parent-child pairing in *The Edge of Heaven* plays up myriad forms of seemingly irreparable differences: a politically active Ayten who refuses to wear a shirt with an American logo and Yeter as prostitute, a bald-faced representative of the capitalistic structures that Ayten abhors; Ali as brothel and race-track customer and Nejat as representative of lofty, canonical ideals; and Susanne's bitter impassivity versus Lotte's impassioned plight to help Ayten. What complicates the process of children separating from parental authority is the manner in which, as Kraushaar has observed, bourgeois structures serve as the "Kernzelle" (core) of the state and the parliament, banks, and industrial and corporate entities that represent it.[58] Not only do these larger institutions reproduce the hierarchies that originate in families, they also magnify them by concentrating power in the hands of a privileged few, those with the correct gender, race, and socioeconomic status. Thus as much as one successfully separates from the family as original "Kernzelle," its shape on a larger macrolevel reproduces and amplifies power structures no longer cast off by a process of individuation.

Rather than critiquing the family as core of an oppressive state, Akin takes a different tack that corrects the excesses of '68, while preserving its utopian aspects in the way he imagines altered familial structures buoyed by forgiveness and solidarity. Both the book that Nejat gives Ali and Lotte's diary, for instance, make it possible to heal deep, familial rifts, even if the rift between Susanne and Lotte only dissolves in the wake of the latter's death. We watch Ali's deeply moved facial expression in a shot late in the film after he has finally read Nejat's book, Selim Özdogan's *The Daughter of the Blacksmith*. The story of a young female Turk's migration, it is characterized, as Mennel observes, by limited agency within historical forces, which certainly resonates for Ali given his deportation from Germany. (Ironically, the male/female fluidity evident in Ali's empathetic response shifts our understanding of him as simply embodying cross-cultural misogyny. In this moment, the cinematic trope of the long-suffering Turkish woman resonates for his identity as well.) After reading Lotte's diary, with its observations about how similar she and her mother are, Susanne goes on to form a deep, if ersatz mother-daughter bond with Ayten. Most important, they have evolved in a manner that challenges the revolutionary imperative to overthrow traditional hierarchies of authoritarian parents and obedient children; unlike the '68ers' unstinting rejection of a parental legacy tainted by fascism, Susanne and Ayten seem capable of forgiveness. When they step into an Istanbul street together at the end of the film, one senses not only acceptance despite difference but also uncompromising solidarity across it. Unlike Nejat's passive stance before the Black Sea, this staging suggests their readiness to usher change into the world beyond his dusty bookstore. If Nejat's caution and passivity throughout have to do with Ali raising him "like a girl," as Ali observes, it is ironically the women who become the agents of an again-altered and attainable revolutionary legacy.

The Edge of Heaven also provides one particularly powerful antidote to the force of paternalistic power as the locus of authoritarianism. Towards the end of the film, Nejat and Susanne observe men in Istanbul walking to the mosque to celebrate Kurban Bayram, the Festival of Sacrifice that celebrates Abraham's willingness to sacrifice his son to appease Allah. In discussing its significance, they discover cross-cultural commonality given the same story's presence in the Bible. While clearly a "Nathan der Weise" moment that underscores a longer humanist tradition of enlightened tolerance, this moment also speaks to Germany's negative perceptions of Turkey as a source of extreme religious fundamentalism, rather than of religious roots not radically different from the Judeo-Christian tradition. More telling, though, is this story's effect on estranged parents and children. In sharing the story, Nejat also recalls his father's response to it, that he would rather make God his enemy than sacrifice his own child. Hierarchical structures that demand unquestioning obedience take a backseat here to the parent-child bond.[59] Fierce solidarity trumps profound difference, which may be the real explanation for Nejat's seemingly passive position on the beach as he waits for a father he had considered dead to him. And if the family is indeed the foundation of larger societal structures, such solidarity sets the terms for larger utopian changes both within Germany, where Turks have been part of the social fabric for generations, and in debates around Turkey's possible admission to the European Union, despite its religious, cultural, and political differences. As much as the family as metaphorical rubric can manifest difference at its core, it also necessitates accepting difference in the name of retaining a life-sustaining bond. A utopian alternative to the European Union in its present form would be a structure built across difference rather than invested in upholding its own version of enlightened democracy.

It should be emphasized, however, how much Fassbinder's influence manifests itself in the film and thus offsets all the more the utopian aspects of *The Edge of Heaven*. Hanna Schygulla's presence in the film as Susanne provides an obvious nod to him, since she was the face of Fassbinder during the 1970s. As much as she plays "typisch Deutsch" in Akin's film, pitting cherries for a "Kuchen" as she argues with Ayten in her kitchen, she also signifies a cinema that dissected and critiqued precisely what it means to be German. And of course the name Ali evokes one of Fassbinder's most famous films, *Ali, Fear Eats the Soul*. This film includes what I would call a Fassbinder "Grundgesetz" or basic law, specifically the manner in which use value defines all relationships, including familial and sexual ones. Several times in the film we see an exchange of money: in the opening scene in a bar, in the very next scene between the female lead Emmi and a neighbor, and most strikingly, in the income she takes from Ali so that they can buy "a piece of heaven." (Initially, she refused to take his first paycheck because, as she put it, "money spoils all relationships.") Like Fassbinder, Akin plays up the economic conditions from which the only escape remains "on the other side" in that final image of an open horizon.

The first and last scene of *The Edge of Heaven* focus on the exchange of money in a Turkish gas station as Nejat travels to the Black Sea to find Ali. Here Nejat appears more interested in making a few random purchases than registering the story the clerk tells him about the singer on the radio, who died of cancer probably caused by Chernobyl. The capitalistic system of exchange subsequently seeps into all of the film's familial and sexual relationships. Ali purchases Yeter for 3,000 euros a month and assumes that Nejat will want her for sex as well. The price of things is constantly discussed, and not only in Ali's first encounter with Yeter in her bordello. Benign examples follow as well when Nejat discusses renting a room in his apartment in Istanbul first to Lotte, then later to Susanne. As soon as Ayten arrives in Germany, she borrows 100 euros from the underground Turks who help her escape, only to find they expect her to be beholden to them. In her first encounter with Lotte, Ayten asks her for money; later Ayten uses her to obtain a weapon and inadvertently sets up the circumstances that contribute to Lotte's murder. Lotte herself uses Susanne for basic housekeeping and later lawyers' fees. Likewise, Nejat's museum-like bookstore, as an oasis from and antidote to the brothel and racetrack, displays many credit card stickers on its door, which one shot captures in medium close-up. In economic terms, there really seems to be no outside space. Just as the film's intertitles announce a particular segment's outcome—most notably those titled "Yeter's Death" and "Lotte's Death"—these economic exchanges resonate along equally inevitable lines. But unlike the neoliberal economic structures that stifle self-realization in *The State I Am In*, identities bound by the basest of societal forces in Akin's film nonetheless have a chance to thrive precisely through their interconnectedness.

This possibility plays out in ways that also speak to more individualistic approaches to feminism, particularly where they close down empathy for oppression beyond personal circumstances. And here I mean the narrow purview of the New German Girls and Alpha Girls who emerged in 2008 and explicitly distanced themselves from the need to address global forms of misogyny. With this backdrop in mind, the film's portrayal of Yeter and Ayten requires additional attention given marked differences between them and the German women. Missed connections pepper the film, and the staging in Yeter's and Ayten's near spatial convergence as they pass each other—Yeter on a streetcar with Nejat, and Ayten in a car that Lotte drives—shows how conditional their mobility remains. Yeter's position behind glass further exemplifies her containment elsewhere in the film, whereas Ayten as passenger underscores that larger forces determine her mobility, notably both the German and Turkish governments. (Interestingly, mother and daughter also mirror each other in framed window shots—Yeter in her bordello and Ayten at a Turkish prison window. And just as the fundamentalists oblige Yeter to repent, Turkish prison authorities grant Ayten her freedom only after she denounces her political activism and cohorts.)

As much as I have underscored menacing Turkish forces around them in Germany—the fundamentalists and manipulative underground radicals—it is equally important to understand a mother's and daughter's plight in relation to Western strictures as well. For Yeter, a global economy articulates itself in the various tricks she performs for customers, or as she tells Ali, "I can do Italian, Greek, and French." As soon as Ayten arrives in Germany, the film captures her sitting on the floor beside a money machine in the university cafeteria. Her rescue comes in the relationship she strikes up with Lotte, who provides her with food and clothing and a room at her mother's house. Ironically, this scenario could be understood as a kinder version of Ali taking Yeter into his own home for sex and companionship, since Lotte and Ayten also develop a sexual relationship.

On the one hand, Ayten and Yeter's struggle to survive in Germany offsets Susanne's and Lotte's economic stability and the ease with which they each traverse national boundaries between India and Germany (Susanne as a '68er) and between Turkey and Germany when each of them takes up residence in Istanbul. More important, however, is that Turkish fundamentalism and/or antidemocratic excesses transplanted onto German soil—that is, seemingly "exotic" problems with which German women potentially cannot identify—exist alongside the barebones dynamic of capitalist exchange. Akin's depiction of Yeter as prostitute and Ayten on the floor beside the money machine plays up global inequities from which Germany is not exempt—the inhumane mechanisms of capitalism beneath its more appealing, neoliberal façade of individual choice. The ease with which a money machine disgorges cash both resembles and belies the coffin on the cargo conveyor belt.

To return to Berlant's rubric, the access to money and education that enables Susanne's and Lotte's mobility perpetuates not only optimism about correcting non-Western injustices; it also makes them blind to the everyday forms of suffering stoked as much by their own social-economic system as culturally transplanted misogyny. "Interconnectedness" in this regard thus has less to do with a dated belief in the political efficacy of a global sisterhood. Instead it manifests itself in the circumstances of Turkish women within a Western context who reveal global capitalism's malignant reach both within and beyond a German Heimat. What remains abstract to Nejat—specifically the metaphor implicit within Chernobyl-related cancer that extends to his family's ancestral home—becomes far more concrete in non-Western female lives in Germany on the verge of calamity. In this sense, Yeter and Ayten are not other and thus superfluous to an individualistic meritocracy but instead make its structures "other" to those who benefit from them via education, professional opportunities, and the pleasures of commodity culture. As Yvonne Tasker and Diane Negra have pointed out, in a postfeminist world too often women assume that such opportunities and values "are somehow universally shared and . . . universally accessible."[60]

At the same time, Akin's utopian politics take a distinctly feminist form if one considers how women seem capable of a kinder, gentler form of exchange that tempers global capitalism's automated, impersonal feel in the film. As I mentioned above, Susanne exchanges her departed daughter for an ersatz mother-daughter bond with Ayten. Their deep connection pointedly counters the many moments when we hear Turks in the film address each other as "uncle" or "sister," which feels less like a form of solidarity than an omnipresent hierarchy that moves back and forth between Turkey and Germany. And though we can hope that Nejat and Ali are in the process, by the end of the film, of repenting for misguided, obstinate behavior, what lingers in memory is Ayten's tear-stained face behind the prison window separation as she implores Susanne, "Forgive me." Here the women strip away the authoritarian underpinnings of religious calls to repent, thereby altering the signifying capacities of a second key force in the film. Even more important, their solidarity extends across seemingly unbridgeable cultural divides. *The Edge of Heaven* ultimately positions women, bolstered by humanist and revolutionary ideals as well as psychic mother-daughter bonds that extend beyond a German frame, as the contemporary agents of '68. Not only are they willing and able to fight the good fight in a landscape more global than that of some contemporary feminists, they also point

Figure 5.3. Still: *The Edge of Heaven* (2007)

Figure 5.4. Still: *The Edge of Heaven* (2007)

the way forward in a contemporary social arena either unable or uninterested in truly addressing and accepting difference.

Conclusion

If we return to the topic of a counter-cinema that speaks to women's circumstances, Petzold's and Akin's films resonate in antithetical ways that nonetheless align with this project. To cite Hake and Mennel's guestworker rubric again, both Petzold and Akin function as "actors on a national and transnational stage" who respond to local and global frames of reference.[61] In terms of local frames, connections to recent forms of German feminism are not hard to make. As much as their films underscore some of its blind spots, Akin proffers the ever more utopian dream of solidarity, especially if one considers the third wave's long-standing (and now popfeminism's) investment in individualist approaches. To break things down into basic categories, Petzold expands the conceptual possibilities of the adjective "counter" beyond narrative depictions of ideological contradictions by conjuring the affective allure but egregiously false promises of neoliberal capitalism. Akin, by contrast, reveals his metaphorical predilection for building bridges, which reverberates all the more in relation to impasses in feminism stoked by generational divides.

Tasker and Negra have argued that postfeminism serves as a rationale for "the brutalities of the emergent 'New Economies,'" with women assimilating to and defining themselves via individualistic choice in cultural, consumerist and economic terms.[62] Strikingly, Petzold targets a girl as the object of such "brutalities," someone who should embody but instead counters postfeminism's emphasis on youthful vitality and the possibility of transformation. By depicting consumerist fantasies' eerie overlap with fairytales, fascism, and failed utopian projects, Petzold continually ruptures the affective rush, itself analogous to the girlish buoyancy underpinning postfeminist assumptions, associated with self-realization within a capitalist meritocracy. Jeanne herself could be understood as the proverbial ghost in the machine—that is, the human fall-out within lifestyle branding that does not "conform to its preferred images" or people who are "too poor to exercise 'control' over their lives through the 'liberation' of consumerism."[63] When the Alpha and New German Girls who emerged in Germany in 2008 conflate "control" with improving individual circumstances via consumer choices and their new, improved signifying capacities, they also embody an optimism at odds with Petzold's ghosts. By this I mean how his liminal spaces extend into everyday worlds, where a Beach Boys poster resonates alongside failed utopian projects, where a luxury villa in the woods points to a fascist past and imperiled fairytale children. With such manifold historical resonances, the future-oriented project of attaching new signifieds to old signifiers begins to take on the chimerical qualities of global capitalism's deferred "good life."

In more overtly hewing to the characteristics of melodrama, Akin activates an artistic license that sanctions precisely this unlikely, unrealistic endpoint. His approach is doubly dated in that he attaches old signifiers, those aligned with melodramatic convention, with old signifieds, or a fifty-year-old utopian project that in a contemporary context has become shorthand for historical naivety. Yet it is precisely this narrative realm that makes it possible, at the very least, to imagine a less discordant future among feminists. As I argued at the end of chapter 1 about the effects of Douglas Sirk's *Imitation of Life* on two deeply divided protagonists, their story suggests that individuality and shifting power relations can coexist with deep bonds and solidarity. And unlike the specious ends that Petzold attaches to exuberant forms of affect, this force could inspire a return to the project that Astrid Henry imagines in her essay "Solitary Sisterhood"—that is, cultivating philosophical and ideological connections among women of varying backgrounds in the pursuit of equality. While Petzold depicts a young girl as a deeply interior and perpetually impeded stand-alone protagonist, Akin makes mother-daughter relations central to his story, offset all the more by a more stymied father-son dynamic. Unlike the ease with which transcultural forms such as music and food build bridges in some of his other films, this configuration, particularly when it also incorporates different nationalities, sets up roadblocks from the start, which the film plays out in varying permutations. Alongside predictable obstinacy on both sides of the mother-daughter dyad, Akin models motherhood, as Oana M. Chivoiu argues, as "a narrative of origins and becoming, with echoes in the past and promises for the future."[64] The latter half of the equation becomes evident in examples of motherhood as a territory of "multiple possibilities," including "transformation, multiplicity, and reinvention."[65] To embody a selfhood that evolves in order to retain and affirm a porous, life-sustaining bond across difference is to model a path forward for rebellious daughters. It both builds a bridge between separate but interconnected entities and opens a door to future alliances that potentially take feminism to a new place.

Notes

1. Claire Johnston, "Women's Cinema as Counter-Cinema," in *Feminist Film Theory: A Reader*, ed. Sue Thornham (New York: New York University Press, 1999), 24. She cites Erwin Panofsky's notion that stereotypes originated in early cinema when audiences had trouble deciphering what appeared on screen, and fixed iconography made it possible to create a cohesive narrative.
2. Ibid., 25.
3. Ibid., 28.
4. Ibid., 29.
5. Johnston uses examples from Dorothy Arzner and Ida Lupino films in which female protagonists are fragmented by wanting to please as well as to find the means for self-expression. In describing the fate of the female protagonist in Arzner's film *Dance, Girl, Dance*, Johnston argues, "Towards the end of the film Arzner brings about her tour de force, cracking open the entire fabric of the film and exposing the workings of ideology in the construction of the stereotype woman" (ibid.). When the main character turns on her audience and tells them how she sees them, Johnston argues that what is "assumed as a one-way process [becomes] a direct assault on the audience within the film and the audience of the film, and that has the effect of directly challenging the entire notion of woman as spectacle" (ibid., 30).

6. *The State I Am In,* directed by Christian Petzold (Schramm Film, 2000). DVD (MC One, 2000). *The Edge of Heaven,* directed by Fatih Akin (Anka Film, 2007). DVD (Strand Leasing, 2008).
7. Rainer Werner Fassbinder, "Imitation of Life: On the Films of Douglas Sirk," in *The Anarchy of the Imagination: Interviews, Essays, Notes. Rainer Werner Fassbinder,* ed. Michael Töteberg and Leo A. Lensing, trans. Krishna Winston (Baltimore: The Johns Hopkins University Press, 1992), 89.
8. Marco Abel points out that a scene in Petzold's *Ghosts,* during which the two female leads do a slow, erotic dance with each other, is also lit with pervasive red coloring. See "Imaging Germany: The (Political) Cinema of Christian Petzold," in *The Collapse of the Conventional: German Film and Its Politics at the Turn of the Twenty-First Century,* ed. Jaimey Fisher and Brad Prager (Detroit: Wayne State University Press, 2010), 23.
9. Fassbinder, "Imitation of Life," 81.
10. Thomas Douherty, "Douglas Sirk: Magnificent Obsession," *Chronicle of Higher Education* 49.12 (15 November 2002), B16.
11. Marco Abel, "Imaging Germany," 261.
12. Quoted in Marco Abel, *The Counter-Cinema of the Berlin School* (Rochester: Camden House, 2013), 92.
13. Abel, "Imaging Germany," 264.
14. Jaimey Fisher, "Globalization as Uneven Geographical Development: The 'Creative' Destruction of Place and Fantasy in Christian Petzold's Ghost Trilogy," *Seminar: A Journal of Germanic Studies* 47.4 (November 2011), 449.
15. Abel, "Imaging Germany," 269.
16. Wolfgang Kraushaar, *1968 als Mythos, Chiffre und Zäsur* (Hamburg: Hamburger Edition, 2000), 311.
17. Quoted in Ali Jaafar, "Flags and our Fathers." *Sight and Sound* 18.3 (March 2008), 9.
18. Although his voice-over guides the fantasies that pass through Jeanne's head, the net effect, as Stephanie Hofer argues, is to sanction this interior world: "In this case the discrepancy between Jeanne's imagination and Heinrich's story establishes an independence in relation to the male narrative voice, or rather power, and grants Jeanne her own dream world." See "'... von der Unmöglichkeit der Gegenwart': Geschlecht, Generation und Nation in Sanders-Brahms' *Deutschland, bleiche Mutter* und Petzolds *Die innere Sicherheit,*" *German Life and Letters* 62.2 (April 2009), 180.
19. As R. G. Renner observes, "The political and social controls that the adults once fought against repeat themselves in the repressive structures that they themselves set up for their child." See "1989 und die Folgen. Deutsche Gegenwartsgeschichte im Nachwendefilm," *Pandaemonium germanicum: Revista de Estudos Germanísticos* 16 (2010), 48.
20. Numerous scholars have pointed out how this scene reprises a similar one in *Marianne und Juliane* (*Die bleierne Zeit*; 1981) when the two protagonists

watch the same film. They also underscore how the teacher embodies a left-wing critique of his young charges because they seem to lack a political consciousness, as well as the ability to be horrified by what they see, unlike the female protagonists in Margarete von Trotta's film. Ilka Rasch, for instance, observes, "With this, Petzold suggests that the Holocaust no longer plays a crucial role in the politicization of Germany's youth or their sense of national identity. Furthermore, the teacher's aggressive verbal attack on the students, which inhibits any fruitful discussion, indicates that the 1968ers are unable to relate to the next generation, to serve as role models and help them analyze the impact of the German past rationally, or to inspire them politically." See "The Generation Gap: The Reappropriation of the Red Army Faction in Contemporary German Film," in *Generational Shifts in Contemporary German Culture*, ed. Laurel Cohen-Pfister and Susanne Vees-Gulani (Rochester, NY: Camden House, 2010), 189.

21. Stefanie Hofer quotes Petzold's description of the family as a "Familienzelle" (family cell) which likely emphasizes the prison-like nature of their coexistence (40). Eric Scheufler also cites Petzold's uses of the word "cell," although he emphasizes its biological implications: "On the one hand, the family can be interpreted as a biological cell, as an organic, self-contained whole. As such the biological cell must guard against the threatening intrusion of foreign elements, but also must be allowed to split and grow in order for life to continue." See "The Ghosts of Autumn Past: History, Memory, and Identity in Christian Petzold's *Die innere Sicherheit*," *Seminar: A Journal of Germanic Studies* 47.1 (February 2011), 108. Similarly, Petzold has described the ending, when Jeanne's parents die in a car accident as she's thrown from the vehicle, as both a birth and a moment when healthy antibodies destroy a foreign body (quoted in Joanne Leal, "Troubled Parents, Angry Children: The Difficult Legacy of 1968 in Contemporary German-Language Film," in *Cinema and Social Change in Germany and Austria*, ed. Gabriele Mueller and James M. Skidmore [Waterloo, ON: Wilfrid Laurier University Press, 2012], 121). As Jens Hinrichsen argues, in this moment "Jeanne is no longer a ghost." See "Im Zwischenreich. Christian Petzolds Gespenster-Trilogie: Passagen in Schattenzonen deutscher Realität," *Film-Dienst* 60.19 (13 September 2007), 8.

22. R. G. Renner has noted the parents' controlling behavior as well, "that leave[s] Jeanne no room for her own development" ("1989 und die Folgen," 47).

23. Here I am echoing Marco Abel's description of Petzold's process: "In Petzold's films it is the staring quality of the camera work that achieves such double-becoming, where simultaneously subject and object become Other to themselves, so that the object stared at becomes available in its immanent becomings, differentiations, or change, just as the subject is affected by these very becomings with regard to his or her perceptual awareness" ("Imaging Germany," 268).

24. Eric Scheufler notes the presence of Brian Wilson in the narrative and argues that he represents a different form of historical consciousness for Heinrich and his generation: "In Heinrich's socialization, the years stretching from Benno Ohnesorg's death to Sartre's visit to Andreas Baader in Stammheim have been replaced with American surfing and the search for the perfect wave. The German Autumn has given way to the "Endless summer" and thereby eliminated in one of the film's primary representatives of the youngest generation the memory of the '68 generation's political influence in favor of sun and escapism" ("The Ghosts of Autumn Past," 111).
25. Quoted in Abel, "Imaging Germany," 268–69.
26. Michael Rutschky, *Erfahrungshunger. Ein Essay über die siebziger Jahre* (Frankfurt a. M.: Fischer, 1982), 225.
27. I am indebted to Francesca Balboni for making this connection.
28. Lauren Berlant, *Cruel Optimism* (Durham: Duke University Press, 2011), 34.
29. Ibid.
30. Ibid., 44.
31. Ibid.
32. See Abel, *The Counter-Cinema of the Berlin School,* 89: "Petzold's cinematic gesture is not a dialectical one: instead of opposing representational (narrative) realism, he intensifies it to such a degree that his images directly affect the realm of the sensible. This cinematic intensification of (narrative) realism impinges directly on our nervous system without having to go through the detour of representation."
33. Elena Del Rio, *Deleuze and the Cinema of Performance: Powers of Affection* (Edinburgh: Edinburgh University Press, 2008), 7.
34. Ibid., 15.
35. Abel argues along similar lines: "For what this *promise* ultimately expresses is [Petzold's] films' *premise* that individual (and collective) happiness can be achieved only if subjects are able to create a place of their own. However, this ability, as Petzold's films repeatedly dramatize, is increasingly thwarted by the sociopolitical conditions to which the economic imperatives of finance capitalism subject contemporary life" (*The Counter-Cinema of the Berlin School*, 69–70). Jaimey Fisher also identifies thwarted states in Petzold's films: "In each film, ascension to the spatial dreams of late capitalism fragments the tenuous alliance formed to foster that ascension. The characters all do enter the wealthy houses of their dreams and fantasies, but their hopes are never fulfilled, and they are invariably led out to drift again" ("Globalization as Uneven Geographical Development," 461).
36. My overall argument about Petzold's film shares strong resonances with Berlant's close reading of two films by the Belgium siblings and filmmakers Jean-Pierre and Luce Dardenne: *La Promesse* (1996) and *Rosetta* (1999). In chapter 5 of *Cruel Optimism*—titled "Nearly Utopian, Nearly Normal: Post-Fordist Affect in *La Promesse* and *Rosetta*"—she traces how "the pro-

ductive instabilities of the contemporary capitalist economy engender new affective practices, in which children scavenge toward a sense of authentic belonging by breaking from their parents' way of attaining the good life" (166). The child protagonists of each film, Igor and Rossetta, live in a world of "so many bad jobs contingently available to so many contingent workers and never enough money, never enough love, and barely any rest, yet with ruthless fantasy abounding" (167). Fantasy refers to the "good life's normative/utopian zone," despite circumstances that trap these children in lives that consist of "struggling, drowning, holding onto the ledge, treading water" (169).

37. Smith-Prei and Stehle, "The Awkward Politics of Popfeminist Literary Events: Helene Hegemann, Charlotte Roche, and Lady Bitch Ray," in *Women's Writing in the 21st Century,* ed. Hester Baer and Alexandra Merley Hill (Camden House, 2015), 135.
38. Sabine Hake and Barbara Mennel, eds., *Turkish German Cinema in the New Millennium: Sites, Sounds, Screens* (New York: Berghahn Books, 2012), 13.
39. Ibid., 1.
40. Ibid., 2.
41. Ibid., 4.
42. Ibid., 5.
43. For instance, see Mah El Hissy's "Transnationaler Grenzverkehr in Fatih Akins *Gegen die Wand* und *Auf der anderen Seite,*" in *Von der nationalen zur internationalen Literatur: Transkulturelle deutschsprachige Literatur und Kultur im Zeitalter globaler Migration,* ed. Helmut Schmitz (Amsterdam: Rodopi: 2009). Citing Akin's documentary film *Crossing the Bridge: The Sound of Istanbul* (2006), in which music serves as a binding element between East and West and the possibility of repeated crossings, she states more generally, "In toto one could say about Akin's films that they allow no room for the discussion about rational spaces and ethnic dividing lines. Instead the protagonists appear in his films as border crossers and are characterized by their mobility in a global world. In the course of their development they upset cultural assumptions and categories" (171). In *The Edge of Heaven* she senses an intensification of this process insofar as "boundaries are dissolved and a melting occurs between the presumably separate worlds in Germany and Turkey" (171).
44. Deniz Göktürk, "Mobilitat und Stillstand im Weltkino Digital," in *Kultur als Ereignis. Fatih Akins Film* Auf der anderen Seite *als transkulturelle Narration,* ed. Özkan Ezli (Bielefeld: transcript Verlag, 2010), 17.
45. Hake and Mennel, *Turkish German Cinema in the New Millennium,* 7.
46. Stefan Volk also sees evidence of multiple genres in the film: "*Auf der anderen Seite* doesn't fit into any drawer; it oscillates between romance, road movie, political and psycho drama, and a cultural study." See "Von der Form

zum Material. Fatih Akin's Spiel mit dem Genrekino in *Gegen die Wand* und *Auf der anderen Seite,*" in Ezli, *Kultur als Ereignis,* 154.

47. Deniz Göktürk cites the late seventeenth-century roots of melodrama in Italian opera and in French theater a century later. She underscores how it corresponded with a post-revolutionary class consciousness, "where expressive excess served as a means to unsettle hierarchies." See "Sound Bridges: Transnational Mobility as Ironic Melodrama," in *European Cinema in Motion: Migrant and Diasporic Film in Contemporary Europe,* ed. Daniela Berghahn and Claudia Sternberg (New York: Palgrave Macmillan, 2010), 216. Racial and ethnic tensions, of course, provide a logical corollary in the twentieth century.
48. Quoted in Mine Eren, "Cosmopolitan Filmmaking: Fatih Akin's *In July* and *Head-On,*" in Hake and Mennel, *Turkish German Cinema in the New Millennium,* 181.
49. See Roger Hillman and Vivian Silvey, "Remixing Hamburg: Transnationalism in Fatih Akin's *Soul Kitchen, In July* and *Head-On,*" in Hake and Mennel, *Turkish German Cinema in the New Millennium,* 187. Deniz Göktürk's various essays on Akin's films, particularly *The Edge of Heaven, In July, Head On,* and his documentary *Crossing the Bridge: The Sound of Istanbul,* have exhaustively mined Akin's cross-cultural reference points, which extend beyond Germany and Turkey to world cinema as well. In filmic terms, she argues, *The Edge of Heaven* provides a meta-reflection on national cinema in the digital age, "where localization and delocalization, place-bound specificity and universal comprehensibility overlap in varying configurations" ("World Cinema Goes Digital: Looking at Europe from the Other Shore," in Hake and Mennel, *Turkish German Cinema in the New Millennium,* 210).
50. In a similar vein, opening shots of Labor Day activity in Germany capture what looks like a marching band parade, a tame alternative to the violent confrontations we soon witness between political activists and SWAT teams in Istanbul.
51. One is reminded here of the transgendered qualities of Maria Braun—i.e., her business smarts and fetishized feminine appearance—given that Hanna Schygulla played both her and the character of Susanne.
52. Kraushaar, *1968 als Mythos, Chiffre und Zäsur,* 320.
53. Barbara Mennel, "Criss-Crossing in Global Space and Time: Fatih Akin's *The Edge of Heaven* (2007)," *Transit* 5.1 (2009), 15.
54. Ibid., 16.
55. Ibid., 3.
56. Ibid.
57. Wolfgang Kraushaar, *Achtundsechzig. Eine Bilanz* (Berlin: Ullstein Buchverlage, 2008), 62–64.
58. Ibid., 64.

59. Oana M. Chivoiu also understands the bond between Susanne and Nejat in parental terms and reads his final position before the sea in terms of traditional metaphors that associate women with fluidity. Just as she provides an ersatz maternal figure for his long-dead mother, Nejat, in traveling to Turkey to find Ayten and support her education, attempts to perform the role with which Yeter had defined her own maternal position. See "Childless Motherhood: The Geopolitics of Maternal Bliss in Fatih Akin's *The Edge of Heaven*," in *Disjointed Perspectives on Motherhood*, ed. Catalina Florina Florescu (New York: Lexington Books, 2013), 98, 100–1.
60. Yvonne Tasker and Diane Negra, *Interrogating Postfeminism: Gender and the Politics of Popular Culture* (Durham: Duke University Press, 2007), 2.
61. Hake and Mennel, *Turkish German Cinema in the New Millennium*, 4.
62. Tasker and Negra, *Interrogating Postfeminism*, 13.
63. Imelda Whelehan, quoted in Tasker and Negra, *Interrogating Postfeminism*, 7.
64. Oana M. Chiviou, "Childless Motherhood: The Geopolitics of Maternal Bliss," 92.
65. Ibid., 93.

CHAPTER SIX

Mutable Mädchen
On Screen and in the Streets

I began chapter 1 of this volume with attention to the FrauenMediaTurm as a metaphorical touchstone for feminist aims across an expanded historical frame, from the medieval "Beguine" movement to generational antagonisms in the 2000s. In doing so I emphasized its visual and patriarchal clout in past centuries, as well as its status as a reclaimed "master's house" given the battles to acquire and maintain Germany's largest gender studies archive. Equally important are its ties to Karneval—the "Kölle Alaaf" cry that originated in power struggles over the tower and now the repetitive refrain from the masses during yearly festivities. It is here that cultural underdogs enact the performative means for claiming power, particularly in opening ceremonies during which women cut off men's neckties. In these ways the FrauenMediaTurm symbolizes women's achievements over the last forty years, while also evoking contemporary feminists' impetus to manipulate the symbolic terms with which female identity is construed. "Taking back the tower" as a claim to supremacy has thus played out across different generations in both concrete and imaginative form. By extension, the FrauenMediaTurm resonates in relation to a central conceit in this volume: that of simultaneous affinities and differences among various forms of feminism. Even as its resonances evoke divergent approaches, the tower's stalwart presence on the Rhine across centuries also solidifies and conjoins them.

Less generously, however, its medieval architecture also handily aligns with the "pastness" that, according to Tasker and Negra, younger feminists associate with second-wave feminism. Likewise its battened-down façade, as well as Alice Schwarzer's presence in the editorial offices of *EMMA* on the tower's second floor, suggests protective retrenchment rather than engagement with the altered landscape of young women's lives. But insofar as the tower also invokes Karneval battle cries and raucous bodies filling the streets, demanding to be seen and heard, it is in fact very much in the spirit of contemporary feminist activism. Now globally connected, its various manifestations have begun appearing in public spaces in Germany and around the world. Equally important, the "media" component of the tower's name points to digital means of shoring up feminism in a world of proliferating screens. Here the "master's house" continually changes shape and thus exceeds concretely spatial parameters that can be acquired, dismantled, and reconstructed according to egalitarian imperatives. Significant in this regard is that not only street-based but also digital forms of activism have boomed in Germany in recent years. As a consequence, the FrauenMediaTurm as evocative of blended second- and third-wave approaches becomes less relevant, ironically, as an actual repository of gender studies artifacts. It perhaps goes without saying that digitally inclined younger feminists no longer necessarily need actual physical structures to archive their legacy. Most important, contemporary circumstances require a return to the terrain I mapped out in chapter 1, as well as the search for other metaphorical frameworks to understand what entwined differences and affinities might look like now.

This aim is complicated by the fact that solidarity has become increasingly desirable among younger feminists. Metaphors alone as the means for understanding possible paths to solidarity are tricky because they resonate, like the tower, in various and not necessarily cohesive ways. They complicate not so much "why" stories matter, to cite Clare Hemmings work on generationally inflected narratives of a shared feminist history, but the "way" they matter.[1] By closely examining various novels and films that depict women's lives in relation to feminism, this volume has highlighted artistic depictions of individual psyches as they process political mandates. And it is in this psychological realm that we witness the push and pull of egotistical and enlightened impulses, as well as the force of capriciously elastic identifications. Above all, we witness a selfhood perpetually at odds with itself as it nonetheless struggles to attain a unified, cohesive sense of self. The way my literary and filmic stories matter—specifically in terms of always fragmented, dichotomous elements within—in turn offers metaphorical possibilities for understanding contemporary conflicts among feminists, particularly those invested in conjuring solidarity. Most obviously, were we to understand competing forms of feminism simply as a normative foundational condition, conflict would likely be less a cause for recrimination or frustration. At the same time, a perpetually divided selfhood may provide a too neat metaphor for conflicts in feminism that, as Birgit Mikus and Emily Spiers have documented, date back to its very inception in Germany. Significantly though, thinking about the foundational role of the past for identity more generally adds important nuance to a comparative framework with feminism.

The kinds of condensations and displacements we associate with dreams keep the past present as a foundation that cannot be cast off, for better or worse. Our psyches perpetually reimagine the past in relation to the present, as well as the present in relation to the past, often in only partially conscious and self-serving ways. Likewise, a longer historical past is foundational to feminism and cannot be simply repressed or rejected in the name of cultivating an autonomy that is as much self-serving as it is future-oriented. Whatever new strategies feminists evolve will always resonate in relation to the past, and in dialogical fashion will also continually reshape our sense of both the past and present. Topless activism provides one example. Once a tactic of female university students, it has lately become means by which the Ukrainian group FEMEN calls attention to global forms of misogyny. As much as FEMEN activists appear to have evolved beyond an earlier feminism concerned only with white women's circumstances, their act, when staged in Berlin in 2012, also stoked various forms of critique from Muslim women and people of color. Ironically, this circumstance actually echoes the aftermath of topless student activism in the late 1960s, which prompted its own kinds of negative reception. As I underscored in the introduction to this volume, the press and public, according to Barbara Becker-Cantarino, found their act "shameless, immoral, and reprehensible," even as their image nonetheless appeared on various magazine covers, no doubt to bolster sales.[2]

Yet dialogical relations do not necessarily preordain adverse, unpredictable outcomes. If we think of such relations as a kind of mechanistic given, they can fuel attempts among women to continually reimagine the divisions that plague feminism, as well as to foster politically transformative scenarios "that intervene to change the way we tell stories."[3] In my introduction I also cited Chandra Talpade Mohanty's work, specifically her attempts to imagine what solidarity among feminists could look like.[4] Within a synchronic frame, recognizing differences in all their particularities—to which I would add accepting them as a normative baseline—also sets the terms, she argues, for perceiving connections and commonalities.⁵ This model creates the conditions for mutually affirming relations across difference, what could be understood metaphorically, as I will discuss further below, as a self-sustaining feminist ecosystem. In what follows I will trace feminism's trajectory in Germany since 2008, beginning with print venues and moving to street-based and digital activisms. Throughout I will assess the extent to which metaphors of fractured psyches and thriving ecosystems are useful in understanding the complexities of achieving solidarity.

EMMA, Missy Magazine, and the Return of the Same

Towards the end of a July/August 2008 *EMMA* editorial, penned at the height of generational debates, Alice Schwarzer threw down the gauntlet, admonishing her media critics to found their own publications.⁶ Funding had already been obtained, in fact, to launch *Missy Magazine*, subtitled *Popkultur für Frauen*, in February of the same year. The first issue appeared the following October, an almost too pert response to Schwarzer's rebuke. In their opening editorial, Chris Köver, Stefanie Lohaus, Julie Steinbrecher, Nicole Ibele, and Sonja Eismann positioned themselves, however, in relation to journalism on popular culture, a "playground" occupied, they argued, by 80 percent boys.⁷ In this manner they may have been speaking back to long-running magazines such as *Spex* as much as to antiquated feminists.⁸ Yet despite articles on the Austrian musician Anja Plaschg of Soap&Skin, female rappers against the "hiphop-patriarchy," and Kamasutra positions, the first issue also looked at topics such as genital mutilation and the discomforts of high-heeled shoes. As I observed in the introduction to this volume, these latter two articles could just as easily have appeared in *EMMA*.⁹ They also anticipated a 2010 editorial decision to drop the subtitle and extend the magazine's focus beyond pop culture as object of feminist critique to politics more broadly. Other examples of a subsequently expanded purview include, as cofounder Sonja Eismann observed in *Missy's* April 2013 five-year anniversary issue, attention to the situation of female refugees in Germany and politics surrounding the family.

Even though such topics also overlap with *EMMA*'s political concerns, gender researcher Stevie Schmeidel observed in a 2015 Deutschlandfunk interview that the two magazines, each with 40,000 subscribers, have very little in common with each other.¹⁰ Her statement may reveal, on the one hand, the kind of selective perception needed to stoke the illusion of autonomy. On the other, it also belies *Missy*'s use of a second-wave vernacular to speak back to the boy's club of pop culture. For instance, Eismann pays tribute in the anniversary issue to the American magazine *Bust* as "big sis" and interviews its editor Debbie Stoller in her New York office. If evocative of a second-wave sisterhood, Eismann's epithet betrays more than either a younger generation unwittingly borrowing from the past or consciously trying to make old forms resignify in new and improved ways. Rather, "sisterhood" in a pop-inflected context obliges us to think about how the past and present continually speak to and alter each other, rather than the latter simply evolving beyond and improving upon the former. In the process, our understanding of female solidarity across a longer history is necessarily reconfigured. As much as the idea of sisterhood once inspired women to rebel against mass culture dictates, it also required, as Alice Schwarzer's varied print venues over time have made clear, "Boulevardjournalismus" publications such as *Stern* and more recently *Bild Zeitung* to rally support for legal abortion and against celebrities charged with rape. Likewise, the kinds of performative-style demonstrations that have recently emerged in Germany reveal how playfulness constitutes a hook for what remain powerfully visceral concerns about women's sociopolitical circumstances. Just as *Missy Magazine* has blended pop with politics, we need to be aware of both entities' evolving fluidity and how it continually rewrites our understanding of a larger genealogy of feminism.

Here and there in Eismann's retrospective musings for *Missy*'s anniversary issue, she does appear to stoke divides by talking back, however unwittingly, to Schwarzer's earlier churlishness. She deemed *Missy*'s 2008 appearance, for instance, as "insolent" and something that had been "terribly missed" in the German print media. Its aim was to provide the "the ultimate styling tips for the totally contemporary popfeminist look."[11] Along similar surface-oriented lines and in the spirit of other popfeminist voices of 2008, *Missy* was highly invested in demonstrating that "feminism still shines."[12] Though Eismann sets up in her introductory text an alternative feminist genealogy rooted in Riot Grrrl culture, her rhetoric, as the example above demonstrates, remains embedded in a longer and more varied history of feminisms.

Suffice it to say, the complicated terrain of common ground and blatant partitions remains a compelling object of analysis, even if feminism in Germany has evolved in dramatically new directions less overtly invested in "talking back" to older forms of feminism. Instead, what compels is the desire for solidarity, on the one hand, and unwitting exclusions, on the other, when feminism operates in digital platforms and/ or globally influenced, performance-style demonstrations. Russian feminist and LGBT activists Pussy Riot, who since 2011 have staged guerrilla performances in unusual locations and disseminated them on video, provide an obvious example of globally connected activism. German support of them culminated in an August 2012 march in Berlin during which participants wore Pussy Riot accoutrements such as colorful balaclavas to express solidarity. Yet the now Paris-based FEMEN, which has staged topless protests against sexism, homophobia, and religious structures since 2008, inspired the critique I mention above, which exposed fracturing along ethnic and racial, as opposed to generational, lines.

Given that discord continues to divide the feminist field into disgruntled factions, one wonders if it is at all possible to harness contradictory aims to a larger solidarity. This is particularly the case if we use partitioned psychic elements unable to speak to or even recognize each other as a point of comparison. At the same time, basic, persistent divisions could serve as a starting point for a new form of feminist politics, which, like the dialogical energy I describe above, challenges the notion of teleological progression towards ever-smarter approaches and the chimerical end point of union and solidarity. Part of the larger aim of this final chapter is to situate the notion of simultaneous difference and affiliation in relation to a possible emergent form of feminist politics.

This chapter examines how German feminism presently positions itself, often subtly, in relation to preceding generations as it confronts and works through new divides. On the one hand, I have called upon the idealistic notion of bridge building, evident in a special 2008 issue of *EMMA* that brought together *Bitch* editor Lisa Jervis, ur-Riot Grrrl and Bikini Kill front woman Kathleen Hanna, and American second-wave icon Gloria Steinem. More recently, a spring 2011 issue of *EMMA* featured on its cover Alice Schwarzer with members of the editorial team of *Missy*. The text below reads: "*EMMA* Meets Mädchen. Not into division. We have to talk." In an eight-page article, she and another *EMMA* editor, two *Missy* editors, and a blogger had a very congenial conversation, initiated with glasses of champagne.[13]

As I argued in relation to the "contradictions and hybridity" that Hester Baer identifies in the third wave, bridges may be less necessary if different feminisms, as both *EMMA* issues appear to demonstrate, share an equitable coexistence. Valerie Renegar and Stacey K. Sowards's essay "Contradiction as Agency: Self-Determination, Transcendence, and

Figure 6.1. *EMMA*, Spring 2011. Source: www.emma.de

Counter-Imagination in Third Wave Feminism" also provides a useful reference point for unifying impulses.[14] Though they argue for multiplicity within the field of feminism—for women understanding their identities and feminism in their own terms—activism should remain, they suggest, embedded in a larger historical context of feminist aims and practices. Such embeddedness, as I will demonstrate, becomes evident when digital platforms reprise an ethics of caring that recalls second-wave values. Likewise, some of the more raucous voices in the blogosphere find their roots, as Emily Nussbaum has observed, in feminist manifestos of the 1970s. In the best possible scenario, contemporary feminism consists not so much of tangled-up factions that stifle growth, but rather a rich variety of voices sustained by the dialogical dynamism of a long, rich history as living substratum. Equally important, as conditions change, some varieties of feminism may be more noxious than salutary in achieving a particular aim. Whatever the outcome, this model shifts expectations of ever-more efficacious strategies to considerations of how suited different approaches are for achieving goals at different moments in time.

Missy Magazine and Popfeminist Dreams of Solidarity

In some respects *Missy Magazine's* 2013 anniversary issue retains traces of earlier attempts to separate popfeminism from feminist precursors wary of commodity culture as an oppressive arena of patriarchal mandates. Featuring Kathleen Hanna—the "patron saint of all Riot Grrrls"—on the cover, the issue included a dossier of queer-feminist voices tasked to provide an interim assessment on the state of feminism.[15] *Missy's* use of the label "queer-feminist" throughout bears mention up front as evidence of altered parameters. It invokes a more disruptive force than feminism alone insofar as queerness potentially undermines the traditional male/female categories by which progress has typically been measured. Along similar lines, the editorial board's opening statement stoked expectations for alternative perspectives when they enthused over dossier perspectives "they could have only dreamed of five years earlier."[16] But Hanna's cover image and feature story constitute an unexpected déjà vu for readers who may have followed *EMMA*'s coverage of the debates of 2008.

On the one hand, Hanna's appearance in *Missy's* anniversary issue clearly aligns with the popfeminist history that Eismann traces in her introduction to the dossier. In it, she cites the preexistence of the term "popfeminism" already in some 1990's circles and identifies a diverse range of popfeminist voices extending back to female authors such as Jutta Koether and Clara Drechsler writing in the magazine *Spex* in the 1980s.[17] Five years before Hanna spoke with the Canadian musician Peaches in the pages of *Missy*, however, she engaged in a congenial dialog with Gloria Steinem in *EMMA*.[18] If the embodiment of insolence as catnip to *Missy's* readers, Hanna had thus already participated in *EMMA's* bridge-building efforts between wounded mothers and recalcitrant daughters. The *Missy* editorial board's admission that it took years to get Hanna to pose for the cover also deflates the force of insolent gestures. Instead one gets a sense of competing camps coopting an affable rather than impudent girl for their own purposes. Perhaps not surprisingly, Hanna once again articulated a magnanimous stance: "I don't care how kids come to feminism, whether they discover it through the Riot Grrrls, Spice Girls, Lady Gaga or 'Spring Breakers,' as long as they do. That's all just a launchpad and from there they'll find their own way."[19]

In a similar vein, many of the dossier voices in *Missy's* anniversary issue struck their own kinds of ameliorative tones. Given this volume's focus on generational rifts, I examined content that responded to one rubric among several that Eismann set up for assessing their viewpoints: what "feminist solidarity looks like today, locally and globally."[20] In brief texts of a few paragraphs, the women in *Missy's* dossier spoke more anecdotally than authoritatively, their observations as much about what still needs to change as progress actually made. Yet the de facto existence or self-evident desirability of solidarity repeatedly appeared in their musings, signaling an important sea change since the debates of 2008.

Blogger and philosopher Antje Schrupp, for instance, asserted that "fewer people would say today than five years ago that feminism is dead or superseded," and "different streams of feminism" now have more contact with each other.[21] Rapper and hip-hop activist Sookee cited early German feminist Clara Zetkin, among others, for inspiring her continued participation in an extensive range of activism. Examples include the feminist panels, campaigns, workshops, concerts, info-events, Ladyfests, salons, discussions, readings, and demonstrations to which she was invited in the preceding five years. When she argues for promoting "the widest possible consciousness for an intersectional approach within feminist politics," she may, in fact, be invoking the kind of energy that had already fueled these various events.[22] Other dossier voices provided evidence of intersectionality in antithetical but congruent tonalities. In reflecting on the "aufschrei" (outrage) Twitter campaign which she co-initiated against sexism, Kathy Meßner, for instance, described both militant and less strident voices: "Aufschrei inscribed feminist concerns, angrily and gently, in screams and in whispers, but above all continually into the public discourse."[23] Her observation resonates all the

Figure 6.2. *Missy Magazine,* April 2013. Source: www.missy-mag.de. Photo by Katharina Poblotzki

more if one recalls a younger generation's distaste for earlier, more truculent forms of feminism.

Other women promoted volume in both acoustic and tangible form as the means to achieve further solidarity. Nancy Haupt and Elisa Gutsche, organizers of Barcamp Frauen, argued, "As a movement we have to grow stronger and bigger, maybe also more compatible.... we have to achieve more solidarity among ourselves. We have to learn to accept and support one another. And we can't forget to build strong networks and look for strong coalitions."[24] Evidence of continued divisiveness, however, became apparent when Stevie Schmiedel observed, "I think we can achieve more if there weren't so many hostilities and exclusions within the scene.... even if we all have a different opinion, there is always overlap."[25] Haupt and Gutsche's use of the word "Netzwerke" of course takes both concrete and virtual form, yet it was in the latter realm that "hostilities and exclusions" often articulated themselves. Meredith Haaf, one of the Alpha Mädchen authors and subsequent cofounder of the website Mädchenmannschaft (Girl's team), provided a salient observation in this regard. She pointed out that for feminist digital networking to be more than a trend, to be a revolution instead of simply "Medien machen" (making news), feminists need to go beyond platforms where everyone can speak but in the end each woman can and only wants to speak for herself. To achieve something more requires a unified aim: "If feminists can't concentrate on a shared opponent, in the end it will only be a media revolution."[26] As I will discuss further below, her words no doubt reflect the fracturing that characterized Mädchenmannschaft's evolution from 2007 to 2012, as well as the singular energy of the 2013 #aufschrei campaign, which united women against sexism after *Stern* journalist Laura Himmelreich revealed sexist comments FDP (Freie Demokratische Partei) politician Rainer Brüderle made to her during an interview.[27]

Second Wavelengths

Whether speaking hypothetically or anecdotally, *Missy Magazine*'s dossier voices conjured solidarity reminiscent of the second wave, but one also complicated by evolving forms of activism in a digitally connected world. Web-based activism and actual demonstrations are intricately entwined, particularly if one considers how the former foments the latter but also creates an echo chamber that subsequently eclipses real events in space and time, especially when they spawn controversy. Some early and recent scholarship on feminism in the blogosphere, however, has emphasized the front end of this relationship, or more generally the manner in which blogs have indeed, as Antje Schrupp observed, made it possible for different streams of feminism to come together, as well as to realize Sookee's hope for intersectional approaches that stoke a broad consciousness among feminists.[28]

In "Searching for a Home Place: Online in the Third Wave," Barbara Duncan compares letters written to Ms. magazine between 1972 and 1987, compiled in the volume Letters to Ms. Magazine, with exchanges on the website for Bust magazine between August 1999 and March 2001.[29] Wittingly or not, Duncan embeds the website's discussions in a historical feminist context via a familial rubric reminiscent of second-wave philosophical underpinnings. While acknowledging Ms. magazine's unifying effects on women, she views Bust's website in more exalted terms, deeming it "a family home" that conjures a "sense of belonging and ... obligation" and "where participants can replenish and sustain themselves for their everyday and ongoing activist goals."[30] The exchanges that Duncan quotes provide evidence, however, not only of supportive familial structures, but also a specifically feminine form of caring. When Bust.com participants express support in the face of illness or offer rides to demonstrations, one is reminded of philosopher Carol Gilligan's argument in In Another Voice: Psychological Theory and Women's Development (1982) about a different moral voice among women that prizes relationships, empathy, and compassion.[31]

Important to note as well is the absence of the hierarchy that structures parent-child relations, since "leaders are not visible" on the website and activism happens spontaneously around temporary political events, with a diverse range of women responding. Such improvisation provides one of the blog's advantages over Ms.'s epistolary interconnectivity, which Duncan argues was more about self-revelation than fomenting activism.[32] It also points to theatricality more generally, though with different aims than, for instance, FEMEN's topless activism. Duncan borrows Benedict Anderson's notion of an "imagined community," a space bound together by a collective imagination rather than a geographical location. Along similar simulated lines, role-playing constitutes part of Bust.com's virtual space. While leaders may remain invisible, Duncan conjures fluid female hierarchies which maximize an ethics of caring:

> Participants can act out the roles of mothers or sisters with each other, providing much needed advice and concern, similar to what a home is supposed to provide. Indeed, this electronic space allows even younger members to take on the role of "mother" as the technology hides physical characteristics. As a result, traditional roles of older and younger relationships can be easily reversed. In doing so, Bust online web space can act as a family and an important home where stereotypes and

standard roles can be circumvented and turned around. There is no longer a clear distinction between learner and teacher or mother and daughter; both happen simultaneously online and with much more flexibility.[33]

Ultimately, Bust.com provides a virtual space "not so much about doing feminism as . . . being a feminist in a safe and respectful place."[34]

As much as Duncan reactivates caring as a feminist value, her perspective may also reveal another form of embeddedness, in this case in relation to historical events less conducive to community-building. By this I mean the divisions that characterized Anglo-American feminism in the 1990s, or the effect of identity politics and postcolonial perspectives, as well as individualistic performativity, in the wake of Judith Butler. Responses by Muslim women and people of color to FEMEN's topless activism in Berlin in 2012 provide another example as well. This incident alone might explain why *Missy*'s dossier participants appear so invested in the possibility of solidarity. Even if Duncan puts an idealistic spin on digital connectivity, she adds, at the same time, important contours to the complicated mesh I mentioned earlier between the Internet and activism on the streets. As much as the digital "echo chamber" muddies our sense of actual events, it also can serve as retroactive salve for divisions that play out among feminists in various arenas.

In 2011 Emily Nussbaum published an essay in *New York Magazine* titled "The Rebirth of the Feminist Manifesto," which was largely celebratory of recent performative forms of activism and a raucous female blogosphere. Yet unlike Duncan, she also acknowledged the unsisterly aspects of both realms. Above all, she expressed her admiration for SlutWalk demonstrations, which originated in Canada in response to a police officer who admonished students to "avoid dressing like sluts." Ultimately, SlutWalks spread across the globe to settings as diverse as Mexico, Germany, Manhattan, and South Africa. (FEMEN's 2012 topless activism in Berlin was also part of a SlutWalk demonstration.) Like Duncan, Nussbaum uses *Ms.* magazine as a point of comparison, again to favorable ends for the next generation. But rather than serve as an early unifying force or caring space for self-revelation, it constitutes to her a tame, liberal-feminist mainstream venue when compared to 1970's manifestos written by Audrey Lorde, Shulamith Firestone, and Valerie Solanas. It is their spirit that she identifies in SlutWalk activism and raw blogosphere voices, as well as pop-culture memes that put Judith Butler's words into Ryan Gosling's mouth. Though she cites blogger Shelby Knox, who compares virtual connectivity with early consciousness-raising, Nussbaum nonetheless emphasizes, like Duncan, more evolved feminist aims now, in this instance in contemporary lobbying efforts for gay marriage and transgender rights. Most important, Duncan's and Nussbaum's essays reveal how teleological trajectories of ever-improving feminism, whether defined in terms of caring or rabble-rousing, require selective comparisons to different aspects of the second wave. At the very least, the gap between Gloria Steinem and Valerie Solanis demonstrates a less monolithic view than that activated by the Alpha and New German Girls in 2008.

If Nussbaum's buoyant stance resembles Duncan's idealistic take on Bust.com, she does acknowledge continued divisiveness, evident in the sharper, crueler exchanges among women on the Internet. While emphasizing how "feminist solidarity has never been a simple matter," she nonetheless sees value in acrimony insofar as it obliges women to hone their ideas in ever-evolving debates.[35] In different locations, for instance, the "slut" in SlutWalk signs was crossed out or the title changed entirely, as in a "Stomp and Holler" demonstration in Northampton, Massachusetts. Tapped into the same energy and outrage as early feminists, SlutWalk participants nonetheless mutated the demonstration's initial contours in response to their own local contexts.[36] Yet Nussbaum ends her essay with a quote from a manifesto written by Molly Lambert that prizes belligerence over reconfigured approaches. Contending that discomfort is a necessary part and not the death of the conversation, Lambert then muses on the possibility of resulting exclusion. If you're cut from the club, she says, "start your own fucking club. I'll come! I'll bring a lovely bottle of orange soda."[37]

As much as Lambert's magnanimous offer points towards solidarity, the "start your own fucking club" mentality underscores how individual parts of the whole—the varieties of feminism at a given moment—will continue to assert their own needs and aims. Additionally, the knowledge each "club" has of feminist history will always at best be partial and self-serving, like Nussbaum highlighting 1970's manifestos in order to promote contemporary forms of raucous activism. As Hemmings has observed, the story one tells about the past "is always motivated by the position one wishes to occupy in the present."[38] If feminists understood division as a basic component of a larger group identity, as well as the notion of solidarity as at best an enabling fiction, some of the inevitable shock and chagrin each time splintering occurs could be mitigated. Equally important, solidarity needs to be imagined not as an end point in time and space but rather in ways elastic enough to accommodate repetitions of the same, or contrary needs that will always assert themselves.

Such perpetual reconceptualization obliges us to think about the "and" between the poles of difference and affinity, or the various ways one could stitch together otherwise binary terms. As I have argued elsewhere in this volume, feminist conflicts have often been understood in dyadic terms, like the mother-daughter rubric Astrid Henry critiques in *Not My Mother's Daughter*. The stakes in this particular model are formidable given how it situates conflict in relation to biological mechanisms that preprogram extinction. When applied to mothers and daughters, this dyad evokes reproductive cycles and the psychological imperative of separation. Yet one could think of the fleeting temporalities that inform this model in less menacing form. They also underpin Jenny Warnecke's concept of "Bindestrich" or hyphenated feminism, which I referenced in this volume's introduction. She describes scenarios in which temporary, strategic alliances among different feminist groups form in order to react to problems as they occur. In the process, the notion of "collectivity" continually reshapes itself into loose confederations, each consisting of individual components that vary over time.

Given dialogism's roots in the linguistic theories of Russian philosopher Mikhail Bakhtin, however, dialogism entails more than such alliances' synchronic temporalities. It also describes a broader engagement with earlier forms of language and thought in which the past and the future converse with and continually alter each other. This process differs from a dialectical approach in which new combinations aim for the resting point of synthesis, a goal less likely for feminism given its consistently multiple, incongruent forms over time. Equally important, the past and present can speak to and alter each other in myriad ways, not all of which constitute a more evolved form of feminism or a carefully conceptualized amalgam of different approaches. This process can just as easily reveal contemporary feminists using the past in misguided ways that belie altered circumstances. This possibility, in turn, constitutes a negative outcome to the project of making old forms signify in new and subversive ways. Instead, historical forms revived in contemporary contexts may reveal previously unrecognized blind spots that resonate more fully in the present moment. In this sense "affinities and differences" refer to semiotic import that continually reshapes itself, and not in a manner as easily managed as hyphenated feminists uniting to achieve a particular aim.

Mädchenmannschaft and Sour Sisters

In 2007, Meredith Haaf and her Alpha Girl coauthors Barbara Streidl and Susanne Klingner founded Mädchenmannschaft as a German version of the American blog feministing.com, or a space for articulating feminist responses to politics and the media. Haaf also emphasized the blog's intention to focus on sexism so that women who experienced it would not feel so alone. Incorporating the perspectives of journalists, psychologists, political scientists, cultural critics, and sociologists, among other professions, the blog became, according to a *taz* article, "the prize-crowned flag ship of web feminism."[39] In 2008, it received the Deutsche Welle BOB (Best of the Blogs) Award, and a year later was nominated for the Grimme Online Award and the Alternativer Medienpreis. Both *taz* and the online magazine *Breitband* characterized the blog as an "opinion leader" in the realms of cyberfeminism and women's politics. Citing Nussbaum's *New York Magazine* essay, *Süddeutsche Zeitung* journalist Niklas Hofmann identified in both Mädchenmannschaft and *Missy* a German counterpart, or a female-centric blogosphere which had cultivated a newly born, young, and self-confident feminism.[40] Interestingly, his article features a photo of women running in high heels, captured from the waist down, the perfect condensation of pop stylishness and second-wave boots-on-the-ground activism.

Yet unity among the contributors eventually gave way, a development that the remaining Mädchenmannschaft bloggers linked to historical displacements of feminist conflicts and blind spots. Between 2010 and 2012, all of the original bloggers left the website, prompting scrutiny from mainstream newspapers and alternative blog venues. In attempting to understand tensions within the organization, a *taz* article observed that Mädchenmannschaft had grown more political and "theory saturated."[41] This direction culminated in the site's engagement with "Critical Whiteness," meaning unconscious notions of supremacy among whites towards nonwhites. Evidence thereof emerged in the wake of the 2012 Berlin SlutWalk demonstration, attended by 3,500 participants, during which three German FEMEN activists drew black robes on their skin, including eye slits, that imitated hijabs. They positioned themselves in front of the Brandenburg gate and held up signs that read "Unveil Women's Right to Unveil" and "There is a War on Women." Muslim woman, in turn, reacted with a "Muslimah Pride" demonstration, and their slogans touted freedom of choice and multiple ways of "being free." People of color also responded to FEMEN's display later the same month by critiquing the racism of white women attempting to free Islamic women from misogynistic structures, comparing FEMEN's performance to "blackfacing" in early twentieth-century theater. When asked by SlutWalk participants to clarify their position, they reacted with the query, why should those discriminated against always have to explain things to the discriminators?[42]

Though Mädchenmannschaft, which had been associated with the protesters, responded with self-critique,[43] Meredith Haaf soon after left the website, offering the following observations: "I thought it was good to talk about possible racism. I thought it was good to move away from a naively friendly feminism a la Alphamädchen, which I, too, would now criticize. But the self-incrimination was once again a dictate and not a discussion ... now it's a radical queer-feminist blog with exclusionary language. That's not accessible for most people."[44]

Emphasizing her own evolution beyond Alpha Mädchen parameters, Haaf nonetheless prefaces the word "racism" with the adjective "possible," signaling her distance from the website's apology. Though the words "self-incrimination" refer to the website in toto, Haaf underscores hierarchical tensions within the organization by characterizing the forces that prompted it as a "dictate." Similarly, when she describes elsewhere the "aggression and destructive anger" that characterized the critiques from people of color, she also implies its impact, which effectively silenced them. Ironically, the charges of the "exclusionary" and "inaccessible" language articulated by queer feminists echo the manner in which nonwhite feminists felt excluded when popfeminism had the podium. These kinds of problems constitute a basic "repetition of the same," and within a very short time frame if one considers how recently younger feminists had challenged older feminists such as Schwarzer for setting the agenda. And if we keep historical circumstances in mind, specifically the forms of identity politics that emerged in the 1990s and appear to reassert themselves in Mädchenmannschaft's trajectory, concrete differences between then and now deserve mention. Such differences have more acute effects than the semiotic fallout when older strategies reemerge in new contexts, in this case topless, 1960s-style activism that mistakenly assumes an exposed/reclaimed female body signifies power in all cultural contexts.

On the one hand, digital connectivity now bridges geographical boundaries, in this instance linking Ukrainian and German feminists. Yet since the 1990s, diminishing economic stability has bolstered neoliberal structures that promote individual achievement. Those with less access to education, who are subject to shrinking social benefits and/or mandates about embracing a "Leitkultur," find themselves increasingly disadvantaged. As I argued in my analysis of *The Edge of Heaven*, Turkish women's difficult circumstances in Germany highlight global inequities, or the inhumane mechanisms of capitalism beneath its more appealing neoliberal façade of individual choice. As much as German feminists fighting misogyny within Islamic culture constitutes a powerful and positive form of global interconnectivity, their efforts divert attention from the structural advantages that enable them to speak out in the first place. These include not only access to education but also professional opportunities, as well as the financial stability to partake of commodity culture's pleasures, with or without feminist intent. What has resulted for many minorities in Germany is an escalating precariousness, rendered less visible when meritocratic ideals tout a level playing field. As I argued in my introduction regarding purely semiotic approaches to feminism, they do not necessarily change the social field. Whatever conceptual approaches feminism evolves to move forward, they need to remain rooted, now more than ever, in the realities of a divided socioeconomic world.

The remaining members of Mädchenmannschaft responded to Haaf's critique by underscoring the media's predictable frames for feminist debate, meaning in terms of scandals and cat fights. Asserting that none of them were interviewed for the *taz* article in which Haaf expressed her frustrations, Mädchenmannschaft also pointed out that by 2012 many of the original bloggers had already left the blog—amicably—to pursue other projects. While these observations downplay fraught divisions, the remaining bloggers also offered a highly analytic, trenchant critique of "Alphamädchen-Feminismus," which bears extended quotation:

> Displacement: away from Alpha-Mädchen feminism that benefits primarily well-situated straight women and doesn't question structures anymore—toward critiques of power, incorporation of feminist discourses and fault lines that were already around 20, 30, 40, 100 years ago.... This does not lead to either isolation or an elitist conceit, rather it enables all constructive, productive feminist work.... Fault lines among feminists have always appeared when those with a higher social standing weren't willing to cede a part of their privileges. Instead they have installed an historical consciousness that continues to obfuscate, negate, and repress many important historical struggles. This historical consciousness calls itself a "three wave model".... I wonder

> how a feminism can respond to a highly complex and diverse society with simplistic answers which pertain to only a fraction of the population. It may even open itself up to repression and backlash that have become dominant in Germany in recent years, with every feminist project looking over its shoulder in order to stay around. I wonder how this is not elitist and exclusive. I wonder how this is feminism at all. This fluffy skirmishing with its outdated understanding of politics, without a trace of solidarity.[45]

Her use of the word "displacement" is telling because it links occluded historical events—those conflicts that have played out in feminism at various intervals over the last hundred years—with a partitioned human psyche alternately unable or unwilling to recognize the repetitive nature of its own internal discord. Being "unable" underscores the difficulty of recognizing the partly unconscious needs that program behavior, such as, for instance, the narcissistic theatricality that fueled Valerie Solanas's radical approaches to activism, as I discussed in chapter 3. "Unwilling" describes more a defensive response in the face of repetitive patterns clearly in need of correction, as when one faction within feminism continually ignores the concrete conditions other kinds of feminists need in order to flourish. Whatever shape the dominant form of feminist discourse takes in a given moment—whether against concrete forms of sexism that affect all women or against other power structures that subject different kinds of women to different "isms"—it will always remain only partially aware of its blind spots. White privilege in the realm of feminism is the most obvious example, which the text above powerfully critiques. At the same time, the charge of "theory-saturated" language among queer feminists reprises the student movement's arcane Marxism and its attendant problems. Just as it remained disconnected from the working classes it sought to champion, feminism's theory-saturated language may also fail to inspire minority women in Germany.

The most oft-cited solution, which appears above as well, is to use conflict to spur "constructive, productive feminist work." Nussbaum essentially argues along the same lines by linking acrimony with an ever more precisely honed feminism. And as I quoted in the introduction to this volume, *Bitch* editor Lisa Jervis observed in *EMMA's* bridge-building issue that feminism has always profited from and evolved via internal debates, which refine its strategies and propel the movement forward. In more pointedly spatial terms, the authors of the 2012 Femfuture report on online feminism observe, "The more radical versions of feminism will continue to push the feminist center, the center will push the margins to be more strategic, those of us who dance in between will continue to be challenged and nurtured by it all."[46] While it would seem churlish to critique such a fair-minded stance, its anodyne nature deserves comment. Again, one senses a more dialectical than dialogical approach—specifically the need to achieve some form of quiescent synthesis. And it presumes that one can stand outside of one's self and relinquish narrowly beneficial aims. Political goals will never perfectly align given the uneven effects of power structures on women's lives, with their differing sexual and racial identities and economic circumstances. Depending on the contours of a particular aim among feminists, women will be variously obliged to claim or forsake power. White feminists will sometimes need to cede the platform to minority groups, and western Muslim women enjoying the benefits of choice vis-à-vis the hijab will need to acknowledge the truly oppressive circumstances of many Muslim women in both the East and West.[47]

Muddled Aims and Building on the Cracks

If recent events within a now globally interconnected feminism are any indication, theatrical display and its affective aftermath has become a powerful tool for spawning reflection and self-awareness. In "WiG-Trouble: Awkwardness and Feminist Politics," Carrie Smith-Prei and Maria Stehle use seeming "failure" within feminist politics—for which FEMEN's unwanted critique of Islam seems exemplary—to initiate a new model of politically engaged feminist scholarship. Citing not only the rise of FEMEN, Pussy Riot, and SlutWalks, but also feminist approaches to the Occupy movements and the Arab Spring, they examine the interplay between digital technologies and activism, which they describe as both fleeting and messy.[48] "Trouble," they argue, describes more than playful, performative means for destabilizing gender normativity. It also refers to the fallout when normativity in all its evolving forms, including prescriptive forms of feminism, is undermined rather than bolstered by repetitive iterations. More specifically, awkwardness ensues when, for example, choice and agency motivate *both* FEMEN and Muslim manifestations of feminism.

Compounding the awkwardness of women rebuffing other women for trying to help them is the "misquoting" by both groups, as Smith-Prei and Stehle assert, of second-wave feminism for their own purposes. FEMEN's topless activism no longer undermines an authoritarian university system but imposes a western notion of female agency on another culture. Muslimah Pride protesters transpose "repressive" power structures from a patriarchal to a feminist context. In this sense, past and present do indeed speak to each other dialogically, and in the process our sense of originary contexts is altered along muddled lines. Did topless students in Theodor Adorno lectures, for instance, imagine themselves speaking for all women as well? How did Marxist-oriented feminists respond to their exhibitionism? Were blind spots already apparent then or was it only in a contemporary context that they were revealed? From our present day vantage point, do we automatically assume naivety on their part that underestimates the impact that topless activists actually had?

Strikingly, Smith-Prei and Stehle also use the metaphor of an ecosystem, though not in relation to historical feminist practices alone, but more in synchronic terms, in the complicated mix of creation, reception, audience, and medium in popfeminist acts. Particularly in the digital afterlife of such events, Smith-Prei and Stehle argue, "political messages percolate and create politics that can be excessive, troubling, and out of control."[49] This observation speaks to what I referenced earlier as the "complicated mesh" between digital activism and actual demonstrations. While the Internet disseminates information both before and after an event takes place, its endless proliferations can create again an obfuscating echo chamber. Our task as scholars, they argue, is to confront the circularities cited above in joyful, collaborative ways that also communicate "hyper-self-awareness, self-parody, and subversion."[50]

Recently I witnessed these elements dramatically and uncomfortably displayed in an unexpected venue: an episode of the American TV sitcom *Louie*, starring comedian Louis C.K. In the first half, he does a stand-up routine about the superiority of women to men, undone in ancient times, he observes, when men realized they could physically abuse them. In the second half, he aggressively manhandles a female friend he wants to kiss, literally dragging her across the room as she desperately grabs onto and pulls furniture along in their wake. Eventually he traps her in a corner and achieves his aim. The episode bothered me so much I had to watch it twice and gain some distance from my conflicting affective responses, specifically smug satisfaction during his stand-up routine and then disbelief that a good liberal could act like such a Neanderthal towards a woman. As I watched it again, however, it became clear that contradiction was precisely the point: our conscious and better selves only partially rule the day, and it would be arrogant to assume otherwise. The fact that each half of the show exists as its own separate entity, with no narrative resolution that plays up insight and growth, underscores all the more the psychic partitioning. I was a little chagrinned that I failed to see this point the first time around, probably because my emotions got the better of me. Of course, when theatrical display generates powerful affect, it provides a launch pad for considered discussion, reflection, and self-awareness. Again, no matter how progressive our feminist agendas are, individual needs—what Louie shows us in their basest form—will always mitigate our actions.

Moving feminist discourse in this direction means altering a basic reflex, specifically using contradiction as a starting point for critiquing the patriarchy, not our own identities. As I underscored in chapter 4, Claire Johnston advocated a feminist film practice that reveals the dislocation between sexist ideology and the text of the film, most evident in the way filmic icons stand in relation to the myths they represent. Riot Grrrl approaches took a slightly different tack by revealing their own cultural inscription within the structures otherwise raucously protested. Smith-Prei and Stehle's politics of awkwardness feels related, though the cultural inscription they spotlight is less about the patriarchy per se than always-shifting power structures that at any given moment benefit some but not all. Acknowledging and displaying the cracks in an otherwise collective identity, then giving our creative and intellectual energy to the reactions they provoke, is, for starters, a far more productive approach than the "start your own publication/club" mentality I referenced earlier. It cultivates our better selves beyond a purely academic context in its fair-mindedness and generosity of spirit.

At the same time, this process should in no way inhibit the possibility of building on the cracks. By this I mean perpetually reimagining ways to keep differences and affinities stitched together in the name of a larger whole. If Hemmings has retained a "dogged optimism" regarding the utopianism of feminist theory, she predicates this aim on a "feminist accountability that shuttles back and forth between past and present in order to imagine a future that is not already known."[51] The latter part of this statement—the future that is "not already known"—points back to her rubric of the familiar narratives that structure a history of feminism, chiefly those of progress, loss, and return. My examination of literary and filmic works in this volume has also been predicated on a search for unpredictability, articulated in stories in which the idiosyncrasies of subjectivity meet up with varied political and conceptual forms of feminism. Perhaps not surprisingly, only two of the works I examined—Elke

Naters's *Lies* and Fatih Akin's *The Edge of Heaven*—provide narratives that gesture towards utopian aims. Not only is it difficult to imagine something entirely new within the conventions of literature and film, the outcome could be nothing more than a kitschy happy ending. Yet somehow both of these works use familiar familial structures, particularly feminism's clichéd mother-daughter trope, to imagine forms of solidarity entirely within our reach. All it requires is mothers and daughters, whether biologically or symbolically tethered, who continually reinfuse and sustain each other across difference. This model of separate but interconnected entities should be the foundation for a future in which feminist alliances perpetually reshape themselves to provide the ties that bind across difference.

Conclusion

Whether we use metaphors of echo chambers, with their insular, narcissistic qualities, or ecosystems and digital interconnectivity as analogues of the ties that bind and invigorate, feminism remains an always contentious and contradictory, but nonetheless pervasive, force. At the same time, the simultaneity implied by the "and" that connects affinity to difference could also undermine the binary of individual needs versus collective aims. To wit: in a recent series of articles in *Die Welt*, all of which began with the tagline "Feminism has gotten boring. We want to change that with radical positions," editor Ronja von Rönne declared up front in her contribution, "I'm not a feminist. I'm an egotist."[52] Thus in two wisp-thin sentences containing only subject and predicate adjective, she erected and cemented a wall between individual and collective selfhood.

Rönne then went on to echo the playbook of postfeminism by belittling "senile Birkenstock feminists" and their "disturbed" online daughters, underscoring that Germany's highest power possesses a vagina, and emphasizing that "We live in a land in which individuals fight for themselves."[53] Her unvarnished articulation of basic postfeminist tenants—what Angela McRobbie critiqued in more subtle forms already a decade ago—could simply be written off as another return of the same, in this case women comfortably ensconcing themselves within a larger meritocracy, with nary a look beyond its exclusionary parameters. Rönne's emphatic divide, however, attests to the foundational presence of feminism, in that there is no way around defining her identity other than in relation to it. More important, her defiantly self-aware egotism actually does provide a necessary and pragmatic vantage point for feminism. The trick is to replace the wall with some more permeable edifice, the architectural equivalent of a conjunction, not a period.

New German and Alpha Girls lacked self-awareness as they nudged feminism in the direction of narrowly defined aims, what Schwarzer exposed with the palliative label "wellness feminism." Though she explicitly critiqued a narrow purview, Schwarzer also provided a label that hints at the chimerical nature of feminism as once and future cure-all for patriarchal ills. Conflicting aims/approaches and differing social/economic/racial/sexual circumstances, of course, provide the most obvious and insurmountable roadblocks. In delving deeply into the complexities of literary and filmic selves impacted by feminism in a variety of contradictory forms, this volume has also tracked the complicated interplay of egotism and enlightened imperatives, a dynamic which potentially fires up as much as it stymies feminism. While neurosis may be the underside of individualist approaches, and while it may sometimes betray misguided perceptions of feminist aims, it does emphatically display the full spectrum of selfhood that feminism needs to acknowledge and respond to.

Second- and third-wave forms of feminism provide the discursive parameters with which Helen Memmel works through childhood trauma in *Wetlands,* resulting in an unruly body sustained by a thriving feminist ecosystem, not bounded by narcissistic insularity. In *Wrecked,* Elizabeth Kiehl, by contrast, shows us how trauma can just as easily articulate itself via a scorch-and-burn approach to a larger feminist legacy, a circumstance that exposes a personality disorder far more than a movement's political shortcomings. The lying, theatricality, and egotism on display in texts such as *The Pollen Room, Relax,* and *Lies* add important dimensions to a performative model of selfhood that typically plays up the political advantages of artificiality and mutability. Instead we see base imperatives articulating themselves within feminist rubrics, but ultimately and more importantly the kinds of "lies" that conjure an enabling narrative of feminist solidarity.

Representing iconic women such as Ulrike Meinhof and Uschi Obermaier according to second-wave, coming-to-consciousness models occludes the fragmented, incongruous selfhood that fuels the feminist project, for better or worse, as my literary examples show. Christian Petzold takes a more compelling approach in *The State I Am In* by exposing a young girl's search for "inner security" within speciously optimistic neoliberal structures that proffer unattainable forms of success. To the extent that feminism conceptualizes itself in terms of endpoints rather than ever-evolving dialogical dynamism, it, too, rides on empty promises. Yet the utopian nature of Fatih Akin's bridge-building in *The Edge of Heaven* helps us to conceptualize continual movement between all points—East and West, gendered and queer, mothers and daughters—in a dynamic where origins and becoming perpetually reinvigorate each other. If one views feminism in such terms, its history will always provide a rich substrata, one that alternately sustains and is sustained by evolving feminist forms. Whatever differences emerge as feminism evolves, particularly between more narrowly defined and collective aims, cannot undo the abiding affinities of shared origins.

Notes

1. Claire Hemmings, *Why Stories Matter: The Political Grammar of Feminist Theory* (Durham: Duke University Press, 2011).
2. Barbara Becker-Canterino, "The Politics of Memory and Gender: What Happened to Second-Wave Feminism in Germany?" *German Life and Letters* 67.4 (October 2014), 609.
3. Claire Hemmings, *Why Stories Matter*, 2.
4. See Chandra Talpade Mohanty, *Feminism without Borders: Decolonizing Theory, Practicing Solidarity* (Durham: Duke University Press, 2003).
5. Mohanty, *Feminism Without Borders*, 226.
6. She writes, "If any of these female colleagues, who apparently don't want to work anymore in editorial offices dependent on corporations and advertising, would like to have their own publication, I have some good advice: you start it yourselves. Like I founded EMMA in 1977" (Alice Schwarzer, "Worum geht es wirklich?" *EMMA* [July/August 2008], 5).
7. Eismann observes, "If journalism on popular culture is a playground, then 80 percent of it is taken up by boys. They sit on the swing, the see-saw, the jungle gym, they block the slide and the sand box. We didn't feel like watching the boys play anymore, we wanted to play ourselves. Missy is something like our Double Dutch, reserved for girls" (Chris Köver, Stefanie Lohaus, Julia Steinbrecher, Nicole Ibele, and Sonja Eismann, "Editorial." *Missy Magazine* [January 2008]: 1).
8. In a dialog between *EMMA* and *Missy Magazine* editors, which included Alice Schwarzer, *Missy* cofounder Stephanie Lohaus described the original concept of their magazine as a combination of *EMMA*, the music magazine *Intro*, with a little bit of the fashion magazine *Maxi*. She also observed that since *Missy Magazine*'s appearance, the top male editor at *Spex* was

joined by a female editor. The first issue they published together featured articles, according to Lohaus, that could have just as easily appeared in *Missy*. "EMMA Meets Mädchen. Kein Bock auf Spaltung. Wir müssen redden." *EMMA* (Spring 2011), 23.
9. Conversely, since *Missy Magazine* has been on the newsstands, *EMMA* featured Lady Gaga on its fall 2010 cover. It has also included articles on performance artists such as Tracy Emin, other artists archived by the re.act. feminism project and exhibit, and the Ukrainian performance-oriented protest group FEMEN.
10. More pointedly, she also observed that both magazines "can't stand each other": "Both are probably representative of feminism but can't stand each other, are very, very different and have only very minimal overlap." See "Viele unterschiedliche Strömingen in Deutschland. Stevie Schmeidel im Gespräch mit Berthold Schossig," *Deutschlandfunk*, 4 June 2015, http://www.deutschlandfunk.de/debatte-ueber-feminismus-viele-unterschiedliche-stroemungen.691.de.html?dram:article_id=321766.
11. "Dossier: Auf einer Welle," *Missy Magazine* (April 2013), 60.
12. "Editorial 4/13," *Missy Magazine*, April 2013, 5.
13. In it they expressed consensus up front that the debates of 2008 and the generational tensions that provided a frame were largely hyped up by the media. *Missy Magazine* cofounder Chris Köver stated that her team never defined itself in opposition to *EMMA*, and even if differences exist between the two magazines, media attention to that alone constitutes a form of backlash. Schwarzer described the two magazines as different but "ergänzend" (complementary). *Missy Magazine* coeditor Stephanie Lohaus distanced herself from the feminist voices of 2008 by proclaiming that she found Jana Hensel's and Elisabeth Raether's *New German Girls* "awful." Most of those present also distanced themselves from the label "Mädchen." Strikingly, *Missy Magazine* includes a rubric entitled "Generationsgespräch" (Generational dialogs). The article ended with Chris Köver's suggestion that they organize events together. See "EMMA Meets Mädchen. Kein Bock auf Spaltung! Wir müssen reden," 20–27.
14. Valerie Renegar and Stacey K. Sowards, "Contradiction as Agency: Self-Determination, Transcendence, and Counter-Imagination in Third Wave Feminism," *Hypatia* 24.2 (Spring 2009), 1–20.
15. "Dossier: Auf einer Welle," 65–67.
16. "Editorial 4/13," *Missy Magazine*, April 2013, 5.
17. Other examples of premillennial popfeminist roots, she argues, include more generally American third-wave feminism and queer-feminist debates in academia, as well as (1) the participation of authors such as Kerstin and Sandra Grether and Barbara Kirchner in debates about the importing of pop culture from England and America; (2) a special issue of the journal *testcard* titled "Beiträge zur Popgeschichte," edited by Tine Plesch and Martin

Büsser; (3) the 1999 founding of the Viennese magazine *Nylon. Kunststoff zu Feminismus und Popkultur*; (4) the 1998 founding of "Electric Indigo female pressure," a platform for women in electronic music; (5) Christiane Rösinger and Almut Klotz's creation in 1998 of the female-centered record label "Flittchen Records"; (6) Gudrun Gut's creation in 1997 of her label "Monika Enterprizes"; (7) the first Ladyfests in Hamburg (2003) and Vienna (2004); and (8) millennial electronic and performative bands such as La Tigre, Chics on Speed, and Peaches, female role models who embodied "corporeality, queerness, theatrical strategies on stage and protest." Eismann ends her cataloging with the observation, "We need this kind of Herstory in order to avoid always reinventing the feminist wheel" ("Dossier: Auf einer Welle," 62–63).

18. Strikingly, on the subject of fashion, Steinem emphatically stated her belief that women should be able to wear what they want; for her part, Hanna described dressing during her Riot Grrrl years like a young girl as a statement for those whose childhoods were destroyed by abuse. Since then she has abandoned this look.

19. Peaches, "Fuck yeah, Kathleen Hanna!" *Missy Magazine* (April 2013), 78. *Spring Breakers* is a 2012 film directed by Harmony Korine. In it, four college women travel to Florida on their spring break and become involved with a drug dealer and his world of crime, eventually murdering him and his gang at the end of the film. Hanna points out that they wear red balaclava masks in one scene, which she herself had worn in an interview in a scene from the film *The Punk Singer*. This look may have also inspired Pussy Riot.

20. "Dossier: Auf einer Welle," 64. Other questions: What perspectives have white women developed in relation to their privileges, and how can they share them with women of color? How can one live equally and in a feminist and queer way after having children? What happens if you reject the "enforced matrix" of heterosexual or homosexual? What does sexual self-determination look like today? How do we deal with the challenge of sex work? How do we react to sexism today? (ibid.).

21. Ibid., 65.
22. Ibid.
23. Ibid., 66.
24. Ibid.
25. Ibid.
26. Ibid., 67.
27. Himmelreich describes him looking at her breasts and observing that she could "fill out a dirndl," as well as kissing her hand and stating that politicians always fall for journalists. He remained silent in the wake of the controversy, during which thousands of Twitter users, including Alice Schwarzer, began documenting everyday sexism. The hashtag #aufschrei appeared the night after the article was published and went viral. Though

Stern was criticized by some for promoting a scandal, Himmelreich was praised by other female journalists for educating the "Altherrenrunde" (gentleman's club) among politicians about the need to maintain professional distance and for making it possible for other female journalists to reveal the sexism they have confronted. A speaker for the Ministry of the Family subsequently revealed statistics from a 2004 study that 58 percent of women have been sexually harassed at least once, 42 percent of them at work. Green politician Claudia Roth observed, "Sexism is demeaning, injurious, discriminatory and not acceptable in any form." See "Sexismus-Aufschrei nach einem Politiker-Portrait," *Welt*, 25 January 2013, http://www.welt.de/newsticker/news3/article113144790/Sexismus-Aufschrei-nach-einem-Politiker-Portraet.html.
28. "Dossier: Auf einer Welle," 65.
29. Barbara Duncan, "Searching for a Home Place: Online in the Third Wave," in *Different Wavelengths: Studies of the Contemporary Women's Movement*, ed. Jo Reger (New York: Routledge, 2005).
30. Barbara Duncan, "Searching for a Home Place: Online in the Third Wave," 167, 161.
31. More recently, Donna Haraway's work *When Species Meet* (2008) understands the practice of care in a much broader context—i.e., across species. Her model focuses as much on the object as the caregiver and requires us to cultivate extensive knowledge of the former, as well as of our own political, ethical, and affective investments in it. In a related vein, Gilligan's work was motivated by the universalizing tendencies among philosophers that bracketed attention to individual subjectivities, as well as the kinds of particularities that Haraway calls attention to. See Donna Haraway, *When Species Meet* (Minneapolis: University of Minnesota Press, 2008); Carol Gilligan, *In Another Voice: Psychological Theory and Women's Development* (Cambridge: Harvard University Press, 1982).
32. Duncan, "Searching for a Home Place," 175.
33. Ibid., 168.
34. Ibid., 164.
35. Emily Nussbaum, "The Rebirth of the Feminist Manifesto," *New York Magazine* (7 November 2011), http://nymag.com/news/features/feminist-blogs-2011-11/.
36. Hester Baer has emphasized the importance of both the translocal and transnational in the articulation of feminist actions relating to body politics. Specifically, such actions "reveal the pervasive, structural nature of sexual violence, linking the specific, local stories of individual women to larger narratives of inequality." Equally important, Baer argues for recent German feminist activism in digital and street-based form making visible "the precarity of feminism itself" in a neoliberal world, thus establishing the grounds for a "collective feminist politics beyond the realm of the self-styled individ-

ual." See "Redoing Feminism: Digital Activism, Body Politics, and Neoliberalism," *Feminist Media Studies* 16.1 (2016), 18, 19.
37. Nussbaum, "The Rebirth of the Feminist Manifesto."
38. Hemmings, "Why Stories Matter," 13.
39. "'Mädchenmannschaft' ausgewechselt," Zerstrittenes Feminismus-Blog, *taz.de*, 23 October 2012, http://www.taz.de/!5081236/.
40. Despite this positive outlook, a *taz* article documented continued inequities in online forums. Women bloggers in Germany apparently write less about topics that speak to a wide audience, such as politics, economics, technology, and the media, and 75 percent of female bloggers write instead in diary form. Cultural theorist Klaus Schönberger argues that "women feel less empowered to speak publicly.... That is the result of years of cultural influence" ("Wie im echten Leben," *taz.de*, 17 August 2010, http://www.taz.de/!5137261/). In "Frauen klicken anders," a *Süddeutsche Zeitung* journalist Ron Steinke described the audience at the 2010 web conference "Re-Publica" as consisting of only 20 percent women. He cites media critic Jan-Hinkrik Schmidt's observation that "almost exclusively male bloggers receive wider attention," and that of the top one hundred blogs in Germany about media, the politics of the web, and technology, hardly twenty are run by women ("Frauen klicken anders," *Süddeutsche Zeitung*, 15 April 2010, http://www.sueddeutsche.de/digital/weibliche-blogger-frauen-klicken-anders-1.16001).
41. "'Mädchenmannschaft' ausgewechselt."
42. Beverly M. Weber's work on Muslim women in German culture is very relevant here. She argues that racialized constructions of them always in relation to gender violence obscures and even limits their participation in politics, economics, and knowledge production. Equally important, only when it becomes possible to imagine "minoritized and racialized women as political and economic actors who produce knowledge does potential exist for wide-ranging political alliances that can organize around economic and political issues that impact women of immigrant heritage and Muslim women in Germany." See *Violence and Gender in the "New" Europe: Islam in German Culture* (New York: Palgrave Macmillian, 2013), 5, 10. Elsewhere she has written about Muslim women's digital activism, particularly by the journalist Kübra Gümüsay, the first "hijabi columnist" in Germany. As Weber argues, her digital activism "functions by taking the risk to both expose and reconfigure the very conditions under which she is visible and comprehensible to her publics." See "Kübra Gümüsay, Muslim Digital Feminism and the Politics of Visuality in Germany," *Feminist Media Studies* 16.1 (2016), 101.
43. After people of color angrily left a podium discussion on September 22 to celebrate Mädchenmannschaft's fifth birthday, five bloggers apologized, observing, "There were a whole number of racist incidents in the discussion about slutwalks, whereupon women of color left the room and the

discussion was finally broken off... we are sorry for tolerating these events, our inappropriate response and our inability to establish a safe place for people of color. That was completely unacceptable and representative of limited awareness and preparation." ("Eine ganz eigene Diktion," http://jungle-world.com/artikel/2012/42/46413.html).
44. "'Mädchenmannschaft' ausgewechselt." The original German reads, "Ich fand es gut, über möglichen Rassismus zu diskutieren. Ich fand es gut, das wir von einem etwas naiven freundlichen Feminismus a la Alphamädchen wegkamen, den ich heute auch kritisieren würde. Aber die Selbstbezichtigung war mal wieder ein Diktat und keine Diskussion.... Das is jetzt ein radikal queerfeministischer Blog mit ausschließender Sprache. Das ist für die meisten Menschen schwer zugänglich."
45. See Nadine Lantzsch, "Stellungnahme zum *taz*-Artikel über die Mädchenmannschaft," Medienlite (blog), 23 October 2012, http://medienelite.de/?s=Stellungnahme+zum+taz&submit=Suche. The original German reads, "Weg vom alphamädchen-feminismus, der in erster linie gut situierten heteras zugute kommt und strukturfragen nicht mehr stellt, zu mehr machtkritik, zu mehr aufnahme von feministischen diskursen und konfliktlinien, die es bereits vor 20, 30, 40, 100 Jahren gab... dies führt weder zu einer abschottung, noch zu elitärem gedünkel, sondern ermöglicht in erster linie konstruktives und produktives feministisches arbeiten... konfliktlinien des feminismus traten schon immer dort auf, wo die mit besserem sozialen stand nicht mehr bereit waren, ein teil ihrer privilegien abzugeben. Für die sache stattdessen haben die leute ein geschichtswissen installiert, das bis heute viele wichtige kämpfe unsichtbar macht, negiert und gewaltvoll unterdrückt. Dieses geschichtswissen nennt sich "drei-wellen-modell"... ich frage mich, wie ein feminismus auf eine hoch komplexe und widersprüchliche gesellschaft reagieren will, der mit einfachen antworten daherkommt, die nur ein bruchteil der bevölkerung überhaupt tangieren, wenn nicht gar sich anschlussfähig macht für repressionen und backlash, die seit mehreren jahren auch in Deutschland vorherrschen und jedes feministische projekt zusehen muss, dass es arbeitsfähig bleiben kann. Ich frage mich, was daran nicht elitär und ausschließend sein sollte. ich frage mich, was das noch mit feminismus zu tun hat. Dieses gepuderte kleinklein mit einem konservativen politikverständnis ohne einen funken solidarität."
46. See Courtney E. Martin and Vanessa Valenti, "The Future of Online Feminism," Infographic, *FemFuture: Online Revolution*, vol. 8, Valenti Martin Media, 2012, http://bcrw.barnard.edu/publications/femfuture-online-revolution/.
47. Alice Schwarzer made a useful observation in this regard by emphasizing the difference between Islam and "Islamismus," the latter being a "misuse of the religion Islam as part of a strategy for political power" ("Wieder mal zurück auf Null?" *EMMA* [January/February 2013], 7). When both entities are conflated, any critique of Islam becomes a form of racism. In the same

editorial she also posits sexism as the basic grid upon which all forms of inequality rest. Should this foundation be disturbed, she argues, all other kinds of contradictions would "fall like a house of cards" (ibid.). Here one can't help but think of male activists during the student movement who posited class relations as the central problem and everything else, including gender equality, as secondary.
48. For a comprehensive view of these arguments, see Carrie Smith-Prei and Maria Stehle, *Awkward Politics: Technologies of Popfeminist Activism* (Montreal: McGill-Queen's University Press, 2016).
49. Carrie Smith-Prei and Maria Stehle, "WiG-Trouble: Awkwardness and Feminist Politics," *Women in German Yearbook* 30 (2014), 217.
50. Ibid., 213.
51. Hemmings, "Why Stories Matter," 3
52. See Ronja von Rönne, "Warum der Feminismus mich anekelt," *Welt,* 8 April 2015, http://www.welt.de/kultur/article139269797/Warum-mich-der-Feminismus-anekelt.html.
53. Other invidious claims include that advertising with naked women is simply a response to market demands, that the sexism that led to the #aufschrei campaign feels too trifling to warrant a vituperative response, and that feminists see themselves as victims and have become "charity" workers for the underprivileged.

Bibliography

Abel, Marco. *The Counter-Cinema of the Berlin School*. Rochester: Camden House, 2013.
——. "Imaging Germany: The (Political) Cinema of Christian Petzold." In *The Collapse of the Conventional: German Film and Its Politics at the Turn of the Twenty-First Century,* ed. Jaimey Fisher and Brad Prager. Detroit: Wayne State University Press, 2010.
Akin, Fatih, dir. 2007. *The Edge of* Heaven. Anka Film. DVD, Strand Leasing, 2008.
Althen, Michael. "Polit-Porno: 'Der Baader-Meinhof-Komplex.'" Frankfurter Allgemeine Zeitung, 24 September 2008. http://www.faz.net/aktuell/feuilleton/kino/video-filmkritiken/video-filmkritik-polit-porno-der-baader-meinhof-komplex-1105334.html.
Ayim, May. "Das Jahr 1990: Heimat und Einheit aus afro-deutscher Perspektive." In *Euer Schweigen schützt euch nicht. Audre Lorde und die Schwarze Frauenbewegung in Deutschland,* ed. Peggy Piesche. Berlin: Orlanda Frauenverlag, 2012.
Baer, Hester. "Redoing Feminism within and outside the Neoliberal Academy. *Women in German Yearbook* 30 (2014), 197–208.
——. "German Feminism in the Age of Neoliberalism: Jana Hensel and Elisabeth Raether's *Neue deutsche Mädchen*." *German Studies Review* 35.2 (May 2012), 355–74.
——. "Digital Activism, Body Politics, and Neoliberalism." *Feminist Media Studies* 16.1 (2016), 17–34.
——. "Sex, Death, and Motherhood in the Eurozone: Contemporary Women's Writing in German." *World Literature Today* 86.3 (May 2012), 59–65.
Baldauf, Anette, and Katharina Weingartner, eds. *Lips. Tits. Hits. Power? Popkultur und Feminismus*. Vienna: Folio, 1998.
Bartel, Heike. "Porn or PorNO: Approaches to Pornography in Elfriede Jelinek's *Lust* and Charlotte Roche's *Feuchtgebiete*." In *German Text Crimes: Writers Accused, from the 1950s to the 2000s,* ed. Tom Cheesman. Amsterdam: Rodopi, 2013.
Baßler, Moritz. *Der deutsche Pop-Roman. Die neuen Archivisten*. München: Verlag C. H. Beck, 2002.

Baumgardner, Jennifer, and Amy Richards. *Manifesta: Young Women, Feminism, and the Future.* New York: Farrar, Straus and Giroux, 2000.

———, eds. *Grass Roots: A Field Guide for Feminist Activism.* New York: Farrar, Straus and Giroux, 2005.

Becker-Cantarino, Barbara. "The Politics of Memory and Gender: What Happened to Second-Wave Feminism in Germany?" *German Life and Letters* 67.4 (October 2014), 604–15.

Bell, James. "After the Revolution." Interview with Bernd Eichinger. *Sight and Sound* 12.26 (December 2008).

Berger, Melody, ed. *We Don't Need Another Wave: Dispatches from the Next Generation of Feminists.* Emery, CA: Seal Press, 2006.

Berlant, Lauren. *Cruel Optimism.* Durham: Duke University Press, 2011.

Borcholte, Andreas. "Eichingers 'Baader-Meinhof-Komplex': Die Terror-Illustrierte." *Spiegel Online,* 18 September 2008. http://www.spiegel.de/kultur/kino/eichingers-baader-meinhof-komplex-die-terror-illustrierte-a-578786-2.html.

Bornhak, Achim, dir. 2007. *Eight Miles High.* Babelsberg Film. DVD, MPI, 2007.

Brady, Kate. "Sexism is Germany's Hidden Secret." *Women Talk Online.* 10 February 2015. http://blogs.dw.com/womentalkonline/2015/02/10/opinion-sexism-is-germanys-hidden-secret/.

Bräunert, Svea. *Gespenster Geschichten. Der linke Terrorismus der RAF und die Künste.* Berlin: Kulturverlag Kadmos, 2015.

Butler, Judith. *Excitable Speech: A Politics of the Performative.* New York: Routledge, 1997.

———. *Gender Trouble: Feminism and the Subversion of Identity.* New York: Routledge, 1999.

———. *The Psychic Life of Power: Theories in Subjection.* Stanford: Stanford University Press, 1997.

Chivoiu, Oana M. "Childless Motherhood: The Geopolitics of Maternal Bliss in Fatih Akin's *The Edge of Heaven.*" In *Disjointed Perspectives on Motherhood,* ed. Catalina Florina Florescu. New York: Lexington Books, 2013.

Colvin, Sarah. *Ulrike Meinhof and West German Terrorism: Language, Violence, and Identity.* Rochester, NY: Camden House, 2009.

Degler, Frank, and Ute Paulokat. *Neue Deutsche Popliteratur.* Paderborn: Wilhelm Fink Verlag, 2008.

del Rio, Elena. *Deleuze and the Cinema of Performance: Powers of Affection.* Edinburgh: Edinburgh University Press, 2008.

Detloff, Madelyn. "Mean Spirits: The Politics of Contempt between Feminist Generations." *Hypatia* 12.3 (Summer 1997), 76–99.

Dicker, Rory, and Alison Piepmeier. *Catching a Wave: Reclaiming Feminism for the 21st Century.* Boston: Northeastern University Press, 2003.

"Die 68erinnen." *EMMA* (May/June 2008), 74–101.

"Die Täter leben in absoluter Inzucht. Spiegel-Interview mit der Frankfurter Kriminologin Professor Helga Einsele." *Der Spiegel* 31.33 (8 August 1977), 28–29.
Disch, Peter. "Alice Schwarzer verkauft ihre Seele." *Badische Zeitung*, 5 September 2010. http://www.badische-zeitung.de/debatte-x3x/alice-schwarzer-verkauft-ihre-seele--35085994.html.
Dittgen, Andrea. "Radical Chic." *Sight and Sound* 18.12 (December 2008), 24–26.
Doherty, Thomas. "Douglas Sirk: Magnificent Obsession." *Chronicle of Higher Education* 49.12 (15 November 2002), B16–B18.
Dorn, Thea. *Die neue F-Klasse. Wie die Zukunft von Frauen gemacht wird.* Hamburg: Piper, 2007.
Douthat, Ross. "I Love Lena." *New York Times*, 4 October 2014. http://www.nytimes.com/2014/10/05/opinion/sunday/ross-douthat-i-love-lena.html?_r=0.
"Alice Schwarzer zu Charlotte Roche. Du hast nicht die Lösung. Du hast das Problem." *Der Tagesspiegel*, 16 August 2011, http://www.tagesspiegel.de/kultur/alice-schwarzer-zu-charlotte-roche-du-hast-nicht-die-loesung-du-hast-das-problem/4504560.html.
Duncan, Barbara. "Searching for a Home Place: Online in the Third Wave." *Different Wavelengths: Studies of the Contemporary Women's Movement*, ed. Jo Reger. New York: Routledge, 2005.
Dünnebier, Anna. "Die Stadt, der Turm, die Frauen." FrauenMediaTurm, 28 January 2012. http://www.frauenmediaturm.de/frauenmediaturm/bayenturm/geschichte/.
"Editorial 4/13," *Missy Magazine* (April 2013), 5.
Edel, Uli, dir. 2008. *The Baader Meinhof Complex*. Constantin Film. DVD, mpi media group, 2010.
Eismann, Sonja. "Big Sis." *Missy Magazine* (April 2013), 71–73.
———. "Dossier: Auf einer Welle." *Missy Magazine* (April 2013), 60–70.
———, ed. *Hot Topic: Popfeminismus heute*. Mainz: Ventil, 2007.
El Hissy, Maha. "Transnationaler Grenzverkehr in Fatih Akins *Gegen die Wand* und *Auf der anderen Seite*." In *Von der nationalen zur internationalen Literatur: Transkulturelle deutschsprachige Literatur und Kultur im Zeitalter globaler Migration*, ed. Helmut Schmitz. Amsterdam: Rodopi: 2009.
El-Tayeb, Fatima. *European Others: Queering Ethnicity in Postnational Europe*. Minneapolis: University of Minnesota Press, 2011.
"EMMA Meets Mädchen. Kein Bock auf Spaltung! Wir müssen reden." *EMMA* (Spring 2011), 20–27.
Eren, Mine. "Cosmopolitan Filmmaking: Fatih Akin's *In July* and *Head-On*." In *Turkish German Cinema in the New Millennium: Sites, Sounds, Screens*, ed. Sabine Hake and Barbara Mennel. New York: Berghahn Books, 2012.
Ernst, Thomas. *Popliteratur*. Hamburg: Europäische Verlagsanstalt, (2002) 2005.
Fassbinder, Rainer Werner. "Imitation of Life: On the Films of Douglas Sirk." In *The Anarchy of the Imagination: Interviews, Essays, Notes*. Rainer Werner

Fassbinder, ed. Michael Töteberg and Leo A. Lensing; trans. Krishna Winston. Baltimore: The Johns Hopkins University Press, 1992.

Ferree, Myra Marx. *Varieties of Feminism: German Gender Politics in Global Perspective*. Stanford: Stanford University Press, 2012.

"Feuchtgebiete am Theater—vom Terror der Körperlichkeit." *Süddeutsche Zeitung*, 30 September 2008. http://www.sueddeutsche.de/kultur/feuchtgebiete-am-theater-vom-terror-der-koerperlichkeit-1.698205?img=4.0.

Fisher, Jaimey. "Globalization as Uneven Geographical Development: The 'Creative' Destruction of Place and Fantasy in Christian Petzold's Ghost Trilogy." *Seminar: A Journal of Germanic Studies* 47.4 (November 2011), 447–64.

Freeman, Elizabeth, *Time Binds: Queer Temporalities, Queer Histories* (Durham: Duke University Press, 2010).

Freund, Andrea. "Echt der Hammer." *EMMA* (March/April 2003), 88–89.

Frey, Mattias. *Postwall German Cinema: History, Film History, and Cinephilia*. New York: Berghahn Books, 2014.

Fuss, Diana. *Identification Papers*. New York: Routledge, 1995.

Gebhardt, Miriam. *Alice im Niemandsland. Wie die deutsche Frauenbewegung die Frauen verlor*. Munich: Verlagsgruppe Random House, 2012.

Gemünden, Gerd. *Framed Visions: Popular Culture, Americanization, and the Contemporary German and Austrian Imagination*. Ann Arbor: University of Michigan Press, 1998.

Genz, Stephanie. "Third Way/ve: The Politics of Postfeminism." *Feminist Theory* 7.3 (2006), 333–53.

Gilligan, Carol. *In Another Voice: Psychological Theory and Women's Development*. Cambridge: Harvard University Press, 1982.

Gleba, Kerstin, and Eckhard Schumacher. *Pop seit 1964*. Cologne: Kiepenheuer & Witsch, 2007.

"Gleichstellung. 'Ziemlich lässig.'" *Der Spiegel* 9 (27 February 2012). http://www.spiegel.de/spiegel/print/d-84162299.html.

Götürk, Deniz. "Mobilität und Stillstand im Weltkino digital." In *Kultur als Ereignis. Fatih Akins Film Auf der anderen Seite als transkulturelle Narration*, ed. Özkan Ezli. Bielefeld: transcript Verlag, 2010.

———. "Sound Bridges: Transnational Mobility as Ironic Melodrama." In *European Cinema in Motion: Migrant and Diasporic Film in Contemporary Europe*, ed. Daniela Berghahn and Claudia Sternberg. New York: Palgrave Macmillan, 2010.

———. "World Cinema Goes Digital: Looking at Europe from the Other Shore." In *Turkish German Cinema in the New Millennium: Sites, Sounds, Screens*, ed. Sabine Hake and Barbara Mennel. New York: Berghahn Books, 2012.

Haaf, Meredith, Susanne Klingner, and Barbara Streidl. *Wir Alphamädchen. Warum Feminismus das Leben schöner macht*. Hamburg: Hoffmann und Campe Verlag, 2008.

Hage, Volker. "Die Enkel kommen." *Der Spiegel* 41 (11 October 1999), 244–54.

Hake, Sabine, and Barbara Mennel, eds. *Turkish German Cinema in the New Millennium: Sites, Sounds, Screens*. New York: Berghahn Books, 2012.
Haraway, Donna. *When Species Meet*. Minneapolis: University of Minnesota Press, 2008.
Harding, James M. "The Simplest Surrealist Act: Valerie Solanas and the (Re)Assertion of Avantgarde Priorities." *TDR: The Drama Review: A Journal of Performance Studies* 45.4 (Winter 2001), 142–62.
Hark, Sabine. "Disputed Territory: Feminist Studies in Germany and Its Queer Discontents." In *Queering America*, special issue of *Amerikastudien / American Studies* 46.1 (2001), 87–103.
Harris, Anita. *Next Wave Cultures: Feminism, Subcultures, Activism*. New York: Routledge, 2008.
Harvey, David. *A Brief History of Neoliberalism*. Oxford: Oxford University Press, 2005.
Hemmings, Clare. *Why Stories Matter: The Political Grammar of Feminist Theory*. Durham: Duke University Press, 2011.
Hennig von Lange, Alexa. *Relax*. Hamburg: Rowohlt Verlag, 1999.
Henry, Astrid. *Not My Mother's Sister: Generational Conflict and Third-Wave Feminism*. Bloomington: Indiana University Press, 2004.
———. "Solitary Sisterhood: Individualism Meets Collectivity in Feminism's Third Wave." In *Different Wavelengths: Studies of the Contemporary Women's Movement*, ed. Jo Reger. New York: Routledge, 2005.
Hensel, Jana, and Elisabeth Raether. *Neue deutsche Mädchen*. Reinbek bei Hamburg: Rowohlt, 2008.
Hermann, Eva. *Das Eva-Prinzip. Für eine neue Weiblichkeit*. Munich: Goldmann, 2007.
Heywood, Leslie, and Jennifer Drake, eds. *Third Wave Agenda: Being Feminist, Doing Feminism*. Minneapolis: University of Minnesota Press, 1997.
Hillman, Roger, and Vivian Silvey. "Remixing Hamburg: Transnationalism in Fatih Akin's *Soul Kitchen*." In *Turkish German Cinema in the New Millennium: Sites, Sounds, Screens*, ed. Sabine Hake and Barbara Mennel. New York: Berghahn Books, 2012.
Hinrichsen, Jens. "Im Zwischenreich. Christian Petzolds Gespenster-Trilogie: Passagen in Schattenzonen deutscher Realität." *Film-Dienst* 60.19 (13 September 2007), 6–8.
Hofer, Stefanie. "'Memory Talk': Terrorism, Trauma, and Generational Struggle in Petzold's *The State I Am In* and von Trotta's *Marianne and Juliane*." *Film Criticism* 34.1 (2009), 36–57.
———. "'... von der Unmöglichkeit der Gegenwart': Geschlecht, Generation und Nation in Sanders-Brahms *Deutschland, bleiche Mutter* und Petzolds *Die innere Sicherheit*," *German Life and Letters* 62.2 (April 2009), 180.
Hoffmann, Christiane, and Rene Pfister. "A Feminist View of Cologne: 'The Current Outrage is Very Hypocritical,'" Interview with Alice Schwarzer and Anne

Wizorek. *Spiegel Online*, 21 January 2016. http://www.spiegel.de/internati onal/germany/german-feminists-debate-cologne-attacks-a-1072806.html.
Hofmann, Niklas. "Neu, jung, selbstbewusst." *Süeddeutsche Zeitung*, 7 November 2011. http://www.sueddeutsche.de/kultur/netzdepeschen-neu-jung-selbstbewusst-1.1182508.
Illies, Florian. *Generation Golf. Eine Inspektion*. Frankfurt am Main: Fischertaschenbuch Verlag, 2000.
Jaafar, Ali. "Flags and our Fathers." *Sight and Sound* 18.3 (March 2008), 9.
Jakob, Christian. "Eine ganz eigene Diktion." *Jungle World* 42.12 (18 October 2012). http://jungle-world.com/artikel/2012/42/46413.html.
Jenny, Zöe. *Das Blütenstaubzimmer (The Pollen Room)*. Munich: btb Verlag, 1999.
———. "Meine Lehrer waren pädophile Weltverbesserer." *Welt*, 14 October 2013. http://www.welt.de/kultur/literarischewelt/article120887193/Meine-Leh rer-waren-paedophile-Weltverbesserer.html.
Jervis, Lisa. "Die Dritte Welle?" *EMMA* (May/June 2008), 44–45.
Johnston, Claire. "Women's Cinema as Counter-Cinema." In *Feminist Film Theory: A Reader*, ed. Sue Thornham. New York: New York University Press, 1999.
Kauer, Katja. *Popfeminismus! Fragezeichen! Eine Einführung*. Berlin: Frank & Timme Verlag, 2009.
Kätzel, Uta. *Die 68erinnen. Porträt einer rebellischen Frauengeneration*. Berlin: Rowohlt, 2002.
Kohaut, Susanne, and Iris Möller. "Führungspositionen in der Privatwirtschaft. Frauen kommen auf den Chefetagen nicht voran." Institut für Arbeitsmarkt- und Berufsforschung, June 2010. http://www.iab.de/194/section.aspx/Pub likation/k100412a01.
Köver, Chris, Stefanie Lohaus, Julia Steinbrecher, Nicole Ibele, and Sonja Eismann. "Editorial." *Missy Magazine* (October 2008), 3.
Kracht, Christian. *Faserland*. Cologne: Kiepenheuer & Witsch, 1995.
Kraushaar, Wolfgang. *1968 als Mythos, Chiffre und Zäsur*. Hamburg: Hamburger Edition, 2000.
———. *Achtundsechzig. Eine Bilanz*. Berlin: Propyläen, 2008.
Kriest, Ulrich. "'Action Speaks Louder than Words.' Oder: Warum niemand den Film *Der Baader Meinhof Komplex* braucht. *Film-Dienst* 20 (25 September 2008), 6–9.
Kullmann, Katja. *Generation Ally. Warum es heute so kompliziert ist, eine Frau zu sein*. Frankfurt am Main: Eichhorn, 2002.
Lantzsch, Nadine. "Stellungnahme zum *taz*-Artikel über die Mädchenmannschaft." Medienlite (blog), 23 October 2012. http://medienelite.de/?s=Stell ungnahme+zum+taz&submit=Suche.
Leal, Joanne. "Troubled Parents, Angry Children: The Difficult Legacy of 1968 in Contemporary German-Language Film." In *Cinema and Social Change in*

Germany and Austria, ed. Gabriele Mueller and James M. Skidmore. Waterloo, ON: Wilfrid Laurier University Press, 2012.
Lee, Nathan. "The Life of a World-Class Sex Kitten." *New York Times*, 11 July 2008. http://www.nytimes.com/2008/07/11/movies/11eigh.html?_r=0.
Liebrand, Claudia. "Pornographische Pathografie. Charlotte Roches *Feuchtgebiete*." *Literatur für Leser* 34.1 (2011), 13–22.
Levy, Ariel. *Female Chauvinist Pigs: Women and the Rise of Raunch Culture*. New York: Free Press, 2005.
Lohaus, Stefanie, and Anne Wizorek. "Immigrants Aren't Responsible for Rape Culture in Germany." *Vice*, 8 January 2016. https://www.vice.com/read/rape-culture-germany-cologne-new-years-2016-876.
"'Mädchenmannschaft' ausgewechselt." Zerstrittenes Feminismus-Blog, *taz.de*, 23 October 2012. http://www.taz.de/!5081236/.
Marazzi, Christian, "Neoliberalism is Destroying Europe," *The Guardian*, 14 September 2010, https://www.theguardian.com/commentisfree/2010/sep/14/neoliberal-europe-union-austerity-crisis.
Martin, Courtney E., and Vanessa Valenti. "The Future of Online Feminism." Infographic. *#FemFuture: Online Revolution*, vol. 8. Valenti Martin Media, 2012. http://bcrw.barnard.edu/publications/femfuture-online-revolution/.
Mayers, Susanne. "Oh Muschilein. Charlotte Roche schreibt ein Sexbuch, und das Feuilleton vibriert. Warum die Feuchtträume einer TV-Moderatorin der Hit sind." *Zeit Online*, 6 March 2008. http://www.zeit.de/2008/11/Glosse-Literatur-Roche.
McClelland, Sara I., and Michelle Fine. "Rescuing a Theory of Adolescent Excess: Young Women and Wanting." In *Next Wave Cultures: Feminism, Subcultures, Activism*, ed. Anita Harris. New York: Routledge, 2008.
McRobbie, Angela. "Postfeminism and Popular Culture: Bridget Jones and the New Gender Regime." In *Interrogating Postfeminism: Gender and the Politics of Popular Culture*, ed. Yvonne Tasker and Diane Negra. Durham: Duke University Press, 2007.
Mehrfort, Sandra. *Popliteratur. Zum literarischen Stellenwert eines Phänomens der 1990er Jahre*. Karlsruhe: Lindemanns Bibliothek, 2008.
"Meine naive Art ist eine Marktlücke." *Süddeutsche Zeitung*, 22 April 2008. http://www.sueddeutsche.de/leben/verona-pooths-geburtstag-meine-naive-art-ist-eine-marktluecke-1.188488.
Melzer, Patricia. "Maternal Ethics and Political Violence: The 'Betrayal' of Motherhood among the Women of the RAF and June 2 Movement." *Seminar* 47.1 (February 2011), 81–102.
Mennel, Barbara. "Criss-Crossing in Global Space and Time: Fatih Akin's *The Edge of Heaven* (2007)." *Transit* 5.1 (2009). http://transit.berkeley.edu/2009/mennel/.
Merley Hill, Alexandra. "Motherhood as Performance: (Re) Negotiations of Motherhood in Contemporary German Literature." *Studies in 20th and 21st Century Literature* 35:1 (Winter 2011), 74–94.

Mikich, Sonia. "Triumph des Willens." *EMMA* (July/August 2008), 20–21.
Mikus, Birgit, and Emily Spiers, eds. "Fractured Legacies: Historical, Cultural and Political Perspectives on German Feminism." Special issue of *Oxford German Studies* 45.1 (2016).
Minioudaki, Kalliopi. "Other(s') Pop: The Return of the Repressed of Two Discourses." In *Power Up: Female Pop Art*, ed. Angela Stief and Martin Walkner. Vienna: Kunsthalle Wien, 2010, 134–43.
———. "Proto-Feminisms: Beyond the Paradox of the Woman Pop Artist." In *Seductive Subversion: Women Pop Artists 1958–1968*, ed. Sid Sachs and Kalliopi Minioudaki. New York: Abbeville Press, 2010, 90–143.
Mitchell, Juliet. *Psychoanalysis and Feminism: Freud, Reich, Laing and Women*. New York: Pantheon Books, 1974.
Mitscherlich, Margarete. "Sündenböcke." *EMMA* (November 1977), 5.
———. "Sind Frauen masochistisch?" *EMMA* (November/December 1977), 11–13.
Mohanty, Chandra Talpade. *Feminism without Borders: Decolonizing Theory, Practicing Solidarity*. Durham: Duke University Press, 2003.
Mohr, Christina. "Wie sich's für ein normales Mädchen anfühlt. In *Madonna und wir. Bekenntnisse*," ed. Kerstin Grether and Sandra Grether. Frankurt am Main: Suhrkamp, 2008.
"Monogamie—ein riesiger Fehler." *Süddeutsche Zeitung*, 21 May 2008. http://www.sueddeutsche.de/kultur/bildergalerie-nimm-mich-jetzt-auch-wenn-ich-stinke-1.218176-2.
Morgan, Robin. "Mein heimlicher Garten." *EMMA* (November/December 1977), 8–11.
Naters, Elke. *Lügen* (*Lies*). Munich: List Taschenbuch, 1999.
Nussbaum, Emily. "The Rebirth of the Feminist Manifesto." *New York Magazine*, 7 November 2011. http://nymag.com/news/features/feminist-blogs-2011-11/.
Obermaier, Uschi, and Olaf Kraemer. *High Times. Mein Wildes Leben*. Munich: Wilhelm Heyne, 2008.
O'Brien, Mary-Elizabeth. *Post-Wall German Cinema and National History: Utopianism and Dissent*. Rochester, NY: Camden House, 2012.
"Ohne dich wäre ich nicht ich." Alice Schwarzer interview with Charlotte and Liz Roche. *EMMA* (May/June 2001), 56–61.
Opitz, Michael, and Carola Opitz-Wiemers. "Vom 'literarischen Fräuleinwunder' oder 'die Enkel kommen.'" In *Deutsche Literaturgeschichte: von den Anfängen bis zur Gegenwart*, ed. Wolfgang Beutin, Klaus Ehlert, and Wolfgang Emmerich. Stuttgart: Metzler, 2001.
Pankau, Johannes G. *Pop Pop Populär. Popliteratur und Jugendkultur*. Bremen: Universitätsverlag Aschenbeck & Isenee, 2004.
Peaches. "Fuck yeah, Kathleen Hanna!" *Missy Magazine* (April 2013), 74–81.
Petzold, Christian, dir. 2000. *The State I Am In*. Schramm Film. DVD, MC One, 2000.

Piesche, Peggy, ed. *Euer Schweigen schützt euch nicht. Audre Lorde und die Schwarze Frauenbewegung in Deutschland.* Berlin: Orlanda Frauenverlag, 2012.
"Questions for Katha Pollitt: Women's Studies." Interview with Deborah Solomon. *New York Times Magazine* (23 September 2007), 17.
Rasch, Ilka. "The Generation Gap: The Reappropriation of the Red Army Faction in Contemporary German Film." In *Generational Shifts in Contemporary German Culture,* ed. Laurel Cohen-Pfister and Susanne Vees-Gulani. Rochester, NY: Camden House, 2010.
Reger, Jo, ed. *Different Wavelengths: Studies of the Contemporary Women's Movement.* New York: Routledge, 2005.
Renegar, Valerie, and Stacey K. Sowards. "Contradiction as Agency: Self-Determination, Transcendence, and Counter-Imagination in Third Wave Feminism." *Hypatia* 24.2 (Spring 2009), 1–20.
Renner, R. G. "1989 und die Folgen. Deutsche Gegenwartsgeschichte im Nachwendefilm." *Pandaemonium germanicum: Revista de Estudos Germanísticos* 16 (2010), 22–52.
Ritter, Andrea. "Die Zotenköniginnin von MuschiLand. Provokation oder neues Selbstbewusstsein—was steckt hinter dem Erfolg des Bestsellers von Charlotte Roche? Eine Expedition in die 'Feuchtgebiete' des Feminismus." *Stern,* 12 May 2008. http://www.stern.de/kultur/buecher/3-charlotte-roche-die-zotenkoenigin-von-muschiland-619765.html.
Roche, Charlotte. *Feuchtgebiete (Wetlands).* Cologne: Dumont, 2008.
———. *Schoßgebete (Wrecked).* Munich: Piper, 2011.
von Rönne, Ronja. "Warum der Feminismus mich anekelt." *Welt,* 8 April 2015. http://www.welt.de/kultur/article139269797/Warum-mich-der-Feminismus-anekelt.html.
Russo, Mary. "Female Grotesques: Carnival and Theory." In *Feminist Studies: Critical Studies,* ed. Teresa de Lauretis. Indiana: Indiana University Press, 1986.
Rutschky, Katharina. "Der Poproman-Merkmale eines unerkannten Genres." *Merkur: Deutsche Zeitschtift für Europäisches Denken* 57.2 (February 2003), 106–17.
Rutschky, Michael. *Erfahrungshunger. Ein Essay über die siebziger Jahre.* Frankfurt am Main: Fischer, 1982.
Ryzik, Melena. "A Feminist Riot That Still Inspires." *New York Times* (5 June 2011, Arts and Leisure), 20.
Sachs, Sid, and Kalliopi Minioudaki, eds. *Seductive Subversion: Women Pop Artists 1958–1968.* New York: Abbeville Press, 2010.
Scharff, Christina. *Repudiating Feminism: Young Women in a Neoliberal World.* London: Routledge, 2012.
Scheufler, Eric. "The Ghosts of Autumn Past: History, Memory, and Identity in Christian Petzold's *Die innere Sicherheit.*" *Seminar: A Journal of Germanic Studies* 47.1 (February 2011), 103–20.

Schilt, Kristen, and Elke Zobl. "Connecting the Dots: Riot Grrrls, Lady Fests, and the International Grrrl Zine Network." In *Next Wave Cultures: Feminism, Subcultures, Activism,* ed. Anita Harris, 171–92. New York: Routledge, 2008.

Schirrmacher, Frank. *Das Methusalem-Komplott.* Munich: Karl Blessing Verlag, 2004.

———. *Minimum. Vom Vergehen und Neuerstehen unserer Gemeinschaft.* Munich: Karl Blessing, 2006.

Schlaffer, Hannelore. "Die Göre—Karriere einer literarischen Figur." *Merkur: Deutsche Zeitschrift für europäisches Denken* 65.3 (March 2011), 274–79.

Schmid, Barbara. "Emanzipation. Unter Frauen." *Der Spiegel* 5 (30 January 2012). http://www.spiegel.de/spiegel/print/d-83774689.html.

Schröder, Kristina, *Danke, emanzipiert sind wir schon selber! Abschied vom Diktat der Rollenbilder.* Munich: Piper Verlag, 2012.

Schroeder, Vera. "Feminismus Light." *EMMA* (July/August 2008), 28–29.

Schumacher, Eckhard. *Gerade Eben Jetzt. Schreibweisen der Gegenwart.* Frankfurt am Main: Suhrkamp, 2003.

Schwarzer, Alice. "Die Folgen der falschen Toleranz." AliceSchwarzer.de, 5 January 2016. http://www.aliceschwarzer.de/artikel/das-sind-die-folgen-der-falschen-toleranz-331143.

———. "Ein Turm für Frauen allein." FrauenMediaTurm, July 1994. http://www.frauenmediaturm.de/frauenmediaturm/publikationen/ein-turm-fuer-frauen-allein/.

———. "Im Inneren des Walfisches." AliceSchwarzer.de, 1 May 2009. http://www.aliceschwarzer.de/artikel/unsichtbar-im-inneren-des-walfischs-263966.

———. "Mein persönliches 68." *EMMA* (May/June 2008), 76–81.

———. "Terroristinnen." *EMMA* (October 1977), 5.

———. "Worum geht es wirklich?" *EMMA* (July/August 2007), 8.

———. "Wieder mal zurück auf Null?" *EMMA* (January/February 2013). 6–7.

"Sexismus-Aufschrei nach einem Politiker-Portrait." *Welt,* 25 January 2013. http://www.welt.de/newsticker/news3/article113144790/Sexismus-Aufschrei-nach-einem-Politiker-Portraet.html.

Sichtermann, Barbara. "Ohne Kampf geht nichts." *EMMA* (September/October 2008), 42–44.

Smith-Prei, Carrie. "'Knaller-Sex für alle': Popfeminist Body Politics in Lady Bitch Ray, Charlotte Roche, and Sarah Kuttner." *Studies in 20th and 21st Century Literature* 35.1 (Winter 2011), 18–39.

———. "Satirizing the Private as Political: 1968 and Postmillennial Family Narratives." *Women in German Yearbook* 25 (2009), 76–99.

Smith-Prei, Carrie, and Maria Stehle. "The Awkward Politics of Popfeminist Literary Events: Helene Hegemann, Charlotte Roche, and Lady Bitch Ray." In *German Women's Writing in the Twenty-First Century,* ed. Hester Baer and Alexandra Merley Hill. Rochester: Camden House, 2015.

———. *Awkward Politics. Technologies of Popfeminist Activism.* Montreal: McGill-Queen's University Press, 2016.
———. "WiG-Trouble: Awkwardness and Feminist Politics." *Women in German Yearbook* 30 (2014), 209–24.
Stämpfli, Regula. "Die Scham ist vorbei." *EMMA* (January/February 2008), 60–61.
Stefan, Verena. *Häutungen.* Munich: Verlag Frauenoffensive, 1975.
"Steinem meets Riot Grrrl." *EMMA* (May/June 2008), 46–48.
Stehle, Maria."Pop-Feminist Music in Twenty-First Century Germany: Innovations, Provocations, and Failures." *Journal of Popular Music Studies* 25.2 (2013), 222–39.
———. "Pop, Porn, and Rebellious Speech: Feminist Politics and the Multi-Media Performances of Elfriede Jelinek, Charlotte Roche, and Lady Bitch Ray." *Feminist Media Studies* 12.2 (2012), 229–47.
Steinke, Ron. "Frauen klicken anders." *Süddeutsche Zeitung,* 15 April 2010. http://www.sueddeutsche.de/digital/weibliche-blogger-frauen-klicken-anders-1.16001.
Stöcker, Mirja. ed. *Das F-Wort: Feminismus ist sexy.* Königstein/Taunus: Ulrike Helmer Verlag, 2007.
Stocker, Günther. "Traumen des Aufwachsens. Drei Variationen aus der Schweizer Literatur der neunziger Jahre." *Weimarer Beiträge* 48.3 (2002), 380–98.
Strigl, Daniela. "Fräulein- und andere Wunder. Galvagni, Röggla, & Co." In *Geschlechter: Essays zur Gegenwartsliteratur,* ed. Friedbert Aspetsberger and Konstanze Fliedl. Innsbruck: Studienverlag, 2001.
Sundermeier, Jörg. "Neue deutsche Vague: Pop-Romane sind da, wo eine Heimat ist." *Jungle World* 19 (3 May 2000). http://jungle-world.com/artikel/2000/18/27872.html.
Tajder, Ana. "Wir wollten doch nur sexy sein . . . ." *EMMA* (Summer 2010), 24–25.
Tasker, Yvonne, and Diane Negra. *Interrogating Postfeminism: Gender and the Politics of Popular Culture.* Durham: Duke University Press, 2007.
"Die Terroristinnen. Frauen und Gewalt." *Der Spiegel* 31.33 (8 August 1977), 22–33.
Tisdale, Sallie. "Graphic Novel." *New York Times,* 16 April 2009. http://www.nytimes.com/2009/04/19/books/review/Tisdale-t.html?pagewanted=all.
"Unsere masochistischen Sex-Phantasien," *EMMA* (September 1977), 6–13.
"Viele unterschiedliche Strömungen in Deutschland. Stevie Schmeidel im Gespräch mit Berthold Schossig." *Deutschlandfunk,* 4 June 2015. http://www.deutschlandfunk.de/debatte-ueber-feminismus-viele-unterschiedliche-stroemungen.691.de.html?dram:article_id=321766.
Volk, Stefan. "Von der Form zum Material. Fatih Akins Spiel mit dem Genrekino in *Gegen die Wand* und *Auf der anderen Seite.*" In *Kultur als Ereignis. Fatih Akins Film* Auf der anderen Seite *als transkulturelle Narration,* ed. Özkan Ezli. Bielefeld: transcript Verlag, 2010.

Walkerdine, Valerie. *Schoolgirl Fictions*. New York: Verso, 1990.
Warnecke, Jenny. "Das ist mir zu extrem! Eine Generationen-Studie." In *Das F-Wort. Feminismus ist sexy*, ed. Mirja Stöcker. Königstein/Taunus: Ulrike Helmer Verlag, 2007.
Waters, Sarah. "Introduction: 1968 in Memory and Place." In *Cultural History and Literary Imagination*. Vol. 16, *Memories of 1968: International Perspectives*, ed. Ingo Cornils and Sarah Waters. Brussels: Peter Lang, 2010.
Weber, Beverly M. *Violence and Gender in the "New" Europe: Islam in German Culture*. New York: Palgrave, 2013.
Weigel, Sigrid. "'Generation' as Symbolic Form: On the Genealogical Discourse of Memory since 1945." *Germanic Review* 77.4 (Fall 2002), 264–77.
"Wie im echten Leben." *taz.de*, 17 August 2010. http://www.taz.de/!5137261/.
"Wir tragen Größe 46." *Zeit Online*, 9 September 1999. http://www.zeit.de/1999/37/199937.reden_stuckrad_k.xml.
Wolf, Yvonne. "Alexa Hennig von Lange." In *Fräuleinwunder literarisch. Literatur zu Beginn des 21. Jahrhunderts*, ed. Christiane Caemmerer, Walter Delabar, and Helga Meise. Frankfurt am Main: Peter Lang, 2005, 85–107.
Zachau, Reinhard. "Death Images in *The Baader Meinhof Komplex*." *Glossen* 33 (November 2011). http://blogs.dickinson.edu/glossen/archive/most-recent-issue-glossen-332011/reinhard-zachau-glossen-33/.
Zeh, Juli. "Wer schlau ist, spielt mit. Alice Schwarzer, Charlotte Roche und Eva Hermann. Wie Frauen im Feminismus ihr Auskommen sichern." *Süddeutsche Zeitung*, 17 May 2010. http://www.sueddeutsche.de/leben/feminismus-debatte-wer-schlau-ist-spielt-mit-1.194195.
Zylka, Jenni. "Schleimporno gegen Hygienezwang." *taz.de*, 28 February 2008. http://www.taz.de/!13560/.

Index

Abel, Marco, 170, 171, 181, 182, 200n8, 11, 201n23, 202n35
    The Counter-Cinema of the Berlin School, 200n12, 202n32
Ade, Maren, 170
Adorno, Theodor, 226
AK, Party, 188
Akin, Fatih
    Crossing the Bridge: The Sound of Istanbul, 203n43, 204n49
    Head On, 168, 204n49
    In July, 187, 204n49
    Short Sharp Shock, 186
    Soul Kitchen, 187
    The Cut, 168
    The Edge of Heaven, 15–17, 159–60, 168–69, 172–74, 176, 183, 184–99, 203n43, 204n49, 223, 228, 229
Albers, Anni, 69
Albrecht, Susanne, 142
Ally McBeal, 40–41, 60n51
Althen, Michael, 161n17
Anderson, Benedict, 217
Appiah, Anthony Kwame, 187
Arab Spring, 225
Arslan, Thomas, 170
Arzner, Dorothy. *See Dance, Girl, Dance,* 199n5
Ataturk, 188
#aufschrei, 7, 21n4, 214, 216, 232n27
#ausnahmslos, 7, 20n3
Aust, Stefan, 138, 162n26
Axell, Evelyne, 156
Ayim, May, 5, 22n13

Baader, Andreas, 137, 142, 143, 144, 145, 147, 158, 202n24

Bachmann, Ingeborg
    Malina, 127n14
    "Todesartenzyklus", 127n14
Baer, Hester, 4, 22n12, 47, 50; 57n11, 14, 21; 62n68, 63n75, 78; 211, 233n36
Bakhtin, Mikhail, 86, 220
Baldauf, Anette
    Lips. Tits. Hits. Power? Popkultur und Feminismus, 42–43, 46, 60n56, 61n57, 101
Bardot, Brigitte, 153
Bartel, Heike, 127n18
Barth, Nadine, 66, 67
Baßler, Moritz
    Der deutsche Pop-Roman: Die neuen Archivisten, 51, 63–64n79, 72–73
Bates, Norman, 91
Bauhaus, 69
Baumgardner, Jennifer
    Grassroots: A Field Guide for Feminist Activism, 65n91; *Manifesta: Young Women, Feminism, and the Future,* 50, 65n91
Bayenturm, 25–28. *See also* FrauenMediaTurm
Becker-Cantarino, Barbara, 19, 23n21, 24n43, 54, 65n88, 89, 208, 230n2
Beguine movement, 27–28, 206
Bell, James, 162n29
Belmondo, Jean Paul, 142
Berg, Sybille, 68, 95n9
Berger, Melody
    We Don't Need Another Wave: Dispatches from the Next Generation of Feminists, 65n91
Bergman, Ingrid, 91

Berlant, Lauren
    Cruel Optimism, 16, 24n40, 181, 182, 183, 195, 202n28, 36
Berlin School of filmmakers, 170
Bessing, Joachim
    Tristesse Royale, 68, 69, 124
Beuschheuer, Else, 68
Biene Maja, 178
Bild Zeitung, 39, 59n47, 210
Biolek, Alfred, 125n5
Bitch, 46, 211
Bitomsky, Hartmut, 170
Bockhorn, Dieter, 150, 154, 155, 156
Bonnie and Clyde, 142
Borchelte, Andreas, 161n16, 162n27
Bornhak, Achim
    Eight Miles High, 14, 15, 133, 134, 149–59
Boty, Pauline, 69, 153, 156
Brady, Kate, 58n22
Brando, Marlon, 142
Brandt, Willy, 162n23
Bräunert, Svea
    Gespenster Geschichten: Der linke Terrorismus der RAF und die Künste, 161n20
Breathless, 142
Brecht, Bertolt, 169, 182
Breitband, 221
Brinkmann, Rolf Dieter, 68, 95n9
Brüderle, Rainer, 216
Büchner, Georg
    Lenz, 127n14
Bust, 46, 210, 217
Bust.com, 218, 219
Butler, Judith, 11, 44, 50, 73, 93, 111, 124, 134, 151, 218
    Excitable Speech: A Politics of the Performative, 37, 59n36, 41, 61n61, 125n3, 160n9
    Gender Trouble: Feminism and the Subversion of Identity, 10, 12, 34–38, 58n31, 59n33, 37, 65n92, 153
    The Psychic Life of Power, 80, 96n27

Casati, Rebecca, 68, 95n9
Chancer, Lynn, 58n30
Cheesman, Tom
    German Text Crimes: Writers Accused from the 1950s to the 2000s, 127n18
Chesler, Phyllis, 111
Chicks on Speed, 52, 60n53, 232n17
Chivoiu, Oana M., 199, 205n59, 64
Chronicle of Higher Education, 200n10
Close, Glenn, 101
Cobain, Kurt, 75
Cohn-Bendit, Daniel, 101
Cologne Assaults, 1, 4, 5
Colvin, Sarah
    Ulrike Meinhof and West German Terrorism, 164n43
Connell, Raewyn, 57n11
Crimp, Douglas, 10

Dardenne, Jean-Pierre and Luce
    La Promesse, 202n36
    Rosetta, 202n36
Darling, Candy, 148
Dean, James, 142, 153
Debates of 2008, 6, 7, 12, 14, 17, 44, 53, 66, 103, 104, 198, 209, 213, 214, 231n13
Degler, Frank
    Neue deutsche Popliteratur, 73, 83, 95n8, 96n15, 97n32, 98n35
Del Rio, Elena, 183
    Deleuze and the Cinema of Performance: Powers of Affection, 202n33
Delauney-Terk, Sonia, 69
Delay, Jan
    "The Sons of Stammheim," 136
Deleuze, Gilles, 171, 182, 183
Demography Debate, 12, 30–31, 74
Der Spiegel, 136, 140, 141, 142, 162n26
Derrida, Jacques
    Spectors of Marx, 131
Detloff, Madelyn, 6, 23n18, 111, 117, 128n25, 129n42
Dicker, Rory
    Catching a Wave: Reclaiming Feminism for the 21st Century, 58n23
Die Braut, 60n53

Die Welt, 77, 228
Die Zeit, 106
Dietrich, Marlene, 94n1
Disch, Peter, 59n47
Dittgen, Andrea, 162n29
Doherty, Thomas, 170, 200n10
Dohm, Hedwig, 21n7
Dorn, Thea
    The New F-Class. How the Future Will Be Made By Women, 44, 46, 61n59
Dörrie, Doris, 24n39
Douthat, Ross, 74, 96n16
Drake, Jennifer
    Third Wave Agenda: Being Feminist, Doing Feminism, 60n50, 55, 62n67
Drechsler, Clara, 95n9, 213
Duncan, Barbara, 217, 218, 219, 233n29, 30, 32
Dunham, Lena
    Girls, 74
    Not That Kind of Girl, 74
Dünnebier, Anna, 28, 56n1, 6
Dutschke, Rudy, 137–38
Duve, Karen, 66, 68
    Regenroman, 67
Dylan, Bob, 145, 146

Ecriture feminine, 108
Edel, Uli
    The Baader Meinhof Complex, 14, 15, 133, 134–149, 150, 151, 158, 162n25
Effie Briest, 96n15
Eichinger, Bernd, 139, 140, 150, 162n25, 163n40
Einsele, Helga, 163n39
Eismann, Sonja
    Hot Topic: Popfeminism Today, 12, 17, 24n36, 44, 45, 46, 47, 47, 51, 62n65, 103
    Missy Magazine, 46–47, 209, 210, 230n7
El Hissy, Maha, 203n43
El-Tayeb, Fatima
    European Others: Queering Ethnicity in Postcolonial Europe, 5, 22n15
"Electric Indigo female pressure," 232n17

Emin, Tracy, 231n9
EMMA, 12, 17, 21n5, 27, 39, 45, 47, 48, 53, 54, 56n2, 101–04, 113–14, 115, 123, 125, 141, 152, 165n55, 206, 208, 210, 213, 214, 224, 230n8, 231n9, 231n13
Ensslin, Gudrun, 137, 142, 143, 144, 146–47, 148, 158, 164n47, 48, 49
Enzensberger, Hans Magnus, 135
Eren, Mine, 204n48
Ernst, Thomas
    Popliteratur, 95n9
Estrich, Susan
    Sex and Power, 58n23
European Union, 17, 20, 33, 184, 189, 193
Export, Valie
    "Action Pants: Genital Panic", 157
    "Tap and Touch Cinema", 157

Farocki, Harun, 170
Fassbinder, Rainer Werner, 16, 186, 193, 200n7
    Ali, Fear Eats the Soul, 170, 193
    Bundesrepublik-Trilogie, 15, 169
    Die Ehe der Maria Braun, 169, 204n51
    Lola, 169
    Veronika Voss, 169
Feldbusch, Verona, 2, 11, 38, 43–44, 46
    Peep!, 40, 60n49
    Verona's World, 42
Felman, Shoshana, 37, 125n3
FEMEN, 208, 210, 217, 218, 221–22, 225, 231n9
Femfuture report, 2012, 224
Feministing.com, 62n72, 221
Ferch, Heino, 161n23
Fichte, Hubert, 68
Fine, Michelle, 126n13
Firestone, Shulamith, 218
Fisher, Jaimey, 171, 200n14, 202n35
FKK (freikörperkultur), 145, 155
"Flittchen Records," 232n17
Foucault, Michel, 171
Frank, Anne, 175
Frankfurter Allgemeine Zeitung, 39, 161n17
Frauenjahrbuch, 33
FrauenMediaTurm, 25–28, 29, 30, 56n4, 206–07

"Frauenquote," 28
Fräuleinwunder, 66, 75, 94n1
Freeman, Elizabeth
  Time Binds: Queer Temporalities, Queer Histories, 131–132, 133, 160n1
Freud, Sigmund
  "Mourning and Melancholia", 80
Frey, Mattias, 136
  Postwall German Cinema, Film History, and Cinephilia, 161n19, 164n47
Friday, Nancy
  My Secret Garden, 114
Fuss, Diana
  Identification Papers, 9–11, 23n24, 111, 112, 128n27, 134, 160n8

Ganz, Bruno, 161n23
Gebhardt, Miriam
  Alice in No-Man's Land: How the German Women's Movement Lost the Women, 4, 22n11, 61n60
Gemünden, Gerd
  Framed Visions: Popular Culture, Americanization, and the Contemporary German and Austrian Imagination, 51
Gender mainstreaming, 33
Genz, Stephanie, 47
Gerhardt, Christina, 161n14
German Democratic Republic, 135
Ghosh, Palesh, 96n25
Gilligan, Carol
  In Another Voice: Psychological Theory and Women's Development, 217, 233n31
Gleba, Kerstin
  Pop seit 1946, 95n9, 95n11
Goethe, Johann Wolfgang von, 73, 173, 176, 187, 190
  Die Leiden des jungen Werther, 176, 188
Goetz, Rainald, 95n9
Göktürk, Deniz, 185, 203n44, 204n47, 204n49
Gosling, Ryan, 218
Graves, Peter J., 94n2

Green Party, 34, 77
Grether, Kerstin, 68, 95n9, 231n17
  Madonna und wir. Bekenntnisse, 60n54
Grether, Sandra, 231n17
  Madonna und wir. Bekenntnisse, 60n54
Grisebach, Valeska, 170
Groult, Benoite
  Salz auf unserer Haut, 128n24
Gümüsay, Kübra, 234n42
Gut, Gudrun, 232n17
Gutsche, Elisa Barcamp Frauen, 215, 216

Haaf, Meredith, 216, 221, 222, 223
  We Alpha-Girls: Why Feminism Makes Life Nicer, 11, 12, 24n34, 49–50, 53, 62n72, 63n75, 103, 124, 153, 159, 165n57, 174, 194, 219, 222, 223, 229
Hage, Volker, 66, 67, 75, 94n1
Hake, Sabine
  German Cinema in the New Millennium, 184, 185, 197, 203n38, 45; 205n61
Hanna, Kathleen, 213, 232n18
  Bikini Kill, 42, 54, 211
Haraway, Donna
  When Species Meet, 233n31
Hardin, Tim, 178
Harding, James M., 149, 165n50
Hark, Sabine, 59n44
Harron, Mary
  I Shot Andy Warhol, 148–49, 158
"Hartz IV," 30
Harvey, David, 30
  A Brief History of Neoliberalism, 57n11
Haupt, Nancy
  Barcamp Frauen, 215, 216
Hegemann, Helene
  Axotl Roadkill, 126n10
Heisenberg, Benjamin, 170
Hemmings, Claire
  Why Stories Matter: The Political Grammar of Feminist Theory, 8, 9, 11, 23n23, 207, 227, 230n1, 3; 234n38, 236n5
Hennig von Lange, Alexa, 68, 95n9
  Relax, 13, 66, 69, 70–72, 73, 81–82, 83–87, 93–94, 94n3, 111, 229

Henry, Astrid, 2, 3, 6, 8, 23n22, 48, 125, 130n57, 198
  Not My Mother's Sister: Generational Conflict and Third-Wave Feminism, 21n6, 22n10, 39, 59n45, 46; 106, 111, 128n26, 220
Hensel, Jana, 63n73
  New German Girls, 11, 24n34, 47–49, 51, 52, 53, 62n70, 71; 103, 114, 124, 159, 174, 194, 198, 219, 229, 231n13
  Zonenkinder, 47
Hermann, Eva
  The Eva Principle: Towards a New Femininity, 31, 57n16
Hermann, Judith, 66, 67, 94n1, 95n9
Herold, Horst, 163n41
Heywood, Leslie
  Third Wave Agenda: Being Feminist, Doing Feminism, 60n50, 55, 62n67
Hillman, Roger, 187, 204n49
Himmelreich, Laura, 216, 232n27
Hinrichsen, Jens, 201n21
Hirschbiegel, Oliver
  Downfall, 162n23
Hitler, Adolph, 162n23
Hochhäusler, Christoph, 170
Hofer, Stephanie, 200n18, 201n21
Hoffmann, Christiane, 21n4
Hofmann, Niklas, 221
Hornby, Nick, 95n9
Hopper, Dennis, 91
Hummer, Julia, 179

Ibele, Nicole, 209
Illies, Florian
  Generation Golf, 40

Jaafar, Ali, 200n17
Jagger, Mick, 76
Jelinek, Elfriede, 51, 95n9
  Lust, 52
Jenny, Zöe, 66, 94n1, 97n26
  The Pollen Room, 13, 66, 67, 74–81, 88, 93, 94n3, 111, 229
Jervis, Lisa, 54–55, 65n91
  Bitch, 54, 211, 224

Johnston, Claire, 15, 17, 167–68, 169, 180, 199n1, 5, 227
Joplin, Janis, 145, 164n46

Kafka, Franz, 73
Kaminer, Wladimir
  Russendisko, 95n10
Karneval, 25–26, 28, 29, 34, 43, 86
Kätzel, Ute
  Die 68erinnen. Porträt einer rebellischen Frauengeneration, 54, 65n88
Kauer, Katja, 12, 42, 50, 152
  Popfeminismus! Fragezeichen! Eine Einführung, 24n37, 60n52, 61n63, 63n77, 64n86, 114, 129n35
Kikeli, Sibel, 59n47
Kirchner, Barbara, 231n17
Klingner, Susanne, 62n71, 63n73, 221
  We Alpha-Girls: Why Feminism Makes Life Nicer, 11, 12, 24n34, 49–50, 53, 62n72, 63n75, 103, 124, 153, 159, 165n57, 174, 194, 198, 219, 222, 223, 229
Klotz, Almut, 232n17
Knef, Hildegard, 94n1
Knox, Shelby, 218
Koether, Jutta, 213
Köver, Chris, 209, 231n13
Köhler, Ulrich, 170
Kracht, Christian, 69, 95n9, 123
  Faserland, 68, 73, 83, 97n34
  Tristesse Royale, 68, 69, 124
Kraemer, Olaf
  High Times. Mein wildes Leben, 150, 151, 157, 166n60, 165n52
Kraushaar, Wolfgang, 132, 134, 137, 172, 190, 191
  1968 als Mythos, Chiffre und Zäsur, 160n6, 11; 200n16, 204n52
  Achtundsechzig. Eine Bilanz, 160n10, 204n57
Kraft, Hannelore, 56n4
Kriest, Ulrich, 136, 161n15, 162n24
Kristeva, Julia, 111
Kruger, Barbara, 69
Kurban Bayram, 192

Kullmann, Katja
    Generation Ally, 40–41
Kusama, Yayoi, 69

Lady Bitch Ray, 52
Lady Gaga, 214, 231n9
Lager, Sven
    The Buch. Leben am Pool, 67
Lambert, Molly, 219
Langer, Tanja, 66, 67
Langhans, Rainer, 150, 152, 153, 154
Lantzsch, Nadine, 235n45
Lassie Singers, 60n53
LaTigre, 46, 232n17
Leal, Joanne, 201n21
Lebert, Benjamin, 95n9
LeBruce, Bruce
    The Raspberry Reich, 136, 137
Lee, Nathan, 165n54
Leigh, Janet, 181
"Leitkultur," 187, 188, 223
Lemonbabies, 60n53
Levy, Ariel
    Female Chauvinest Pigs: Women and the Rise of Raunch Culture, 98n39
Liebrand, Claudia, 127n14, 127n20, 129n44
Liesegang, Torsten, 68, 95n6
Lohaus, Stephanie, 1, 2, 6, 20n2, 209, 230n8, 231n13
Löhrmann, Sylvia, 56n4
Longstocking, Pippi, 106, 126n10
Lorde, Audre, 5, 218
Love, Courtney, 42
Lucilectric, 60n53
Lupino, Ida, 199n5
Lynch, David
    Blue Velvet, 91

MacKinnon, Catherine
    Feminism Unmodified: Discourses on Life and Law, 33, 58n28
Mad Magazine, 106, 110
Madonna, 73, 89
Mädchenmannschaft, 62n72, 216, 221–23, 234n43
Makatsch, Heike, 53
Mann, Thomas, 73

Maradona, Diego, 179
Marazzi, Christian, 30, 57n12
Marisol, 69
Martens, Helge, 190
Martin, Courtney, 235n46
Marx Ferree, Myra
    Varieties of Feminism: German Gender Politics in Global Perspective, 7, 23n20, 32–34, 36, 52, 56n8, 58n24, 29; 59n40
Mayers, Susanne, 106, 126n9
McClelland, Sara I., 126n13
McRobbie, Angela, 30, 183, 228
    The Aftermath of Feminism: Gender, Culture and Social Change, 57n13, 14
Mean Girls, 60n51
Mehrfort, Sandra
    Popliteratur. Zum literarischen Stellenwert eines Phänomens der 1990er, 95n9, 97n33
Meinecke, Thomas, 69, 95n11
Meinhof, Ulrike, 14, 133, 138, 139, 140, 142–48, 158, 162n26, 163n42, 164n43, 46, 47, 48; 229
Melzer, Patricia, 145, 164n44, 49
Mennel, Barbara, 190, 192, 204n53
    German Cinema in the New Millennium, 184, 185, 197, 203n38, 45; 205n61
Merkel, Angela, 28, 58n22
Merley Hill, Alexandra, 30–31, 57n15
Meßner, Kathy, 214
Mikich, Sonia, 99n50
Mikus, Birgit, 2, 3, 12, 21n7, 22n9, 23n19, 24n35, 160n2, 207
Minioudaki, Kalliopi, 153, 156, 165n58, 59
Missy Magazine, 17, 209–10, 211, 212–16, 218, 221, 230n8, 231n9, 11, 12, 13
Mitchell, Juliet
    Psychoanalysis and Feminism. Freud, Reich, Laing and Women, 110, 128n23
Mitscherlich, Alexander
    The Inability to Mourn, 141
Mitscherlich, Margarete, 113, 142, 163n37
    The Inability to Mourn, 141

Moby Dick, 142, 178
Mobylettes, 60n53
Mohanty, Chandra Talpade
    Feminism Without Borders: Decolonizing Theory, Practicing Solidarity, 17–18, 19, 24n41, 42, 44; 208, 230n4
Mohnhaupt, Brigitte, 144, 147
Mohr, Christina, 60n54
"Monika Enterprizes," 232n17
Monroe, Marilyn, 125n5
Morgan, Robin, 113
Moss, Kate, 75
Ms. Magazine, 50, 217, 218

Naters, Elke
    Lies, 13, 66, 73, 81–82, 87–93, 93–94, 94n3, 95n9, 111, 227–28, 229
    The Buch. Leben am Pool, 67
"Nathan der Weise", 192
Negra, Diane
    Interrogating Postfeminism: Gender and the Politics of Popular Culture, 28–29, 42, 56n7, 9; 60n51, 117, 196, 198, 205n60, 62; 206
Neoliberalism, 29–30, 41, 48, 50, 52, 57n14, 64n83, 230
Neuhaus, Stefan, 95n9
New Subjectivity, 50, 51, 180
New York Magazine, 218, 221
New York Times, 106, 113, 151, 165n54
Nickel, Eckhard
    Tristesse Royale, 68, 69, 124
Night and Fog, 178
Nollau, Günter, 141
Nussbaum, Emily, 213, 218, 219, 224, 233n35, 234n37
Nylon: Kunststoff zu Feminismus und Popkultur, 232n17

Oasis, 72
Obermaier, Uschi, 14, 15, 133–32, 149–160, 229
O'Brien, Mary-Elizabeth, 136, 143
    Post-Wall German Cinema and National History: Utopianism and Dissent, 161n19, 163n41, 42; 164n46

Oedipus, 91
Ohnesorg, Benno, 202n24
Ortgies, Lisa, 56n2
Otto-Peter, Louise, 32
Our Bodies, Ourselves, 128n24
Özdogan, Selim
    The Daughter of the Blacksmith, 192

Pankau, Johannes G.
    Pop Pop Populär. Popliteratur und Jugendkultur, 95n9
Panofsky, Erwin, 167, 199n1
Park, Inwon, 96n17
Paulokat, Ute
    Neue deutsche Popliteratur, 73, 83, 95n8, 96n15, 97n32, 98n35
Peaches, 52, 60n53, 213, 232n17
    "Rub", 157
Petzold, Christian
    Ghosts, 168, 179, 181, 182
    The State I Am In, 15–16, 159, 168–83, 229
    Yella, 168, 181, 182
Pfister, Rene, 21n4
Piepmeier, Alison
    Catching a Wave: Reclaiming Feminism for the 21st Century, 58n23
Piesche, Peggy
    Your Silence Does Not Protect You: Audre Lorde and the Black Women's Movement in Germany, 5, 22n13
Piper, Andrew, 190
Plaschg, Anja, 209
Playboy, 156
Pollitt, Katha, 113, 116, 128n30, 31
Ponto, Jürgen, 142
Pop art by women, 151, 152, 153, 157
Pop literature, 50, 66, 67–74, 75, 83, 91, 92, 115, 116
Presley, Elvis, 104
Princess Diaries, 60n51
Psycho, 181
Puar, Jasbir, 24n33
Pulver, Lilo, 94n1
Pussy Riot, 211, 225, 232n19

Queneaus, Raymond
   Zazie, 126n10

Radisch, Iris, 12
Rasch, Ilka, 201n20
Red Army Faction (RAF) chapter 4, 171, 172, 175, 178
Raether, Elisabeth
   New German Girls, 11, 24n34, 47–49, 51, 52, 53, 62n70, 103, 114, 124, 159, 174, 194, 198, 219, 229, 231n13
Reger, Jo
   Different Wavelengths: Studies of the Contemporary Women's Movement, 58n30, 63n74, 130n57
Renegar, Valerie R., 5, 22n14, 117, 128n28, 129n41, 211, 231n14
Renner, R. G., 135, 140, 148, 161n12, 200n19, 201n22
Reulecke, Ann-Kathrin
   Paradoxie des Begehrens: Liebesdiskurse in deutschsprachigen und koreanischen Prosa Texten, 96n17
Revolution of 1848, 32
Rich, Adrienne, 111
Richards, Amy
   Grassroots: A Field Guide for Feminist Activism, 65n91
   Manifesta: Young Women, Feminism, and the Future, 50
Richards, Keith, 150, 154
Riot Grrrl, 42, 53, 55, 58n30, 60n53, 60n54, 153, 157, 210, 211, 213, 214, 227, 232n18
Ritter, Andrea, 106, 126n10
Roche, Charlotte, 101-04, 105, 107, 113
   Wetlands, 14, 101–03, 104–11, 114, 115–119, 121, 124, 129n35, 159, 229
   Wrecked, 14, 101–03, 104, 105, 106, 115, 118, 119–24, 229
Röggla, Katrin, 68, 95n9
Rösinger, Christiane, 232n17
Rossellini, Isabella, 73, 91
Roth, Christopher
   Baader, 164n45
Roth, Claudia, 77, 233n27

Russo, Mary, 86, 98n43, 108
Rutschky, Katharina, 73, 96n14
Rutschky, Michael
   Erfahrungshunger, 180, 202n26
Rüttgers, Jürgen, 56n4

Sandoval, Chela, 117
Sartre, Jean Paul, 163n40, 202n24
Sassulitsch, Wera, 163n39
Schanelec, Angela, 170
Scharff, Christina
   Repudiating Feminism: Young Women in a Neoliberal World, 57n17, 21; 61n62, 63n76, 64n83
Scheufler, Eric, 201n21, 202n24
Schirrmacher, Frank
   The Methusalem Plot, 31
   Minimum: Regarding the Decay and Resurrection of our Community, 31, 57n18, 19
Schlaffer, Hanalore, 126n10
Schleyer, Hanns Martin, 146, 148
Schlöndorff, Volker
   The Legend of Rita, 135, 140, 148
   The Lost Honor of Katherine Blum, 135, 140, 148
Schmeidel, Stevie, 209, 216, 231n10
Schmidt, Barbara, 56n4
Schmidt, Jan-Hinkrik, 234n40
Schnitzler, Arthur
   Fräulein Else, 73
Schönberger, Klaus, 234n40
Schröder, Gerhard, 69
Schröder, Kristina
   Danke, emanzipiert sind wir schon selber! Abschied vom Diktat der Rollenbilder, 56n4
Schroeder, Vera, 53, 65n87
Schrupp, Antje, 214, 216
Schuhmacher, Eckhard
   Gerade Eben Jetzt, 95n4, 5, 9
   Pop seit, 1946, 95n9, 95n11
Schwarzer, Alice, 1, 2, 3, 4, 5, 6, 7, 11, 12, 14, 20n1, 21n5, 27, 28, 35, 38, 41, 43, 45, 46, 47, 48, 49, 50, 53, 54, 56n3, 4, 5; 59n47, 64n85, 65n90, 103–05, 112, 113, 115, 121, 122, 123, 125n5, 141–42, 150,

163n35, 206, 209, 210, 211, 222, 229, 230n6, 8, 231n13, 232n27, 235n47
  Der kleine Unterschied und seine großen Folgen, 58n32
Schygulla, Hanna, 193, 204n51
Sedgwick, Eve
  Epistomology of the Closet, 10
Sherman, Cindy, 69, 73, 89
Sichtermann, Barbara, 64n84
Sight and Sound, 139
Silvey, Vivien, 187, 204n49
Sirk, Douglas, 15, 73
  All That Heaven Allows, 169–70
  Imitation of Life, 14, 16, 88, 92–93, 169, 186, 198
Singin' in the Rain, 81
Slutwalk demonstrations, 17, 218, 219, 221–22, 225, 234n43
Smith-Prei, Carrie, 31, 57n20, 61n64, 127n17, 183, 203n37, 225, 226, 227, 236n49
  Awkward Politics: Technologies of Popfeminist Activism, 24n33, 38; 236n48
Solanis, Valerie, 149, 158, 218, 219, 224
  "The Society for Cutting Up Men," 148, 164n50
Solomon, Deborah, 113, 128n30
Sookee, 214
Sowards, Stacey K., 5, 22n14, 117, 128n28, 129n41, 211, 231n14
"Spaßgesellschaft," 75
Speer, Albert, 162n23
Spex, 209, 213, 230n8
Spice Girls, 214
Spiers, Emily, 2, 3, 12, 21n7, 22n9, 23n19, 24n35, 160n2, 208
Spring Breakers, 214, 232n19
Sprinkle, Annie, 52
Stämpfli, Regula, 114, 128n33
Stefan, Verena
  Häutungen, 15, 116, 145
Stehle, Maria, 52, 60n53, 64n80, 128n34, 183, 203n37, 225, 226, 227, 236n49
  Awkward Politics: Technologies of Popfeminist Activism, 24n33, 38; 236n48

Steinbrecher, Julie, 209
Steinem, Gloria, 50, 54, 211, 214, 219, 232n18
Steinke, Ron, 234n40
Stendhal
  The Red and the Black, 81
Stephan, Inge
  Paradoxie des Begehrens: Liebesdiskurse in deutschsprachigen und koreanischen Prosa Texten, 96n17
Stern, 39, 106, 210, 216, 232n27
Stocker, Günther, 96n18
Stöcker, Mira, 46
  Das F-Wort. Feminismus ist sexy, 44–45, 47
Stoller, Debbie, 210
Streidl, Barbara, 221
  We Alpha-Girls: Why Feminism Makes Life Nicer, 11, 12, 24n34, 49–50, 53, 62n72, 63n75, 103, 124, 153, 159, 165n57, 174, 194, 198, 219, 222, 223, 229
Strigl, Daniela, 94n1
Student movement of '68, 3, 4, 7, 13, 17, 20, 33, 40, 53, 69, 75, 78, 86, 89, 93, 94, 132, 134–40, 150, 162n31, 173, 174, 184, 189, 190, 191, 192, 195, 196, 202n24, 224, 236n47
Sturm und Drang, 176
Süddeutsche Zeitung, 43, 64n85, 106, 128n29
Suding, Katja, 58n22
Sundermeier, Jörg, 96n13

Tagesspiegel, 130n54
Tanzer, Ulrike, 94n1
Tasker, Yvonne
  Interrogating Postfeminism: Gender and the Politics of Popular Culture, 28–29, 42, 56n7, 9, 60n51, 117, 196, 198, 205n60, 62; 206
Taeuber-Arp, Sophie, 69
Taz, 106, 221, 223, 234n40
The Punk Singer, 232n19
The Wild One, 142
Tic Tac Toe, 60n53

Tisdale, Sallie, 106, 126n12
Topless activism, 19, 208, 222, 225
Treut, Monika, 51–52
Trittin, Jürgen, 77
Tsing, Anna, 185
Tussi Deluxe, 136
Twen, 154

Vagina Monologues, 108
Valenti, Vanessa, 235n46
Vampirella, 67, 71, 72, 82, 84, 85, 86, 87, 96n29, 98n45
Van Bruggen, Coosje, 69
Van de Meiklokjes, Enie, 53
Van Org, Luci, 53
Vedder, Ulrike
    Paradoxie des Begehrens: Liebesdiskurse in deutschsprachigen und koreanischen Prosa Texten, 96n17
Venus Zine, 46
Vergangenheitsbewältigung, 3, 40, 113, 141
Villa Stahl, 175
Viva, 101, 105, 128n31, 129n35
Volk, Stefan, 203n46
Von Rönne, Ronja, 228, 236n52
Von Schönburg, Alexander
    Tristesse Royale, 68, 69, 124
Von Stuckrad-Barre, Benjamin, 69, 95n9, 11; 123
    Soloalbum, 68, 72, 73, 83
    Tristesse Royale, 68, 69, 124
Von Trotta, Margarete
    Marianne und Juliane, 200n20
Vukadinovic, Vojin Sasa, 140, 141, 147–48, 163n33

Waldsterben, 78
Walker, Rebecca, 58n30, 113
Wander, Maxi
    Guten Morgen, du Schöne, 50
Warhol, Andy, 148
Warnecke, Jenny, 45, 46, 62n66, 103, 220
Warner, Ansgar, 96n15
Waters, Sarah, 136, 161n18
Weber, Beverly M., 234n42

Weigel, Sigrid, 40, 60n48
    Paradoxie des Begehrens: Liebesdiskurse in deutschsprachigen und koreanischen Prosa Texten, 96n17
Weingartner, Hans
    The Edukators, 162n31, 165n55
Weingartner, Katharina
    Lips. Tits. Hits. Power? Popkultur und Feminismus, 42–43, 46, 60n56, 61n57, 101
Whelehan, Imelda, 205n63
Wilson, Brian, 179, 202n24
Wizorak, Anne, 1, 2, 6, 7, 20n2, 21n4, 5
Wnendt, David
    Wetlands, 126n7
Wolf, Yvonne, 82, 97n30
Woolf, Virginia
    A Room of One's Own, 27, 29, 41

#YesAllWomen, 7

Zachau, Reinhard, 163n42
Zaimoglu, Feridun
    Kanak Sprak–24 Mißtöne vom Rande der Gesellschaft, 95n10
Zetkin, Clara, 214
Zylka, Jenni, 106, 126n110

www.ingramcontent.com/pod-product-compliance
Lightning Source LLC
Chambersburg PA
CBHW072148100526
44589CB00015B/2140